# Crime and Coercion

## An Integrated Theory of Chronic Criminality

*Mark Colvin*

St. Martin's Press
New York

CRIME AND COERCION

Copyright © 2000 Mark Colvin. All rights reserved. Printed in the United States of America. No part of this book may be used or reproduced in any manner whatsoever without written permission except in the case of brief quotations embodied in critical articles or reviews. For information, address St. Martin's Press, Scholarly and Reference Division, 175 Fifth Avenue, New York, N.Y. 10010.

ISBN 0-312-23389-2

**Library of Congress Cataloging-in-Publication Data to be found at the Library of Congress.**

Design by Letra Libre, Inc.
First edition: July 2000
10  9  8  7  6  5  4  3  2  1

*To the grandchildren*

# Contents

# Acknowledgments

S pecial thanks go to Francis T. Cullen, who gave me valuable advice throughout this project, and to Suzanne Colvin, who read early drafts, discussed and listened to my ideas, and who, over the years, has provided much needed encouragement, love, and moral support. Tom Vander Ven provided insightful comments on the final manuscript of this book.

Any work in criminological theory builds on the ideas of other criminologists who have provided important insights into the causes of criminal behavior. I owe a debt to all the criminologists I cite and discuss in this book. Without their pioneering efforts, this book would not have been possible. I hope that I have (at least partially) lived up to their fine examples.

Many of the original ideas contained in this book grew out of discussions and collaboration with John Pauly with whom I presented an integrated theory of delinquency in an article published in the *American Journal of Sociology* (Colvin and Pauly 1983). John's indispensable contribution to that article continues to greatly influence my thinking about criminal behavior and its relation to larger political and economic structures.

I must also acknowledge the great debt I owe to my first criminology professor, Raymon C. Forston, who taught me respect for careful, logical, empirically-based arguments in developing knowledge about crime and punishment.

My department chair, Joe Scimecca, provided much encouragement and protected my time so that I could complete this book.

While I was in the middle of writing this book, I lost two important friends to cancer. First was my father, Emmett Colvin, a renowned criminal defense attorney who practiced law in Texas. He argued two cases before the United States Supreme Court, winning both appeals. He established a reputation for very high ethical standards and as a champion of poor people caught up in the criminal justice system. He set a strong, worthy example for his children. It was through my father that I first became interested in studying crime and punishment. Beginning in my early teens, he took me to court, let me sit in on interviews with his clients, and allowed me to observe behind-the-scenes workings of the criminal justice process. He taught me compassion and reason, not only through his words but also through his deeds. I miss him greatly.

My other friend who died of cancer in 1999 also had a profound impact on me. I first met Roberto Samora in 1975 when he was my client in a prison education program that I coordinated for the Penitentiary of New Mexico. Roberto, who had been in juvenile institutions and prisons for much of his life from age 12 to age 27, graduated from the prison's college program and earned parole in 1975. He soon became a social worker, focusing his energies on helping abused kids. As someone who himself had been physically and psychologically abused as a child, he understood first-hand the important connection between child abuse and criminal behavior. Roberto established a reputation as an honest, humble, and caring human being. He underwent amazing spiritual growth in the face of horrendous circumstances. Roberto's example gives me enduring faith in the capacity for human beings to reform, change, and overcome the emotional injuries in their backgrounds. Roberto became my closest and dearest friend. I also miss him greatly.

A special thanks to the anonymous reviewer, editors, and staff of St. Martin's Press. Thanks especially to Senior Editor Karen Wolny, her assistant Ella Pearce, and Production Manager Ruth Mannes.

I am solely responsible for any errors of fact or interpretation contained in this book.

# Figures*

---

\* *All figures in this book are original creations of the author.*

# Chapter 1

# Introduction

C hronic criminals are made, not born. They emerge from a developmental process that is punctuated by recurring, erratic episodes of coercion. They become both the recipients and perpetrators of coercion, entrapped in a dynamic that propels them along a pathway toward chronic criminality. Repeated experiences of coercion reinforce social-psychological attributes that make it more likely that an individual will exhibit behaviors that elicit further coercion, which only amplifies the emotional and cognitive traits that produce hostile behaviors. An individual caught up in this social dynamic will have a difficult time disengaging from a trajectory that is speeding toward chronic criminality. Yet individuals are not psychologically hardwired in early childhood to exhibit this dynamic. Changes in context along with timely interventions can alter the path toward chronic criminality that this social dynamic creates. An understanding of what creates this dynamic and how it is perpetuated through micro-processes of control, which are influenced by macro-economic and cultural forces, can help us devise strategies that make effective interventions possible. Such interventions must change the immediate and larger contexts that perpetuate coercion while also altering the individual's social-psychological characteristics that have developed through the dynamics of coercion.

People vary in their propensity to engage in crime. This propensity for criminal behavior, defined as "criminality" (Gottfredson and Hirschi 1990: 4), must be distinguished from acts of crime.[1] A theory that attempts to explain variations in propensity for crime necessarily focuses on the background factors that create potential for criminal behavior. But specific acts of crime are not explained by these background factors alone. A specific criminal event contains dynamics that induce or propel an actor toward committing a crime. These foreground dynamics include various coercive forces (often created in part by the offender) that seem to compel the actor toward a criminal act (Hagan and McCarthy 1997; Katz 1988; Luckenbill 1977; Wright and Decker 1997, 1994). An individual's background may help us understand why certain elements in the foreground of crime are compelling to (and created by) a particular individual, but it is these foreground dynamics, which may or may not come into play during a specific event, that are the immediate cause of a criminal act. Thus a thorough discussion of crime must deal with both the background that produces a potential toward criminal behavior and the foreground in which acts of crime take place.

Three distinct patterns of criminal involvement can be discerned. (1) *Chronic offending* involves frequent and persistent engagement in predatory street crime (homicide, rape, robbery, assault, burglary, and theft). (2) *Exploratory offending* involves infrequent, sporadic, and temporary engagement in street crimes (usually those of a less serious, non-predatory nature). (3) *White-collar crime* involves (sometimes chronic and predatory) criminal violations of trust by a person or group of persons in the course of an otherwise legitimate and respected occupation or financial activity.[2] Since these three types of criminal behavior are qualitatively different, it is often assumed that distinctive explanations for them are needed. The theory developed in this book accounts for all three patterns of criminality as well as non-criminality. The primary focus of this book, however, is on chronic involvement in predatory street crime and delinquency,[3] understanding both the background and foreground factors that lead to this criminal pattern. Frequent and persistent involvement in predatory street crimes, which the public is most concerned about and fears, is quite a different phenomenon than infrequent engagement in street crime or the "crimes in the suites" that make up white-collar crime.

While it is true that the public *should* fear the harms and depredations of many white-collar crimes, especially those that cause death and physical suffering (Reiman 1995), there is still a qualitative difference between these behaviors and chronic involvement in predatory street crime. The differences between white-collar and chronic street crimes in the moral opprobrium attached to each by the public and the state not only influences how these offenders are dealt with by the criminal justice system but also helps us understand their etiology. Self-image plays a role in creating criminal behavior; the public's moral stance toward certain criminal behaviors (while greatly influenced by politics and media) is the context against which moral self-images of criminals are created. Self-images of white-collar criminals contrast starkly with those of chronic street criminals. White-collar criminals do not have an image of themselves as criminal; they can avoid such an image by rationalizing their behavior, a feat accomplished with the help of a public and a criminal justice system that appears less disturbed by their behavior. In contrast, one of the prevailing features of people who persistently engage in street crime is their glorification of criminal self-images (Katz 1988). Exploratory offenders usually do not hold self-images as criminal, so in this sense, they are similar to white-collar offenders, except that the latter often become persistent in their offending.

The distinction between street crime and white-collar crime in the discussion above is a major distinction between types of crime. It is rare that a person becomes both a chronic street criminal and a white-collar criminal. Much of this has more to do with opportunity than with motive. White-collar criminals necessarily have to gain positions of trust in legitimate organizations or business activities before they can commit their crimes. Chronic street offenders, usually quite early on, opt out of any possibility of gaining such positions.

The official categories of property crimes, violent crimes, and drug offenses do not concern us much in this discussion. Chronic street criminals tend not to specialize but are involved in a wide variety of criminal behaviors that cross the boundaries of these legal categories (Blumstein et al. 1986; Elliott et al. 1989; Farrington 1997; Osgood et al. 1988; Tracy and Kempf-Leonard 1996; Visher 1995; Wolfgang et al. 1972). One important characteristic of chronic offenders is that they begin engaging in crime earlier than do other offenders (Farrington 1997; Wolfgang et al. 1972). These "early starters," as they have been labeled in the criminology literature (Simons et al. 1994), become involved in a wide variety of conduct violations and minor delinquency during childhood and early adolescence and, as they age, many add serious violent offenses to their repertoire (Elliott 1994). It is my contention that these offenders have experienced coercive controls early in life and that this coercion has shaped a set of social-psychological characteristics and corresponding behaviors that continue to elicit coercive controls from others. As this dynamic continues, it is eventually reflected in predatory criminal events during which the equation of coercion is reversed.

Chronic street criminals were uncovered in a Philadelphia study in which a cohort born in 1945 was tracked over time through official records (Wolfgang et al. 1972). This study found that a small number of the overall cohort accounted for the majority of arrests, especially those for index crimes. (Index crimes include murder, rape, robbery, aggravated assault, burglary, grand larceny, motor vehicle theft, and arson. These are considered the most serious predatory street crimes against persons and property.) Six percent of the entire cohort (who comprise 18 percent of those in the cohort who had ever been arrested) accounted for 52 percent of all arrests and 63 percent of the arrests for index crimes, including 71 percent of all murders, 82 percent of all robberies, 69 percent of all aggravated assaults, and 73 percent of all rapes. Similar findings were reported in a study of a cohort born in 1955 in Racine, Wisconsin (Shannon 1988) and in a later study from Philadelphia of a cohort born in 1958 (Tracy et al. 1990).

The Philadelphia and Racine birth-cohort studies are based on arrest data, which potentially contain many biases. Arrests may be the result of actual criminal behavior or merely the result of police activity that targets certain groups or individuals for arrest. People who have been previously arrested are often the target of further arrests because they become known to the police, who "round up the usual suspects" when a serious crime occurs. Thus being labeled a chronic offender based on arrest data may not be an accurate gauge of actual criminal behavior.

Self-report studies are an alternative measure of criminal behavior. Samples of individuals are asked by researchers to report, confidentially, on their own criminal behavior. These data are thus independent of the influence of police behavior. Many self-report studies use samples (such as high school students) in which the probability of including chronic offenders is nil (Chernkovich et al. 1985; Hagan and McCarthy 1997). However, one of the most important and sophisticated self-report studies (the National Youth Survey conducted by Delbert S. Elliott and his associates) revealed a category of chronic offenders, comprising about five percent of the study's national sample. This small segment of the sample accounted for 50 percent of all offenses and 83 percent of all index crimes reported for the sample (Elliott 1994: 12). These findings correspond to those of the Philadelphia and Racine birth-cohort studies. Thus with two entirely different measures of criminal behavior, we are able to confirm the existence of chronic offenders who account for the overwhelming majority of predatory street crimes.

This book focuses primarily on chronic offenders because they commit most of the street crimes that the public most fears. But I do not ignore exploratory offenders or white-collar criminals in the theory developed in chapter 2 or in the discussion of the immediate criminal event (the foreground) in chapter 5. These criminal patterns are important to understand because more individuals are caught up in them than in chronic street crime and because they offer important contrasts to chronic criminality in their etiology.

Is the etiology of chronic street crime different from the etiology of other forms of crime? General theories of criminal behavior argue that a common causal element is behind all types of criminal behavior. The most important of these general theories of crime (which are discussed in the next chapter) include Robert Agnew's general strain theory, Michael R. Gottfredson and Travis Hirschi's self-control theory, Ron Akers's social learning theory, Francis T. Cullen's social support theory, and Charles R. Tittle's control balance theory. Each theory offers a distinct explanation of criminal behavior and purports to explain a wide range of deviant behaviors. In chapter 2, I fully delineate each of these theories (along with insights from other theories and studies of crime) and offer a new integrated theory, which combines elements of existing theories to better understand criminal behavior.

I bring into this integrated theory the factor of coercion. Coercion can be direct or indirect. I label direct coercion *interpersonal coercion,* which is the use or threat of force and intimidation aimed at creating compliance through fear. While it often involves the actual use or threat of physical force in an interpersonal relationship, this is not a necessary component. Coercion also involves the actual or threatened removal of social supports, which provide both material and emotional needs for individuals (Cullen 1994). I refer to indirect coercion as *impersonal coercion,* which is the pressure arising from structural arrangements and circumstances that seem beyond individual control, such as economic and social pressure caused by unemployment, poverty, or competition among businesses or other groups. This impersonal coercion creates a sense of desperation that seems to compel an individual toward immediate action (Hagan and McCarthy 1997).

Coercion, it is argued, is an important part of the etiological mix for understanding the production of chronic street criminality. It forms one pole of a dimension of control, ranging from highly coercive to completely non-coercive. Another dimension is the consistency to which coercion is experienced or applied, which can range from highly consistent to highly erratic. These two dimensions (degree of coerciveness and degree of consistency) render four patterns of control, three of which are implicated in deviant outcomes that vary in seriousness, frequency, and type. Thus the theory developed in this book can be understood as a theory of *differential coercion* in that it posits variance in both the strength of coercion and the consistency to which it is experienced or applied.

Other theorists have offered concepts that are similar to coercion in their theories of criminal and delinquent behavior (Agnew 1992; Athens 1992; Colvin and Pauly 1983; Patterson 1982; Regoli and Hewitt 1997; Tittle 1995). In chapter 2, I build on these and other insights in the development of a differential coercion theory of criminality. I use the label *differential coercion theory* since the key independent variable for understanding criminality is the degree of coercion (in both its strength and consistency) experienced by individuals. Gerald Patterson and his colleagues (1980, 1982) use a similar name, *coercion theory,* in their explanation of delinquency.

However, their theory is limited almost entirely to the family context where it is assumed that parents help create children's delinquency through coercive disciplinary practices. The current book makes a more general statement about the effects of coercion and then focuses on multiple contexts in which coercion propels some individuals toward chronic involvement in criminal behavior.

A theory not only must make a general statement about the etiology of crime and account for a wide range of behaviors, it must also define the contexts in which the potentials for criminal behavior are most likely to be produced. In chapter 3, various social contexts including workplaces, families, schools, peer groups, and the bureaucracies of welfare and criminal justice agencies are explored. These are the sites in which *interpersonal coercion* can be experienced to varying degrees. As a person passes through these various contexts, the degree to which interpersonal coercion is experienced will help determine the extent to which his or her life is perceived as a generalized coercive experience. This, it is argued, produces *coercive ideation* in which the world is imagined to be a continuous pattern of coercion that can only be overcome through coercion. This worldview becomes an important element in shaping chronic criminality and is directly acted upon during the commission of predatory street crimes.

These immediate social contexts are shaped by larger economic, historical, and cultural forces, which are discussed in chapter 4. The economy, more so during periods of recession, produces *interpersonal coercion* through its effect on workplace controls and *impersonal coercion* through the economic pressures created by competition, poverty, and structural unemployment. In addition, interpersonal and impersonal forms of coercion are given cultural support through values that encourage competitive individualism and codes that demand the defense of honor. These larger economic and cultural forces influence the immediate contexts of work, family, school, peer associations, and welfare and criminal justice bureaucracies that shape the background of chronic criminality. They also influence the production of *coercive ideation* as these larger impersonal forces combine with more immediate interpersonal ones to make the world in general seem hostile and coercive.

In chapter 5, the foreground of crime is explored. The meanings, calculations, and emotions that are in play in the immediate event of a criminal act are shaped by the background contexts. The situational dynamics of a criminal event, which the offender helps to create, bring to the fore the experiences, meanings, and emotions produced in past episodes of coercion. The criminal act often involves the offender specifically using coercion on victims. The immediate circumstance of a criminal event may also involve provocation from others, which is interpreted by the perpetrator as a coercive attempt to gain the perpetrator's obedience. This perceived coercion (with its potential for humiliation) triggers a coercive response that may take one form or another of predatory crime (Katz 1988). Coercion thus becomes part of the foreground of crime, a response to the immediate situation that reflects the coercion-filled background of the offender. This connection between background and foreground is dynamic and helps explain why these criminal acts become persistent. The foreground also contains perceived opportunities and risks that offenders, to varying degrees, consider during the commission of a crime (Clark and Cornish 1985). These opportunities and risks are shaped by larger social trends that have affected people's "routine activities," making them more or less vulnerable to victimization (Felson 1998). In addition to considering the foreground of chronic street criminals, chapter 5 also explores the foreground of exploratory offending and white-collar crime and connects these to the background dimensions of control out of which these criminal patterns arise.

In chapter 6, the policy implications of differential coercion theory are developed. The response to chronic street crime must be driven by theory if it is to be successful. Successful intervention is predicated upon an understanding of both the social contexts and the social-psychological elements that lead to chronic criminality. Both of these must be altered simultaneously for effective intervention aimed at prevention and rehabilitation. Most current practices of the criminal justice system involve interventions that, from the perspective of the theory developed in this book, can be expected not only to fail but be counterproductive. For the most part these interventions merely reproduce and often exacerbate the dynamics of coercion that led individuals toward chronic criminality in the first place. Chapter 6 also proposes economic and cultural reforms aimed at moving us away from our current coercion-laden society, which produces an overabundance of chronic criminals.

# Chapter 2

# Emergence of a Differential Coercion Theory of Criminality

In this chapter I review several theories of criminality in an effort to develop differential coercion theory. Since the early 1980s theorists have included factors related to coercion in their explanations of crime and delinquency. The first major section of this chapter reviews these previous theories. The second major section lays out the differential coercion theory of criminality.

## THE THEORETICAL TRADITIONS INFORMING DIFFERENTIAL COERCION THEORY

A number of theorists and researchers have contributed insights that I draw upon to develop differential coercion theory. Gerald Patterson (1982) coined the term *coercion theory* in his discussion of family dynamics and delinquency. John Pauly and I (Colvin and Pauly 1983) related coercive control patterns in workplaces, families, schools, and among peers to the production of serious, chronic delinquency. The theories of Robert Agnew (1985, 1992) focus on negative stimuli (which include coercion) as causing strain, which can foster criminal behavior. Francis T. Cullen (1994) implies that coercive environments lack the type of social support that can prevent crime. Lonnie Athens (1992) sees coercion as part of a brutalization process that creates dangerous violent criminals. Charles Tittle (1995) posits a relationship between various degrees of repression and various types of deviant behavior. Robert Regoli and John Hewitt (1997) relate coercive oppression by adults to the coercive behavior and delinquent retaliatory acts of children.

In addition, recent theories and studies have explored social–psychological correlates of crime. Agnew's (1985) work highlights anger as a basic emotion

that is implicated in criminal behavior. Travis Hirschi (1969) relates weak social bonds, such as weak attachment to others, to criminality. Michael Gottfredson and Travis Hirschi (1990) focus on low self-control as a precursor
to criminality. Ronald Akers's (1985) social learning theory argues that criminality is learned partially through behavioral modeling. Studies have also
found that low self-efficacy, negative emotionality, and an external locus of
control are related to delinquency (Caspi et al. 1994; Peiser and Heaven
1996; Shaw and Scott 1991). The differential coercion theory I build in this
chapter draws on and incorporates many of the ideas included in these previous theories and studies; thus I develop an integrated theory (Barak 1998;
Messner et al. 1989). The theory ties different patterns of coercion to the development of social-psychological states that are conducive to criminality.
Before laying out the general elements of differential coercion theory, I provide details of the theoretical developments that inform this new theory of
criminality.

### Patterson's Coercion Theory and Akers's Social Learning Theory

Gerald R. Patterson (1995, 1990, 1982) is a pioneer in both the study and
treatment of family dynamics that cause delinquency. He focuses on family disciplinary patterns as a primary element in the production or prevention of delinquent behavior. He argues that inconsistent but frequent
punitive forms of discipline create a coercive pattern that is reflected in all
family interactions. In these family interactions, discipline is generally
harsh, but is often not directly aimed at misbehavior. "Although the parents of antisocial boys have been observed to threaten, scold, and hit their
sons at significantly higher rates than do control parents, most of these reactions are not contingent on misbehaviors. Observational data have
shown that these parents are also noncontingent in their use of praise and
support for pro-social behavior. The result is that their boys become defi-
cient in their social skills as well as increasingly antisocial" (Larselere and
Patterson 1990: 305–6). Family interactions become "aversive interchanges" in which coercion becomes a primary learned response to adverse situations (Snyder and Patterson 1987: 222). Coercive interchanges
can include physical attacks, which are often the outcome of several non-
physical coercive interchanges including negative commands, critical remarks, teasing, humiliation, whining, yelling, and threats that escalate to
hitting. The child and the parents both contribute to the coercive process
in these interchanges.

Patterson argues that different parental disciplining styles can create different delinquent outcomes. Families that are more harsh, punitive, and restrictive (in a word, coercive) tend to create children who engage in "overt

antisocial behavior" (aggression, assaults, and person-oriented crime) (Snyder and Patterson 1987: 236). These children also tend to become "early starters" in delinquency (Patterson 1995; Patterson et al. 1991; Simons et al. 1994) and are at greater risk of becoming "life-course persistent" offenders (Moffitt 1997). Families that are overly lax and permissive tend to produce children who engage in "covert antisocial behavior" (lying, stealing, and property-oriented crimes) (Snyder and Patterson 1987: 236). These children, who tend to be "late starters" in delinquency, are more likely to experiment with delinquent behavior as they drift toward the influence of peers who encourage such deviant explorations (Patterson and Yoerger 1993; Simons et al. 1994). These children are also referred to as "adolescent-limited" offenders (Moffitt 1997). I will pick up on these themes in the development of differential coercion theory later in this chapter and in the discussion of family context in the next chapter. What is important in the work of Patterson and his colleagues is the identification of coercive family interactions as a primary element in the etiology of predatory delinquency.

Patterson argues that behavioral modeling occurs during coercive interchanges. Aggression in children is "facilitated by the ubiquitous presence of coercive models," especially in the home (Patterson 1982: 93). Coercive discipline by parents is ineffective for two reasons. First, it becomes a model for children to imitate when they encounter conflict or feel irritable. Second, as discussed above, coercive parents' interventions fail to punish children's coercive behavior, or to praise children's pro-social behavior, on a consistent basis. The child learns that coercive behavior is often successful in producing desired outcomes and begins to hone greater coercive skills during repeated coercive interchanges with parents, siblings, teachers, and peers. These coercive interchanges (both physical and non-physical) bring about positive reinforcements (including the attention gained from others, even if this is negative, and the reactions of pain and submission they create in others).

Patterson follows a major tradition of deviance studies: social learning theory. He directly borrows from Albert Bandura (1973), who argues that children learn by modeling the behavior of other people. Ronald L. Akers (1997, 1985), drawing upon the pioneering work of Edwin H. Sutherland and Donald R. Cressey (1978), has become the strongest proponent of social learning theory as an explanation of deviant and criminal behavior.

Akers's social learning theory is a direct descendent of Sutherland and Cressey's differential association theory (Akers 1997: 62). Sutherland and Cressey proposed that criminal behavior is learned like any other behavior during associations with others in intimate groups, such as families, friends, or co-workers. Not only are techniques for committing crime learned but also acquired are the definitions (attitudes, values, rationalizations, and motives) favorable or unfavorable to law violation. Associations with definitions favorable to law violation will have greater impact if they come earlier in life, happen frequently, occur over a long time period, and are with groups or individuals that the person holds in high esteem. In Sutherland's initial conceptualization, it was not clear what the "definitions" consisted of. Were these direct unconditional endorsements of criminal behavior or could they also be implied approval of values and behavior that may be conducive to crime, such as risk-taking or use of aggression to deal with conflict? Other theorists tend to downplay the direct endorsements of criminal behavior and point to the indirect or implied approval of values and rationalizations that may justify crime in certain situations (Agnew 1995; Akers 1997; Sykes and Matza 1957).

Akers (1985) expanded upon differential association theory by bringing in concepts from operant conditioning, which focuses on learning reinforced through rewards and punishments. Akers's contribution was to specify the processes by which the learning of deviant behavior takes place. As he explains, "The groups with which one is in differential association provide the major social contexts in which all the mechanisms of social learning operate. They not only expose one to definitions, they also present them with models to imitate and with differential reinforcement (source, schedule, value, and amount) for criminal or conforming behavior" (Akers 1997: 64). As he further explains, "These definitions favorable or unfavorable to criminal and delinquent behavior are developed through imitation and differential reinforcement. Cognitively, they provide a mindset that makes one more willing to commit the act when the opportunity occurs. Behaviorally, they affect the commission of deviant or criminal behavior by acting as internal descriminative stimuli [, which] operate as cues or signals to the individual as to what responses are appropriate or expected in a given situation" (Akers 1997: 65).

The role of reward and punishment is central to the learning of criminal behavior. The schedule of rewards and punishments for conformity is effective to the extent that it is consistent and fair. The role of positive incentives is important, since these present pleasurable experiences for compliance. Discipline that is based on positive rewards is more effective than one that is based purely on punishment. In fact, punishment that involves violence may have the unintended effect of teaching the individual that violence is an appropriate response to conflict. Coercive relations of control, while creating negative feedback about behavior to the one being controlled, may also model behavior for those instances when this individual attempts to control others. If subjected to control that is predominately coercive, on what basis will the individual learn techniques of positive control? In this sense, relations of control become learning experiences that speak not only to the behavior being reinforced or extinguished but also become the basis upon which behavior is modeled, even if the experience is punishing. Thus the way in which control is carried out over an individual becomes the model the individual imitates when he or she exercises control. For the development of differential coercion theory, the social learning perspective provides the insight that coercive punishment and other coercive interchanges create models for behavior that the individual imitates in his or her relations with others.

The impact of coercive parental discipline and aversive family relations is best demonstrated when family dynamics are changed to a consistent, non-coercive pattern. Patterson established "parent effectiveness training" at the Oregon Social Learning Center where parents of delinquents were trained to discipline their children in consistent and non-coercive ways. The training was aimed at changing the process of coercive family interactions. The program's effectiveness was evaluated using a series of experiments in which delinquents' families were randomly assigned to the training program. A significant difference in subsequent delinquency was found between the experimental and control groups, with a significant lowering of delinquency for the experimental group (Bank et al. 1991; Patterson 1982: 304–8; Patterson et al. 1982). These experiments demonstrate the causal role of coercive discipline and coercive interactions in the production of delinquency.

Patterson's research focuses mostly on the family. He points out that coercive family interactions produce poor social skills and antisocial behavior that children carry into other settings. "When their sons enter school, their abrasive style and noncompliance soon lead to peer rejection and academic failure," which tend to "maintain boys' antisocial behavior into the adolescent years" (Larzelere and Patterson 1990: 306). Although Patterson does not state this explicitly, it can be argued that a child's coercive behavior (learned initially in coercive family interactions) is brought into other social settings and is likely to produce a coercive response from others in these non-family environments. This interaction between coercion in one setting and coercion in another is the focus of the next theory.

### Colvin and Pauly's Integrated Structural Marxist Theory

This book is in many ways a follow-up to an article that John Pauly and I published in the *American Journal of Sociology* (Colvin and Pauly 1983). The key idea discussed in that work was that coercive controls (in various settings) produce an alienated bond between the controller and the one who is being controlled. The theory posits class-based differences in serious chronic delinquency because the workplace is the starting point for understanding control relations.

Workplaces differ in the quality of their control relations. Drawing on the organizational theory of Amitai Etzioni (1970), workplaces are dominated by normative, remunerative, or coercive control. Normative control involves the manipulation of symbolic rewards, such as status and honors and the use of praise and emotional support. Remunerative control involves the manipulation of material rewards, such as the promise of pay raises. Coercive control involves the use of threats and force, including the threat of job loss in which one is deprived the material means of survival.

These three types of workplace controls roughly correspond to the three fractions of the working class posited by Richard Edwards (1979). These working-class fractions are created by the historical and economic trends of capitalism that led to the segmentation of the labor market. Fraction 3 is composed of workers who are under "bureaucratic control," which is similar to Etzioni's normative control. The job experience of fraction 3 workers, in which complex tasks are encountered and greater autonomy and decision-making are exercised, fosters in these workers a more positive bond to their work, to authorities at the workplace, and to their organization in general. Fraction 2 is composed of organized workers who have gained wage concessions and industry-wide unions. They are under "technical control" at the workplace, which corresponds to Etzioni's remunerative control. Technical control is machine-paced and impersonal, often involving assembly lines, and it relies on the worker calculating his or her material self-interest for pay raises and job security. Workers in this type of workplace develop an intermediately intense bond to their jobs, based on the calculation of extrinsic rewards. This is a precarious ideological bond, depending on continual remuneration and advancement up the pay scale; it produces little loyalty on the part of the worker. As long as remuneration is forthcoming, the worker is not alienated from the workplace's authorities or organization. Fraction 1 workers are more likely to be subjected to coercive controls in jobs that are usually dead-end with few prospects for advancement or for organizing into unions. The primary control mechanism is threatened or actual dismissal from the job, which, depending on the state of the labor market (and thus the size of the surplus population competing for jobs), can be an enormously coercive measure. This coercive control produces a highly negative and alienated bond to the workplace, its authorities, and organization.

Since class fractions are a key highlight of the Colvin-Pauly thesis, the theory has been viewed primarily as a class-based theory of delinquency (Brownfield 1986; Paternoster and Tittle 1990; Simpson and Elis 1994). Workplace experiences are class differentiated and are posited by Pauly and

myself to have important effects on family interactions. Following the research of Melvin Kohn (1977) on work and families, the degree of workplace supervision is seen to shape parents' control and disciplining of
children; parents' coercive workplaces tend to correspond to coercive discipline of children in the home. These children develop more alienated
bonds to parents, the initial authority figures in their lives. As they enter
school, they bring with them these alienated bonds and, through behavior
that reflects this alienation, elicit more coercive controls at school, often
being placed in the "non-college" tracks in which obedience to rules is
emphasized over initiative, autonomy, and self-direction. Their initial alienated bonds are only reinforced by the school experience. As alienated children begin to hang out together they tend to create coercive relations
among themselves, which are conducive to producing violent delinquent
behavior. Some of these alienated young people may become connected
to criminal subcultures that offer material rewards through selling drugs or
stolen merchandise. These connections will create a stronger bond to the
criminal subculture based on the expectation of remunerative rewards
from the activities of this subculture.

While the theory is class-based, it is important to note that the connection between class (as specifically defined by control experiences at the
workplace) and chronic delinquency is in Colvin and Pauly's theory entirely mediated by family, school, and peer relations. Thus it is not necessary
for support of the theory to find a direct relationship between class and
delinquency. Larzelere and Patterson (1990) argue that poor parental management (in the form of weak monitoring and coercive patterns of discipline) accounts for social class differences in early on-set of delinquent
behavior. That is, lower socioeconomic class parents are more likely to use
coercive discipline and erratically monitor their children's behavior. This in
turn leads to higher rates of delinquency. Larzelere and Patterson (1990)
tested this hypothesis on a sample of young boys, with parents' socioeconomic status measured in fourth grade, parental management measured in
sixth grade, and self-report and official delinquency measured in seventh
grade. Socioeconomic status was a strong predictor of parental management
skills (beta = .66), which in turn predicted delinquency (beta = -.76). When
controlling for parental management skills, the initial significant statistical
association between social class and delinquency disappeared. Ronald L. Simons and his co-researchers (1994: 261) report similar findings. Thus
parental management appears to mediate the relationship between social
class and delinquency.

Since the Colvin-Pauly thesis was laid out the way it was—with historically created differences in workplace controls producing class fractions that are indirectly connected to chronic delinquency—the theory

is context driven. That is, the theory highlights the historical (and national) contexts of workplaces, families, schools, and peer relations that produce chronic delinquency. This is a problem since buried in the theory's presentation is a general theoretical statement that is really independent of context. The general theoretical statement is that *coercion produces alienated bonds, which, if reinforced by continual coercive relations, produce chronic involvement in serious delinquent behavior.* This proposition should hold for any context in which coercive relations predominate. This is not to deny the importance of context since context always shapes how the coercion - alienated bonds - chronic delinquency relationship will play itself out. (And context is the focus of the next two chapters.) But what I believe to be a key general theoretical point of the Colvin-Pauly thesis was overshadowed in the theory by its highlighting of contexts, starting with workplaces. For that reason, the empirical tests of the Colvin-Pauly thesis have focused on the relationship between class fractions and delinquency, with mixed results (Messner and Krohn 1990; Paternoster and Tittle 1990; Simpson and Elis 1994). In addition, the theory focuses on the effects that coercion has on social bonding, to the exclusion of other possible social-psychological outcomes that may be conducive to criminality. Other theories and studies offer insights into other social-psychological elements that produce crime and delinquency. I turn to a discussion of these theories and studies in an attempt to tie them to the general theme of coercion.

### Agnew's General Strain Theory

Robert S. Agnew's theory is rooted in one of the major traditions in criminology: strain theory. It is important to grasp this tradition to understand how Agnew's work has revitalized strain theory, which by the early 1980s had lost its prominent place in criminological discussions. All strain theories argue that individuals are pressured into crime by negative emotions, such as frustration or anger. The source of these negative emotions, however, is conceived differently by various strain theorists.

Robert Merton (1990 [1938]) borrowed from Emil Durkheim's (1952 [1897]) concept of *anomie* to describe a social order whose value system and social structure are out of sync. A society contains a culture that defines desirable achievement goals. Virtually everyone in the society is influenced by these culturally-defined goals. Yet a society may also contain a structure of opportunity that blocks a segment of the population from achieving these goals. In a society like the United States in which material success is highly prized, the disjunction between goals and means revolves primarily around achievement of financial success. The blocked opportunities to achieve culturally-defined goals create a social-psychological state of strain, which can be understood in Merton's formulation as frustration. This strain creates pressure and motivates the individual to eliminate the source of the strain. This can be accomplished through several adaptations. Conformity involves trying harder to achieve the goal through legitimate means. Innovation involves trying to achieve the culturally approved goal through illegitimate means. Retreatism involves rejecting the goal and escaping strain by withdrawing from life's struggles through illegitimate means (such as drug use). Ritualism involves escaping frustration by rejecting the importance of the goal but continuing to engage (ritually) in legitimate means with no thought of attaining the goal. Rebellion involves rejecting the culturally-defined goal and replacing it with an alternative goal that requires an alternative means, usually illegitimate by the standards of the society, for its achievement.

According to Merton (1990 [1938]: 231), whether or not one or another adaptation to strain is adopted is "determined by the particular personality and thus the *particular* cultural background" of the person under strain. Merton does not proceed from there to develop a theory of these background dynamics and thus he provides an incomplete explanation of criminal behavior. In his theory, strain explains both criminal (innovation, retreatism, rebellion) and non-criminal (conformity, ritualism) behavior. The personality and cultural determinants that lead to one adaptation or another are not spelled out; yet these seem to be the crucial elements in determining a criminal or non-criminal outcome. Since some of the adaptations involve deviance and others do not, understanding the factors involved in determining which adaptation is chosen constitutes a theory of deviance, which Merton does not adequately explore (Cullen 1983). But Merton created an important opening for other theorists.

Richard A. Cloward and Lloyd E. Ohlin (1960) started with Merton's basic idea about strain, arguing that the poor are impacted greatly by the disjunction between goals and means for financial success. How poor people adapt to this strain, argue Cloward and Ohlin, will be determined by the organization of legitimate and illegitimate means in the community in which they live and by the presence of subcultures that provide avenues for particular adaptations to strain. If legitimate means are available, then they will pursue the adaptation that Merton labeled conformity. However, given the nature of economic opportunities in the United States, many poor people will feel that this avenue is blocked. Illegitimate means must be used to pursue economic success. But here the individual may find that these means are blocked as well unless the immediate social environment contains a *criminal subculture* that provides contact with illegal opportunities for economic gain, such as successful drug, gambling, or burglary rackets. Without contacts to this type of subculture and to the illicit opportunities it offers, the person will be cut off from this illegitimate path to economic success. Thus the individual will have to pursue other means to reduce strain. These could include a retreat into drug use. But Cloward and Ohlin argue that chronic drug use also requires contact with a deviant subculture oriented around the use of drugs, especially if the drug use involves heroin. One must know how to obtain, prepare, and use the drugs. These can only be learned from others who are willing to teach you. Without these contacts with a *retreatist subculture,* this path to reducing strain may be more difficult to pursue. Another path may be to reject the goal of financial success and adopt an alternative goal that is contrary to the culturally desired goal. One example might be to adopt the goal of achieving respect, based not on middle-class notions of respect but on fighting skills, courage, and toughness encouraged by a *conflict subculture.* Success and achievement are then redefined in such a way that they become attainable to those who are blocked from other avenues to success. Cloward and Ohlin argue that conflict subcultures, which support the rise and perpetuation of fighting gangs, emerge in socially disorganized areas that contain few legitimate or illegitimate opportunities for economic gain. This adaptation requires certain attributes that only some individuals may possess, including a willingness to place one's body in harm's way. Without these necessary attributes, this adaptation may be blocked as well. In this case, the person may have to adapt to strain by ritually going through the motions of survival by seeking low paying legitimate employment that offers little hope of economic success.

Cloward and Ohlin thus provide a subcultural explanation of why one adaptation to strain is taken and not another. But they share with Merton the thought that the source of strain is the failure to achieve positively valued goals, especially goals of financial success.

Albert Cohen (1955) somewhat refocused Merton's strain theory by de-emphasizing the role of economic success goals and focusing on middle-class status goals. As with Cloward and Ohlin, Cohen argues that strain is more likely to affect the poor and working class, especially the children of these classes. Cohen doubted that economic success goals, which mainly affect adults, would have much meaning for children. Instead, he saw more immediate sources of strain arising from these children's experiences at school. The children are unprepared from their family upbringing to be judged successfully by the middle-class standards of behavior that their middle-class teachers expect of them. Strain is produced by the failure to live up to these "middle-class measuring rods." The "status frustration" pushes these kids toward a delinquent subculture that specifically rejects middle-class standards. Instead of attempting to pursue financial gain, this subculture encourages "negativistic behavior" such as vandalism, petty theft, drinking, and disorderly conduct, which express rejection of the value system they feel has rejected them. Instead of pursuing rational instrumental behavior for economic gain, these juveniles engage in irrational acts of defiance. Cohen is describing an adaptation that is akin to Merton's "rebellion." But he does not see blockage of financial success goals as an important motivating factor in delinquency.

Later conceptualizations of strain also tended to de-emphasize financial success goals, especially when considering juvenile delinquency, and instead focused on any valued goal (good grades, popularity, athletic ability, or physical attractiveness), the achievement of which can become blocked. This reconceptualization overcame a major limitation of the previous strain theories, namely the empirical evidence that delinquency was prevalent in the middle class, not just confined to the lower class. Contrary to the expectations of strain theories, empirical studies reveal that a strong attachment to the idea of achieving legitimate goals, no matter how much one actually expects to reach these, lowers the probability of delinquency (Hindelang 1973; Hirschi 1969; Johnson 1979; LaGrange and White 1985; Massey and Krohn 1986). So the gap between the goal of success (no matter how defined) and the expectation of achievement, the major source of strain emphasized in the strain tradition, does not appear to be a predictor of delinquency.[1] In fact, the studies tend to show that delinquents are those with low aspirations and expectations for achieving success, a finding more consistent with Hirschi's (1969) social control theory, which I discuss later.

By the early 1980s, the strain tradition seemed moribund. Then in 1985, Robert Agnew published an article that gave new life to strain theory. He reconceptulized strain theory by emphasizing a source of strain neglected by earlier strain theorists. Strain could also be caused by negative stimuli. "In particular, it is argued that adolescents are often placed in aversive situations from which they cannot legally escape" (Agnew 1985: 154). In contrast to the strain postulated by Merton and others in which the individual is blocked from achieving a desirable goal, Agnew posits another source of strain in which the individual is blocked from escaping a (physically or emotionally) painful situation. Such aversive situations can include "parental rejection, unfair or inconsistent discipline, parental conflict, adverse or negative school experiences, and unsatisfactory relations with peers" (Agnew 1985: 155). In a later work, Agnew (1992: 50) argued that strain results from negative relations with others "in which others are not treating the individual as he or she would like to be treated." According to Agnew (1985: 155), "aversive situations affect delinquency even when these situations do not seem to interfere with the achievement of valued goals." In the conceptualizations of Merton, Cohen, and Cloward and

Ohlin *frustration* was the emotion acted upon by the individual who was blocked from desirable goals. In Agnew's revised strain theory, *anger* is the emotional response to aversive situations.

> Anger, however, is the most critical emotional reaction for the purposes of the general strain theory. Anger results when individuals blame their adversity on others, and anger is a key emotion because it increases the individual's level of felt injury, creates a desire for retaliation/revenge, energizes the individual for action, lowers inhibitions, in part because individuals believe that others will feel their aggression is justified. Anger, then, affects the individual in several ways that are conducive to delinquency (Agnew 1992: 59–60).

Aversive situations and negative relations that are repetitive create a deep-seated sense of anger that predisposes a person to crime. Chronic strains of this type "increase the likelihood that individuals will be high in negative affect/arousal at any given time" (Agnew 1992: 61). Criminal events themselves may be directly triggered by an aversive situation in which strain is produced. "A particular instance of strain may also function as the situational event that ignites a delinquent act, especially among adolescents predisposed to delinquency" (Agnew 1992: 61).

For the development of a differential coercion theory of chronic criminality, Agnew's insights offer a major contribution. Situations and relations in which *interpersonal coercion* is a major feature constitute the most aversive and negative forces that individuals encounter. These interpersonal forms of coercion are a primary cause of the type of strain that produces a heightened emotion of anger. To the extent that this anger is directed toward others, rather than toward the self, predatory criminal behavior is more likely to result. Aspects of Merton's classic strain theory, which focus on economic pressures, are also important for differential coercion theory. Economic pressures are a major source of *impersonal coercion,* which creates a sense of desperation, reduces a person's sense of control, and often compels an individual toward actions that can be criminal in nature (Agnew et al. 1996; Hagan and McCarthy 1997; Menard 1997, 1995).

### Hirschi's Social Control Theory and Gottfredson and Hirschi's Self-Control Theory

Unlike strain theory, in which the person is pushed into criminal behavior by negative emotions, the social control and self-control theories maintain that individuals are naturally drawn to deviance unless restrained. In social control theory, these restraints are seen as social in nature. In self-control theory, the restraints are psychological.

Travis Hirschi (1969) is the most important theorist in this tradition. He postulates that individuals are prevented from following deviant impulses because bonds to society restrain them. These bonds include attachments, commitments, involvement, and beliefs. Attachments refer to emotional ties one has to others, especially to parents, teachers, and law-abiding, conventional friends. If you are highly attached to others, then you are constrained from considering criminal involvement out of fear of disappointing those you care about and who care about you. If on the other hand, you have no strong ties to others, then these considerations will not hold you back from considering a criminal act. Commitments refer to the investments one has made toward pursuing legitimate goals, such as education. The more you have invested (in time, money, and emotion) in pursuing conventional activities, the more you have to lose by committing a crime. You have developed a stake in conformity that you do not want to risk. On the other hand, if you do not have such a commitment to conventional goals, and your stake in conformity is low, then you may calculate that you have nothing or little to lose by taking a chance by committing a crime. Involvement refers to the time component. Those who pursue conventional activities to a high level have little time left for much else, including deviant behavior. On the other hand, those with much time on their hands may gravitate toward deviant pursuits. Beliefs refer to the moral feelings one gains as conventional attachments and commitments are pursued. These are seen as morally correct paths for action and any alternative produces a sense of guilt that blocks deviant behavior. Someone with low levels of belief in the moral rightness of pursuing law-abiding behavior will experience less guilt when contemplating a criminal act.

The focus of Hirschi's theory is on social relations that produce strong bonds during the socialization process. The absence of these relations produces an individual who is free to indulge in his or her natural impulses to pursue pleasure at any cost. Thus the focus of the theory is not on factors that cause people to deviate, but rather on factors that cause people to conform.

Hirschi does not discuss in much detail the types of relations that produce strong social bonds or weak social bonds. He assumes that someone who is socialized properly has strong social bonds. The origin of social bonds, however, is an important issue. One of the main arguments that John Pauly and I made was that social bonds arise out of relations of control (Colvin and Pauly 1983). As discussed earlier, coercive control was seen as producing weak, alienated social bonds.

Michael R. Gottfredson and Travis Hirschi (1990) extended the social control theory by refocusing on the internalization of self-control. They argue that crime is a direct result of an inability to control impulses for pleasure seeking. They point out that a wide array of behaviors result from low self-control and that criminals are people who generally indulge not only in crime but drugs, promiscuous sex, partying, and spending money well beyond their means. They have life-long problems with forming stable relationships because of their inability to control their impulses. The underlying and immediate source of all of these behaviors is an inability to defer gratification and to control oneself. Low self-control is thus seen as the primary characteristic of all criminals, including both street criminals and white-collar criminals (although application of their theory to the latter type of criminals has been questioned [Steffensmeier 1989]).

The source of low self-control springs primarily from a failure by parents to correct misconduct. Although Gottfredson and Hirschi do not go into much detail about the particular styles of correction that may be most effective for instilling self-control, they do state that consistent correction of misconduct is key and that it need not be harsh to be effective (Gottfredson and Hirschi 1990: 100). Early childhood becomes crucial in their theory because this is where self-control is instilled, or fails to be instilled. This is the key departure from Hirschi's earlier social control theory. In that theory, it can be argued that a person's social bond can change with new life events that create attachments that were previously lacking in the person's life. This change in social bonding would alter the person's behavior (see Sampson and Laub 1993). In self-control theory, however, criminal propensities are set in childhood and the person with such inclinations has problems of misconduct and related problems (such as unstable marriages, inability to hold a job, etc.) throughout the course of his or her life. Thus Gottfredson and Hirschi argue that self-control becomes an embedded personality trait early in life. Failure to instill self-control early in life means that it will never be instilled, and that such an individual will have problems deferring gratification the rest of his or her life. Such people have a greater propensity for committing crimes. In fact, the relation between low self-control and criminal behavior has been demonstrated empirically (Grasmick et al. 1993; Wright et al. 1999).

The connection to differential coercion can be made since coercive family discipline, as discussed by Patterson, can be seen as a major source of low self-control. As I develop more thoroughly later in this chapter, coercive discipline is usually erratic because constant monitoring of behavior is rarely possible and parents who use coercive discipline threaten, scold, and hit on a nearly random schedule that is not always contingent on misbehavior (Larzelere and Patterson 1990; Patterson 1982). So the child may not be able to predict when nothing will happen to him or her (more likely him, as I discuss later) or when severe sanctions may occur. In this erratic schedule, which is punctuated by coercion (at times violent), the child begins to learn that he cannot control consequences, which appear to occur randomly. If a child does not understand which consequences he will face according to which actions he makes, then there is no incentive or pattern for learning self-control. From the child's perception he thinks, "consequences do not arise from my behavior but appear to happen by luck—whether I get caught or not, whether mom or dad is in a bad mood, whether authorities believe my story, whether the teacher, police officer, prosecutor or judge happen to be lenient, overworked, ready to go home, etc." Since, as Gottfredson and Hirschi argue, deviance contains its own rewards, why not take the risk of indulging in impulsive behavior, luck might be on your side? Low self-control can emerge from this pattern of erratic coercive discipline as well as from lax controls in which virtually no discipline occurs. As I discuss latter, these two patterns of control (erratic coercion and that which is overly lenient) can produce different forms of deviance, a point made earlier in the discussion of Patterson's theory.

Early childhood discipline has an obvious effect on self-control. However, it is not clear whether or not once a child develops low self-control that he or she is doomed to have this trait the rest of his or her life. Gottfredson and Hirschi imply that low self-control becomes a hard-wired personality trait. But it is possible that a person's propensity for low self-control is partially sustained through social interactions that reinforce this trait. A person with low self-control invites external control from others, often of a coercive nature. These external controls only enhance the experience of being at the mercy of forces beyond one's control. The initial lessons about one's locus of control are reinforced as low internal self-control creates behavior that elicits high levels of external, coercive control. The cognitive connection between behavior and consequences becomes further broken if these external controls are delivered erratically. Thus someone may be sent on a pathway toward chronic criminality as external controls continually reinforce low self-control.

While this trait becomes a prominent feature of the individual's personality, circumstances and effective interventions can emerge and reverse this mindset. A person may learn that positive consequences can consistently result from behavior if the right situations arise so that he or she can regularly experience this. This can come about through an alteration in the way parents discipline their children (as in Patterson's parent effectiveness training) or through deliberate interventions in schools or treatment centers. But such interventions will inevitably be faced with the personal baggage left over from a life in which positive or negative consequences were thought to occur as a result of good or bad luck, not as a result of one's behavior. Removing such cognitive baggage requires not only a change in circumstances but also a change in perception (Beck 1995; Salkovskis

1996). The change in circumstances occurs when coercive relations are removed and social bonds are strengthened. The change in perception takes place when the individual begins to understand that many of the bad things that occur in life are a result of one's own behavior and that many more good things could occur if the individual could control his or her impulses. This cognitive change in the understanding of reality does not jump immediately from a change in circumstance. It has to be coaxed through a sustained experience (often as part of therapy) in which it becomes clear that this new perception of reality is true, that is, what I do really *does* lead to predictable consequences that I can control. When these circumstantial and perceptual changes occur, then self-control is exercised and slowly becomes a predictable trait.

Thus low self-control can be altered by later social relations in which positive social bonding occurs, but it is likely that once a person begins to exhibit low self-control he or she will become subject to coercive controls, which only sustain both low self-control and weak social bonds. But this is not inevitable. Life courses can and do take different trajectories than the paths initially set in childhood (Sampson and Laub 1993). But such changes require an enhancement of social supports that channel behavior in more positive directions.

### Cullen's Social Support Theory

Whether strain, low self-control, or coercion result in criminal behavior depends partially on social supports. Francis T. Cullen (1994) developed an integrated theory in which he argues that social supports can prevent deviant motivations from arising or they can channel these toward more positive behaviors. Social supports include both instrumental and expressive supports. Instrumental supports include material and financial assistance and the giving of advice and guidance. Expressive supports include the sharing and ventilation of emotions and the affirmation of one's own and others' sense of worth and dignity. Thus social support involves responsiveness to the needs and desires of others. It is not merely the actual delivery of these supports that affect the individual but also the individual's perception that he or she has such social supports. These supports exist at several levels of society, in the immediate interactions within families or among friends and within larger social networks of the community. Social supports are potentially provided during informal relations among families and friends and in formal settings such as schools, workplaces, and government agencies of welfare and criminal justice.

Cullen is able to explain differences in crime rates among nations and communities through the levels of social supports these geographic units provide. National and community policies that provide greater levels of social support enmesh greater numbers of individuals and families in supportive networks that prevent crime. The United States provides less official social supports than the social democracies of Europe (which provide paid family leave, more generous unemployment compensation, and greater financial support for education and welfare [Messner and Rosenfeld 1994]), which may partially account for the higher rates of crime in the United States. The lack of official social supports negatively affects the ability of families (especially poor families) to provide social supports on an informal level. When social supports are greater, the effects of criminogenic strains are lessened. When these are lacking, criminogenic strains are likely to have a greater impact.

The source of social support has a potential impact on criminal and non-criminal outcomes. Following Akers's (1985) social learning theory, the source may help model the behavior of the recipient of the social support. Thus if a law-abiding individual provides social support, his or her conforming behavior will be modeled. If, on the other hand, the provider of social support is deviant (a gang member giving advice or sharing material possessions or emotions with a friend) then this association may expose the recipient of social support to criminal role modeling and other criminogenic influences. Thus Cullen argues that social support from law-abiding sources is most likely to prevent criminal behavior.

Cullen argues that anticipating a lack of social support leads to greater involvement in crime. Here we can begin to connect Cullen's theory to the concept of differential coercion. Anticipation of a general lack of social support would be most likely for a juvenile or adult who has greater experience of coercion in the past. Coercion involves the threat of losing social support. For example, coercive work relations involve the constant threat of losing the instrumental social supports (money) that the job provides. Coercive family relations involve the actual or threatened loss of both instrumental and expressive social supports. (Coercive parents often threaten to throw a child out of the home, a version of the "tough love" approach which is often a precursor to greater involvement in delinquency.) Someone with these coercive relations in their background would be more likely to anticipate the same in the future. They become resigned to fate and lose any confidence in their ability to change the coercive circumstances in which they are seemingly trapped. Such low self-efficacy may contribute to a further weakening of social bonds and render the individual vulnerable to criminogenic influences. They see no way to elicit the social support necessary to remove them from coercive forces. Instead, they act out their anger (or is it *rage?*) through coercive acts of their own, which only invites further coercion and less social support. In addition, if an authority figure, even one who is otherwise law-abiding, fails to provide social support and in addition provides coercion, he or she may be modeling behavior in which nonresponsiveness to the needs of others and coercion as a way of acting toward others are learned.

To the extent that interpersonal relations and social settings lack social support, they can be seen as potentially coercive. The provision of social supports lessens the coercive nature of social relations. Without reducing social supports to mere control relations, we can nonetheless adapt Etzioni's (1970) types of control to Cullen's discussion. Normative controls can be seen as providing a high level of expressive social support in the form of emotional support, status, a positive identity, and a sense of belonging and dignity. Remunerative controls can be seen as providing instrumental support through the satisfying of material needs. Coercion threatens or actually removes these social supports. This is why coercion is such a strong motivator and why it has such deep social-psychological impact, such as the production of anger.

Cullen argues that an individual who gives social support to others is less likely to be involved in crime. These people are caught up in what I see as a virtuous cycle. They give social support to others who in turn give social support to them, which creates the environment for lower crime. Social support can be understood as responsiveness to the needs and desires of others, which Cullen (following Pepinsky's [1988] insight) argues is the very opposite of crime. On the other hand, a person can be caught up in a vicious cycle. The coercion and lack of social support that a person has encountered in the past create an individual who is unresponsive to the needs and desires of others and is more likely to use coercion in his or her relations with others. Such coercive behavior reduces the provision of social supports from others and often elicits coercion from others, thus deepening the vicious cycle of coercion that makes crime more likely. Thus there is a virtuous cycle of social support and vicious cycle of coercion. Much of this book focuses on the production and perpetuation of the vicious cycle of coercion.

Throughout the course of life, social supports may vary. Even someone on a pathway to crime can be turned around if social supports are provided. Current criminal justice policies in the United States for the most part are based on coercion, which undermines social support. A saner criminal justice policy, based on rehabilitation, would gradually enhance social supports as coercion is gradually reduced. As I discuss in chapter 6, the theory developed in this book, based in part on Cullen's social support theory, implies radical change in the way we deal with criminals. The key to reducing crime is to understand how the vicious cycle of coercion can be transformed into a virtuous cycle of social support.

## Athens on Brutalization in the
## Creation of Dangerous Violent Criminals

The vicious cycle of coercion is reflected most dramatically in Lonnie H. Athens's (1992) discussion of the development of dangerous violent criminals. For Athens, the key to understanding the creation of dangerous violent criminals is a careful examination of their social experiences. Drawing on the ideas of John Dewey (1929), Athens (1992: 15) argues that "a social experience emerges from the special interaction that takes place between a human organism and his social environment during the process of living. This interaction takes the form of human beings *acting* toward one another. What makes it special is that it generates both thoughts and emotions." The significant social interactions in the background of violent offenders involve heavy doses of coercion by others that produce in the individual cognitive and emotional states conducive to violence. The significant social experiences that produce dangerous violent criminals consist of four sequential stages through which the individual passes: (1) brutalization, (2) belligerency, (3) violent performances, and (4) virulency. Brutalization can take three forms: the experiences of violent subjugation, personal horrification, and violent coaching.

*Violent subjugation* takes two forms. It can involve (what Athens labels as) *coercion* in which "authority figures employ violence or the threat of violence to force the subject to comply with some command (including to show respect) which the subject displays some reluctance to obey or refuses to obey outright" in an act of defiance (Athens 1992: 29). This coercive subjugation is halted when the subject's defiance erodes into fear and the subject submits. This submission produces humiliation, which becomes the emotional breeding ground for revenge. Violent subjugation can also involve *retaliation* in which "authority figures use violence to punish subjects for past disobedience to them or for a present display of disrespect towards them" (Athens 1992: 31). What distinguishes coercion from retaliation is that submission by the subject ends coercive subjugation, whereas violence continues well beyond the point of submission in cases of retaliation. In the case of retaliation, feelings of dread, terror, and (finally) resignation overtake the subject. Even more than in cases of coercive subjugation, the subject develops an intense desire for revenge, entertaining fantasies of violence toward the subjugator. Coercive and retaliatory subjugation have different goals. In the former, short-term obedience is sought in a specific situation. The latter seeks to create a long-term state of submissiveness.

A second form of brutalization is referred to as *personal horrification* (Athens 1992: 38). In these cases, the brutalization is indirect since the subject does not personally experience violent subjugation, but witnesses someone who is personally close to him or her undergoing this ordeal. Feelings of anger toward the subjugator are suppressed as fear overtakes the subject. In fact, this anger turns inward as the subject castigates himself for his failure to intervene. Personal horrification describes the experience of a child who witnesses his mother being battered by his father. These experiences have long-term emotional effects on the subject. "Thus, although the experience of personal horrification may be less traumatizing than violent subjugation from a *physical* standpoint, it is not less traumatizing from a *psychological* standpoint" (Athens 1992: 44). In addition, such experiences combine with the subject's own experiences of violent subjugation to create a mixture of resignation and vengeful motives.

Both direct and indirect experiences of violent subjugation entail coercive behavioral modeling, which Athens (1992: 46) terms *violent coaching*. This concept derives directly from the social learning theory discussed earlier. Violent coaching is indirect, through the modeling of coercive behavior both observed and personally experienced, and direct, through active encouragement by an authority figure for the subject to respond to others with violence. Such instances as a parent mocking a child for backing down from a fight would be included in this type of coaching.

Brutalization, especially in combination of its three forms, creates a complex of conflicting emotions and thoughts that finally crystallize into a realization on the part of the subject that violence is often necessary for physical and psychological survival. Athens (1992: 60) describes this mind set as *belligerency* in which the subject resolves to use violence if circumstances necessitate this response. The subject is not going to take it anymore *from anyone*. His entire being is attuned to detect any potential for coercion from others that might require a violent response.

This state of belligerency is an immediate precursor of the performance of violent acts. But the connection to a mental resolve to use violence and actual violent behavior is indeterminate. Can the individual organize the emotions (letting anger override fear) and the behavior to create a violent response when strongly or moderately provoked by coercion from others? Are the courage and skills present to carry out such an attack? If these are not present, then belligerency will not lead to action. If they are present, then violent action is more likely in the presence of a strong or moderate provocation. If violent action occurs, many contingencies may prevent it from being successful in fending off another's attempt at coercion. Such failure may make future violent performances less likely. But if successful, the subject gains confidence that future provocations can be successfully combated. The experience of successfully performing violently in the face of coercive provocation facilitates the subject's progression toward the final stage of becoming a dangerous violent criminal.

These successful violent responses to strong or moderate provocations create a sudden and drastic change in the way others see the subject. He is now viewed as not only a "violent individual" but as a "violent crazy man" (Athens 1992: 73), which for some peer groups may be a positive attribute. Success in these violent encounters, especially if the success involved excessive violence well beyond that needed to stop the coercive provocation, helps foster this "crazy man" image that others now hold of the subject. He begins to be treated by others as a dangerous person; they act very cautiously toward him. As the subject experiences this violent notoriety and the trepidation it creates in others, he must decide whether to embrace or reject this violent image. Embracing the image has many immediate advantages that may be difficult, for someone who has a history of being subjugated, to pass up. The newly discovered sense of power is irresistible precisely because it reverses the equation of the subject's entire life up to that point. This revelation creates feelings of invincibility and omnipotence that directly lead to a state Athens (1992: 79) describes as *virulency*. The subject "now firmly resolves to attack people physically with the serious intention of gravely harming or even killing them for the slightest or no provocation whatsoever. . . . The subject is determined not to tolerate any provocation from other people, and, should the whim strike him, to provoke other people" (Athens 1992: 75).

What is important in Athens's theory is the role coercion plays in the background of violent criminals. They move from being the victims of coercive and retaliatory brutalization to being the perpetrators of this brutalization. Their life experience is filled with coercion that paves the way toward chronic violent behavior. Athens provides key insights into the creation of chronic violent criminals. But he offers little help in understanding other criminal behavior patterns. Can criminological theories using concepts similar to differential coercion explain a broader range of criminal and deviant behavior?

### Tittle's Control Balance Theory and Regoli and Hewitt's Differential Oppression Theory

Charles R. Tittle (1995) presents a significant new approach for understanding deviance that incorporates concepts similar to differential coercion and accounts for various types of deviant behavior. The core of control balance theory postulates that deviance is related to the ratio of control a person exercises to that which is exercised over the person. This ratio may be balanced (or equal to 1), in surplus (greater than 1), or in deficit (less than one). The theory postulates a nonlinear relationship between the control ratio and deviance. A balanced ratio of control is most conducive to conformity. A control imbalance is likely to produce a general predisposition to deviance of some type.

Tittle assumes that everyone shares an innate desire for autonomy, which appears in Tittle's theory to be a basic human drive. (In fact, without the postulation of this "autonomy drive," it is not certain that the theory as stated would work.) But this basic desire for autonomy comes into conflict (which can vary from a great deal to very little) with constraints imposed by social structures, physical environments, and other people. A *control balance* allows just enough autonomy and constraint so that you have no more control over other people or forces than they have over you. In such a situation you neither wish to extend greater control over others or fear having others reduce your autonomy. So there is no basis for a deviant motivation. A *control surplus* allows you to have more control over other people or forces (and greater autonomy) than they have over you. Under these circumstances (in which you feel little to no constraint) you will try to extend your control (enhance your autonomy) in ways considered deviant (exploitation, plunder, or decadence). A *control deficit* involves a loss of autonomy to the extent that other people or forces have more control over you than you have over them. Deviance under these circumstances is aimed at redressing or escaping the control deficit through predatory acts, defiance, or submission. Thus a general predisposition for deviance arises at the conjuncture of a control imbalance, the desire for autonomy, and (of less importance) the blockage (which threatens autonomy) of some basic human impulse, including both biological and socially created needs.

This general predisposition for deviance changes to a direct motivation for deviance when situational provocations and experiences of debasement occur. Such provocations emphatically bring into consciousness the control imbalance that underlies the motivation to deviate. If the provocation includes an experience of debasement, belittlement, or humiliation (rude reminders that in the situation you have less control or autonomy than imagined) deviant motivation is even more likely to arise. This deviant motivation will lead to an act of deviance if the opportunity presents itself.

As Tittle argues, the opportunity for some type of deviance is almost always present, but the form this deviance takes is not just a function of motivation and opportunity, it is also a function of constraint. Constraint will block (if it is strong) or allow (if it is weak) certain types of deviance. First, a degree of constraint is built into a control imbalance (either more constraint relative to autonomy in a control deficit, or less constraint relative to autonomy in a control surplus). Thus constraint in a situation of potential deviance is partly a function of the control imbalance that played into the creation of the deviant motivation. Second, situational risks contribute to the constraints on deviance, whether getting caught is high or low is a major risk assessment. Third, deviance can potentially elicit strong counter-control measures from others depending on the degree to which the deviance is considered serious. The interplay of these factors produces a degree of constraint on deviance and will determine the specific type of deviance engaged in.

Control ratios that are in deficit involve greater control experienced than exercised. That is, more repression than autonomy is experienced. The degree of repression is linked to the type of deviance that an individual can engage in. Those with marginal repression are most likely to engage in predatory acts (such as theft, assault, rape, homicide, or "any behavior in which one person directly preys upon another person or entity" including [inexplicably] "when a mother invokes guilt in her children to gain their attention" [Tittle 1995: 189]). The control imbalance and provocation motivates one toward deviance, but since the control imbalance involves only marginal repression, more serious predatory acts are allowed because this marginal repression translates into lower constraint. "The imbalance of control is small enough for people in this situation to sometimes be able to imagine that they can escape control from others. Such people have a low probability of deviance generally, but they are also the ones most likely to commit predation" (Tittle 1995: 189).[2]

Those who are under greater repression have even more constraints on their choices of deviance. Moderately repressed and extremely repressed individuals have a much greater chance of evoking counter-control measures if they were to attempt to redress a control imbalance through predatory behavior. Thus they must engage in less serious forms of deviance. Their larger control deficit gives them a stronger general predisposition to deviance than those marginally repressed, but this larger control deficit also subjects them to greater control and greater likelihood of strong counter measures against serious acts of deviance, such as predatory acts. Thus moderately repressed individuals are constrained to engaging in acts of defiance, which include protests or withdrawal from participation through activities such as drug use. Extremely repressed individuals, who have the highest general predisposition for deviance but are also the most constrained, are cut off from acts of predation and defiance and must submit. Such slavish submission is considered deviant in a culture like ours that prizes freedom and autonomy.

Control deficits are thus inversely related to seriousness of deviance because of the degree of repression involved. The greater the control deficit, the less serious the deviance.

Control surpluses have a positive relation to the seriousness of deviance. The greater the control surplus, the more serious the deviance. A control surplus involves greater autonomy, which means less constraint. Someone (or some social entity, since a corporation or government agency can enjoy a control surplus) may have a control surplus that gives them a minimal level of net autonomy. While they have some freedom from constraint, they cannot entirely escape the control of others, so they must engage in deviance that does not elicit direct counter controls. They will seek to expand their level of autonomy and control over other people or the social or physical environment through exploitation, "which involves indirect predation," such as price-fixing, shakedowns of merchants, bribery of officials, or hiring an agent to kill or discredit someone. A control surplus that Tittle describes as medium involves considerably more autonomy and less constraint. This level of control surplus will allow the person to engage in plunder, including such activities as environmental pollution, which show indifference "to the needs of others or to their potential responses." A control surplus in which an individual or social entity has maximum autonomy, with virtually no constraints on behavior, allows for deviance that Tittle labels decadence, such as an eccentric billionaire who engages in bizarre sexual activities because of boredom.

This basic core of the theory is supplemented by Tittle with discussions of contingencies that inhibit or accelerate the central causal process of the theory or change its manifestations. One of the more important contingencies he discusses is perception. The causal mechanisms will not come into play if an individual does not perceive, for example, a control deficit, even if one is present. Moral commitments may constrain an individual from acting on a control deficit or surplus even if it is obvious to the individual. A person may form certain conformist habits that restrain him from deviant responses or he or she may form deviant habits (through prior deviance) that make the causal process more likely to operate. Certain personality traits, such as self-confidence, impulsiveness, and intelligence, may alter the operation of causal mechanisms of the theory. The extent to which a person lacks skills in criminal techniques may in part determine if an opportunity for deviance can be taken, even if all the causal mechanisms are in place. Organizational contingencies, such as subcultures that encourage deviance, may distort the predictions of the theory because they may create a motivation toward deviance beyond what a control imbalance by itself would create.

Situational contingencies that alter the operation of the theory can also come into play. Clearly, the number and kinds of opportunities for deviance will determine the outcome of deviant motivation as will the perceived risk of being caught and being subjected to counter control. These are elements of the situation in which deviance is being contemplated. Another situational contingency, which is highly relevant for the differential coercion theory I develop in this book, is

> the degree to which individuals are made acutely conscious of their control ratios and of the possibilities for changing them through the use of deviant behavior. Recall that *provocation is an essential part of the control balancing process—with rare exception, deviance does not occur without it*. However, provocation is also a contingency; its intensity and frequency are conditions that influence the extent to which the control balancing process unfolds with greater or lesser force. The greater the provocation, the greater the chances of deviance specified by a particular control ratio, and the weaker the provocation, the lower the chances (Tittle 1995: 223, *emphasis added*).

Thus provocations are in the background helping to form a deviant motivation but they may also be in the immediate situational foreground accelerating the deviant motivation toward actual deviant behavior. This focus on provocation is a key point that I will return to when I connect Tittle's theory to the concept of differential coercion.

There are many elements of control balance theory that fit with differential coercion. Tittle's use of the concept of repression comes close to describing coercion. In a similar vein, Robert M. Regoli and John D. Hewitt's (1997) concept of oppression evokes the theme of coercion. In their differential oppression theory adults' desire to establish order in the home and in school "often lead to oppressive acts directed at children. Sometimes the coercion and force take the form of abuse and neglect, which diminishes the parent-child relationship and ultimately the child's respect for even legitimate authority" (Regoli and Hewitt 1997: 249–50). Children adapt to this coercive oppression by exercising illegitimate coercive power to gain a sense of control and autonomy. Or they retaliate against the adults who they blame for oppressing them. Or they turn inward, "becoming psychotically depressed or attempting suicide" (Regoli and Hewitt 1997: 250). There are some similarities between this theory and Tittle's, but Tittle's theory has the advantage of accounting (through the degree of repression in a control deficit) for why one of the above adaptations will be followed rather than another.

A major problem with Tittle's discussion, however, is that he does not differentiate types of control. A control deficit that accrues from a relationship in which normative or remunerative control is being exercised (following Etzioni's [1970] terminology) is likely to have a much different effect than one arising from coercive control. In Tittle's theory these would all be considered "repressive" since they create a control deficit. However, coercion is much more likely to produce a sense of alienation and other social-psychological states that are conducive to deviance than are the two other types of control. Perhaps, normative and remunerative controls are less likely to provoke *recognition* of a control deficit than is coercive control. In that case, it is possible to reconcile these types of control with Tittle's theory by focusing on their effects on provocation, which Tittle recognizes as an essential step in the production of deviant behavior. What could be more provocative of a deviant motivation or a deviant response than being forced by coercive means to do something against your will? As Tittle argues, such provocations are part of both the motivational background and the immediate social situation in which deviance occurs. Thus if coercion can be seen as one of the most important (if not the most important) forms of provocation, then Tittle's theory can easily accommodate the theme of differential coercion.

In fact, using the concept of coercion as an important element in provoking a motivation toward deviance means that we do not have to rely on an assumption about an underlying autonomy drive to make the theory work. Coercion is a force that motivates because it threatens to cut off instrumental and expressive social supports (Cullen 1994), unlike remunerative and normative controls, which, respectively, provide these. Whether or not there is a drive to autonomy becomes irrelevant when the theory focuses on types of control and the variations in social-psychological outcomes these produce. (But Tittle might counter that social supports are effective because they accommodate the drive to autonomy while coercion conflicts with the drive to autonomy, but this still begs some important questions.) The desire for autonomy may be a culturally produced need that becomes a *contingency,* rather than an underlying cause, in the production of deviant behavior. Some cultures promote autonomy more than others. Walter Miller (1958) recognized autonomy as a focal concern of the urban lower class, which he related to delinquency. The southern culture of honor, which has been linked to higher levels of violence, strongly promoted the value of individual autonomy (Wyatt-Brown 1982). Japan, which has one of the world's lowest crime rates, greatly devalues autonomy (Westermann and Burfeind 1991). (In addition, some people appear to have a need for dependency rather than autonomy. It might be argued that a dependency need arises from an extreme control deficit, but such an argument borders on the type of circular reasoning that Tittle warns against.) Thus the need for autonomy varies more widely than Tittle assumes and it can be understood as a cultural (and thus measurable) rather than a natural phenomenon. In Tittle's theory, desire for autonomy is akin to Freud's id or Nietzsche's will to power. But there is no need to assume such underlying (and thus unmeasurable) drives to successfully build a theory. Rather than conceptualizing desire for autonomy as an underlying natural drive, it can be seen as a culturally produced contingency that accelerates the causal process toward deviance. A person who places great value on autonomy is going to be much more affected by coercion than is someone who does not value autonomy.

A highly useful insight for building differential coercion theory concerns Tittle's discussion of the level of constraint. According to Tittle, someone with a control deficit may encounter marginal to extreme constraint (or repression). Another way of understanding this is that constraint may range from highly erratic to highly consistent. Earlier I discussed the differential impact that erratic and consistent forms of parental discipline have on self-control. With Tittle's theory, we can move this insight to any setting in which control is experienced. On the one hand, a person with a control deficit who encounters extreme constraint is likely to experience a very consistent coercive response to his or her deviance. On the other hand, someone with a control deficit but under marginal repression is likely to experience coercive responses on an erratic schedule when he or she is deviant. I would predict that someone who repeatedly encounters the latter schedule of coercive control is more likely to become a chronic criminal who (as Tittle also argues) engages in predatory crime.

Another important insight provided by Tittle's theory is that control has a nonlinear relation to deviance. That is, too much control and too little control can both produce deviance, though deviance of different types. This is similar to Patterson's (1982) argument, discussed earlier, that different parental disciplining styles can create different delinquent outcomes. Families that are more coercive produce overtly antisocial children (the "early starters" who are aggressive), while families that are overly lax and permissive produce covertly antisocial children (the "late starters" who associate with deviant friends and engage in lying, stealing, and property-oriented crimes) (Snyder and Patterson 1987: 236). Tittle generalizes this insight to all social settings in which control is exercised and experienced, and attempts to generalize it to all types of deviance. Tittle has perhaps extended his theory to too many types of deviance and does not clearly establish his definitions of seriousness and predation (as in his inexplicable example [p. 189] of a mother using guilt to attract attention as a serious predatory act). (See Braithwaite [1997] for a critique of Tittle's deviance categories.) But Tittle's insight concerning the relation between control patterns and variations in seriousness, frequency, and types of deviance is crucial for developing differential coercion theory.

# A DIFFERENTIAL COERCION
# THEORY OF CRIMINALITY

Drawing on the insights of previous theories, we are able to discern two important dimensions of control. First is the degree of coercion, ranging from extremely high coercion to complete non-coercion. Second is the degree of consistency, ranging from highly consistent to highly erratic. With these two dimensions I construct four types of control that have profoundly different effects on criminal and non-criminal outcomes: (1) non-coercive consistent control; (2) non-coercive erratic control; (3) coercive consistent control; and (4) coercive erratic control. I label these, respectively, Type 1, Type 2, Type 3, and Type 4 control (see figure 2.1). Type 1 consistently uses non-coercive control (both normative and remunerative) that provides the subordinate with consistently strong social support and consistent messages about realistic limitations on behavior. Type 2 erratically provides non-coercive control (primarily remunerative) that gives indifferent social support and few if any limits on behavior. This pattern coincides with Patterson's lax and permissive discipline and somewhat with Tittle's maximum autonomy. Type 3 consistently uses coercive controls, providing low levels of social support and myriad restrictions on behavior. This pattern coincides with Tittle's extreme repression. Type 4 erratically uses coercive controls providing low levels of social support and sporadic restrictions on behavior. This pattern coincides with Patterson's description of coercive interaction processes in which highly punitive actions occur erratically and are often not targeted at misbehavior. This section will spell out the nature of each of these control types, their differing effects on a series of social-psychological variables, and their effects on the frequency and types of crime and delinquency.

Coercion occurs when one is compelled to act in a certain way through direct force or intimidation from others or through the pressure of impersonal economic or social forces. Interpersonal forms of coercion may or may not involve the use of violence. Coercion can involve the threat of or actual taking away of something of value, such as a person's job or other social supports. It is punitive in nature. It motivates behavior because it is physically and/or emotionally painful and because it threatens to or actually does remove both expressive and instrumental social supports. Coercion, as I am using the term, encompasses Athens's (1992) definition of coercion and includes his concept of retaliation. Retaliation, in my use of this concept, is an excessively brutal and more unrelenting form of coercion.

Etzioni (1970) includes coercive compliance in his compliance theory, in which he proposes a relationship between certain types of power and

**Figure 2.1   Dimensions of Control: Degrees of Coercion and Consistency**

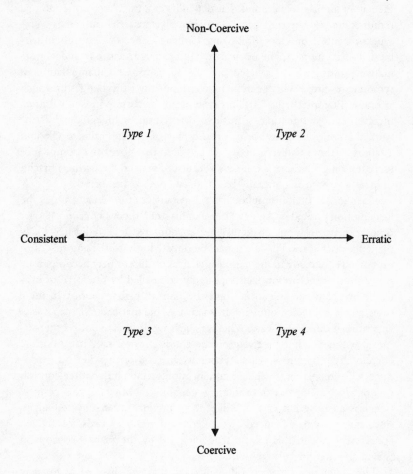

subordinates' orientation toward those who exercise control. A coercive compliance structure includes power that is based on "the application or the threat of application of physical sanctions" that include "controlling through force the satisfaction of needs" (Etzioni 1970: 104). This coercive power tends to create an "alienative involvement," an intense negative orientation (hostility, anger) on the part of the subordinate in the compliance relationship, which constitutes a very weak, alienated social bond.

Etzioni also discusses two other compliance structures. The utilitarian compliance structure is composed of remunerative power in which material rewards are manipulated for control. Subordinates in such a control relationship tend to have a "calculative involvement," which is an inter-mediately intense social bond that depends on a calculation of continual remuneration (or reward or other pleasurable material outcomes). This type of control provides (following Cullen's conceptualization) instrumental social support. The normative compliance structure includes "normative power," which is based on "the allocation and manipulation of symbolic rewards," which can include emotionally satisfying gestures such as praise (Etzioni 1970: 104). This type of power corresponds to a "moral involvement," designating "a positive orientation of high intensity" toward the controlling authority on the part of the subordinate (Etzioni 1970: 104). From Cullen's theory we can posit that normative compliance includes a high level of expressive social support and, following Hirschi, induces a very strong, morally based social bond to authority.

Coercion, as Etzioni implies, has a direct effect of producing anger, the key emotion posited by Agnew (1992) in his strain theory of crime. If, over time, coercive relations of control are encountered repeatedly, it is likely that anger will grow. The anger may be directed toward the authority figures involved directly in the compliance relationship, or may become more generalized as the person feels repeatedly compelled by the force of others or by economic and social forces beyond his or her control. In these cases, anger is directed outward. It is also possible that coercion can create anger that is directed inward. Whether anger is self-directed or is other-directed will depend, respectively, on the consistent or erratic nature of the coercion. Type 3 control, which is coercive and consistent, will tend to produce self-directed anger, since constant monitoring and counter controls do not allow the open expression of anger aimed at others. Type 4 control, which is coercive but erratic, will tend to produce other-directed anger, since anger may be enhanced by the perceived injustice of controls (which appear arbitrary in this erratic schedule) and by the many occasions in which counter controls are not elicited.

This difference between other-directed and self-directed anger may partly explain gender differences in predatory crime; males are more likely to be involved in these behaviors than females (Chesney-Lind and Shelden 1998; Elliott 1994; Tracy et al. 1990). Females who are under coercive relations of control fall more toward the Type 3 pattern, while males who are under coercive controls fall more toward the Type 4 pattern. Studies have demonstrated that girls tend to be more closely monitored than are boys (especially for sexual behavior) (cf., Chesney-Lind and Shelden 1998). This would tend to make these females' anger self-directed and males' anger other-directed when the predominate control structure is coercive. Other factors besides gender may channel anger inward or outward, such as cultural styles and religious beliefs. Certainly, Tittle's insight about constraint points to the impact of consistent versus erratic coercion on the self- versus other-directed nature of anger. In any event, repeated subjection to coercive relations produces anger and if this anger becomes other-directed through erratic application of control, then an individual will have a higher propensity for chronic involvement in predatory street crime.

Coercive control also affects a person's social bond. Repeated exposure to coercive relations creates weak attachments to the figures of authority that exercise control in these relations. In addition, a person's commitment to conventional activities is reduced as one's sense of self-efficacy is diminished. The individual under repeated coercive relations begins to lose confidence that he or she can create positive outcomes or reduce the influence of these outside forces. A commitment to the pursuit of conventional activities entails a belief that one has the self-efficacy (confidence) to reach conventional success goals (Bandura 1982, 1977). Being subordinated to coercive relations and forces on a repeated basis destroys self-efficacy and creates a sense of powerlessness.

Coercion also creates a highly external locus of control for the person who is the subject of long-term coercive control. A locus of control is the perceived source of demands on one's behavior, whether these demands come from within the individual or arise from other people or forces outside the person. Coercion tends to produce an external locus of control, as one must respond to the external demands of authority or outside forces. David Matza (1964: 188–89) relates this external locus of control to a "mood of fatalism" that "neutralizes the legal bind" and "provides a sense of desperation." "The mood of fatalism, it will be recalled, refers to the experience of seeing one's self as effect. It is elicited by being 'pushed around' and yields the feeling that one's self exercises no control over the circumstances surrounding it and the destiny awaiting it." In any context in which autonomy, "manliness," or the capacity to control one's surroundings is considered important, "the mood of fatalism will yield something approximating a sense of desperation." Matza understands delinquency as a willful and desperate attempt to regain potency in the face of fatalism and external control. Matza thus believes that delinquency is triggered by the mood of fatalism and is a desperate attempt to create its opposite. Coercive controls have the effect of creating this fatalistic mood.

If the coercive relation of control (or the experience of coercive impersonal forces) is also erratic then the propensity toward chronic predatory criminality will be even more enhanced. Not knowing for sure when behavior will be ignored or harshly punished leaves the person uncertain about how his or her behavior is related to consequences. In addition to the weak bond, low self-efficacy, and anger created by coercion, the erratic element will also create low self-control. Painful or rewarding consequences do not seem to accrue from behavior but from the arbitrary actions of authorities or the vagaries of circumstances. The person begins to sense that events are beyond his or her control. Thus a strong belief in fate and luck is fostered along with a mindset of "get it now" or "grab it while it's there" rather than deferring gratification. This is what experience teaches a person when he or she is subjected to erratic relations of control. If these also include a strong dose of periodic coercion, then low self-control can be added to weak social bonds, anger, low self-efficacy, and an external locus of control to create a stronger predisposition for chronic predatory criminality.

People who are repeatedly exposed to coercion (by seeing others subjected to it or by being subjected to it themselves) learn a model for controlling others. Following the social learning theory developed by Akers, coercive episodes become learning experiences from which individuals model their own behavior.

Coercive episodes also become events of provocation as the individual rudely comes to recognize his or her deficit in a control situation. This provocation, according to Tittle, directly feeds into the development of a deviant motivation, especially if accompanied by debasement or belittlement. Such humiliating provocations have even more pronounced effects for someone under an erratic schedule of coercion (the Type 4 pattern) because the subordinate is more likely to entertain illusions of autonomy under this erratic schedule than is a subordinate under a consistent regimen of coercive control (Type 3).

Thus coercion can be seen as setting into motion the social-psychological dynamics that the major theories of criminality discussed earlier posit as precursors to chronic involvement in criminal behavior. Coercion creates strain in the form of anger; it contributes to weak, alienated social bonds, low self-efficacy, an external locus of control, and, if delivered on an erratic schedule, low self-control. In addition, it models behavior for the individual when that person exercises control over others. And it becomes a provocation that produces a deviant motivation. These social-psychological variables are altered depending on the degree of coercion and consistency in control relations. In the discussion below, we explore the social-psychological and behavioral outcomes produced by the four types of control.

## THE VARIETIES OF CONTROL EXPERIENCES

As discussed in the previous section, relations of control come in varying forms defined by their degree of coercion and their consistency in application. Non-coercive controls can be either consistent, firm and fair, or they can be overly lenient, permissive, and erratic. I refer to these respectively as Type 1 and Type 2 forms of control. Coercive relations of control can be consistently punitive or erratically punitive. These are labeled Type 3 and Type 4 respectively in the following discussion. The form of control most conducive to chronic predatory criminality is Type 4, a coercive relation that is erratic and punitive. However, as discussed is this section, Type 2 control is also conducive to certain forms of criminality, as to some extent is Type 3.

The control relations described in this section (and this cannot be emphasized too strongly) should be considered as ideal types. Specific individuals, at any point in time, will likely fall somewhere in between these extreme types. Over time, a particular individual may experience a mix of these pure types, but it is likely that one or another will tend to predominate at least for a period of time. Most typically these control types would be applied to parental disciplining patterns, but they can be applied to any authority-subordinate relationship in which control is exercised. Also, impersonal economic and social forces may create differing levels of coercion and consistency experienced by individuals. These impersonal coercive forces have the same social-psychological and behavioral consequences as interpersonal coercive relations. Over time, a person may shift from one predominate type to another. This shift may occur for any number of reasons. Deliberate interventions by schools, social agencies and therapists, a change in the subject-of-control's behavior, or a change in the controller's behavior can alter the type of control. Sudden changes in economic fortune or social circumstances can also alter the pattern and level of coercion experienced by an individual.

Each type of control has different social-psychological outcomes and thus different effects on behavior. Figure 2.2 presents the social-psychological and behavioral outcomes that emerge from each type of control. The following discussion expands upon the relationships presented in figure 2.2 and draws upon the ideas of theorists discussed earlier in this chapter.

### Type 1: Consistent, Non-Coercive

This is a non-coercive type of control in which strong social support of both expressive and instrumental needs are provided. It utilizes a combination of normative and remunerative control. It involves no provocation that could become the basis for recognizing a control deficit. It produces the following social-psychological outcomes:

> Low anger
> High self-control, based on internalization of norms
> Internal locus of control
> High self-efficacy
> Strong, positive, moral social bond

No modeling for coercive behavior
No perceived control deficit or control surplus (control balance)

And it produces the following behavioral outcomes:

Generally non-criminal, non-delinquent
Strong tendency to engage in pro-social behavior

This type of control involves consistent, assertive interventions for non-compliance that are neither lenient nor overly harsh and punitive. (In the child discipline literature, this has been described as "fair but firm" [Loeber and Stouthamer-Loeber 1986; Wells and Rankin 1988]. Obviously I apply it beyond family relations.) It usually entails appeals to reason and persuasion rather than direct punitive measures; it rarely if ever involves physical punishments or threats. Subtle, rather than overt, coercion lays in the background, since the threat of punitive or negative consequences is the implied result when voluntary compliance fails to materialize. (Joan McCord [1995] argues that this subtle coercion is an essential element of successful socialization.) Rewards and positive feedback are consistently given for pro-social or compliant behavior and strong messages about the individual's worth and dignity are recurrently given. Rules are not overly strict but do place reasonable limits on behavior, and are often determined in consultation with the subordinate. Generally, a certain degree of autonomy is given the subordinate, who internalizes compliance norms and has a realistic understanding of limits. Constant monitoring of behavior becomes unnecessary since the internalization of norms produces effective self-monitoring. Since interventions are consistent, the person learns that his or her behavior can predictably lead to either rewarding or negative consequences. The individual develops a positive connection to the idea that one's own behavior can predictably produce positive life events and rewards. This leads to a high level of self-control in which an internal locus of control is produced. The person develops high self-efficacy because he or she gains confidence through experience that his or her voluntary pro-social behavior can consistently create positive outcomes. This becomes further reinforced when larger economic and social structures provide consistent positive outcomes. Such individuals enjoy conventional pursuits because of the emotional, social, and economic rewards they bring. Since authorities' interventions are aimed at correcting in a firm but gentle and fair way, anger is not produced. Respect for authority is instilled because of the consistency and firmness of the intervention and thus the social bond is highly positive, based on a moral commitment.

**Figure 2.2 Social-Psychological and Behavioral Outcomes Predicted by Four Control Types**

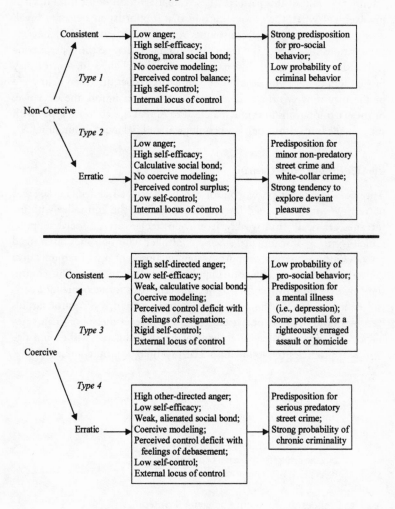

Type 1 control is the least likely to produce a propensity for criminal or delinquent behavior and is the most likely to insulate the person from exploring the pleasures of deviance. This is not to say that a person emerging from such control relations will be completely non-deviant and law-abiding. But deviant explorations will require rationalizations that "neutralize" the guilt that would otherwise hold these individuals back from deviant activities (Sykes and Matza 1957). Some white-collar criminals (usually of a less chronic variety) and short-term exploratory offenders would fit this pattern. These offenders soon desist from deviant involvement when the rationalizations that support their behavior break down and internal moral constraints reassert themselves. Such deviant explorations may, under the right circumstances, change the type of control under which the person has operated. This change in control may move them toward one or another of the three types discussed below. He or she may move to the lenient type if controllers ignore the deviance, or these explorations in crime may lead to one of the coercive types with subsequent impact on social-psychological and behavioral outcomes.

### Type 2: Erratic, Non-Coercive

This non-coercive type of control can be described as lenient, lax, and permissive with a detached interest on the part of the controller who intervenes erratically and weakly. It provides feeble, erratic social support, which is mostly instrumental since a controller who becomes disengaged provides little expressive support. At best, inconsistent use of remunerative control is used in attempts to manipulate a subject's behavior. This control type involves no provocation that becomes the basis for recognizing a control deficit; in fact, it often involves situations in which a control surplus becomes evident as the purported controller ignores the subordinate's behavior or is manipulated to accede to the subordinate's wishes and demands. It produces the following social-psychological outcomes:

> Low anger
> Low self-control
> Internal locus of control
> High self-efficacy
> Intermediate, calculative social bond
> No modeling for coercive behavior
> Perception of a control surplus

And it produces the following behavioral outcomes:

> Strong tendency to explore pleasurable deviant activities
> Manipulation of authority figures and of rules and procedures
> Lying
> Strong predisposition for less predatory, minor street crime
> Predisposition for white-collar criminality (if opportunity arises)

In this form of control, the person is usually ignored when non-compliant or is only mildly reprimanded when interventions do happen. On an erratic basis the controller may also attempt to bribe the subordinate into compliance. The person can readily predict that serious interventions will not arise from behavior, so the pursuit of pleasure or financial gain is not constrained and thus self-control is not induced. Erratic monitoring of behavior by external authorities means that the person is free to experiment and take risks. Such individuals are not driven by the compulsion of others or of events, and in fact they try to shape these to allow for greater pursuit of personal pleasure or profit. Thus they have an internal locus of control in which they direct their own pursuit toward maximization of pleasure or gain. Rules are ill defined, vague, and subject to change through persistent manipulation. Thus the person develops little in the way of appreciating limits on behavior and in this sense may exhibit distorted (even grandiose) self-efficacy (confidence) in his or her abilities to take on and overcome risks. The lenient nature of interventions (when they do occur) means that anger is not produced, although respect for authority (which presents itself as weak, detached, and apathetic) is not induced either. It is more likely that such individuals become indifferent to the demands of authority. The social bond is intermediate, based on calculation of reward through pleasure seeking.

Type 2 control predisposes the person to crime and delinquency that is generally less predatory, since it is not anger-driven. With low self-control, they are highly likely to explore deviant, pleasurable experiences, such as drug use, petty theft, sexual promiscuity, drinking, and other minor delinquent acts. Their combination of low self-control, intermediate calculative social bond, and high self-efficacy allows them to calculate pleasurable outcomes without having to neutralize guilt, while feeling confident in their abilities to manipulate circumstances to reduce risks. Some may become chronically involved in these types of activities as long as pleasurable rewards outweigh negative costs of continuing in these behaviors. When negative costs (to health, social relations, or freedom) begin to accumulate, the person is likely to desist from criminal involvement out of rational calculation that these deviant pursuits are no longer worth it. This type is congruent with the "adolescent-limited" pattern of delinquency in which juveniles engage in deviance for a period of time and then desist from deviant involvement (Moffitt 1997). Since the Type 2 pattern promotes chronic lying and manipulation, it also applies to the background of many white-collar criminals, especially to the more chronically involved ones. The patterns of control and crime emerging from Type 2 (which accounts for the majority of *offenders*) are most congruent with arguments from control theory since individuals in this pattern are acting free from external and internal constraints.

## *Type 3: Consistent, Coercive*

Coercive control in this pattern is delivered on a consistent schedule and creates a highly punitive relationship between the controller and the sub-ordinate. The relationship provides weak instrumental and expressive social support. In fact, to the extent that they exist at all, these social supports are constantly under threat of removal. It continually provokes recognition of a control deficit, which is obvious to the subordinate who develops a posture of resignation. The Type 3 pattern produces these social-psychological outcomes:

> High level of self-directed anger
> Rigid self-control, based on constant fear of a painful response
> External locus of control
> Low self-efficacy
> Weak, calculative social bond
> Strong modeling for coercive behavior
> Perception of a control deficit accompanied by resignation

And it produces these behavioral outcomes:

> Low probability of criminal behavior
> Low probability of pro-social behavior
> High probability of mental health problems, such as chronic depression
> Some potential for a righteously enraged assault or murder

In this form of control, the person is consistently met with a punitive response when not complying with rules, which are usually highly restrictive. Behavior is rarely ignored and rewards are rarely given for compliance. This control relation produces a highly external locus of control, as the person becomes fearful, submissive, depressed, and powerless. Anger tends to be directed inward since outward expressions of anger are met immediately with punitive responses. A sense of resignation to the demands of authority leads to few displays of defiance. The consistency of coercion tends to produce someone who *rigidly* monitors his or her behavior out of fear in order to avoid negative consequences, which they learn can be avoided only by very careful monitoring of behavior and following rules to the letter. The social bond lies between intermediate and negative, based on a calculation of avoiding pain. Self-directed anger focuses the negative feelings of alienation inward rather than outward.

Type 3 control is not likely to create a predisposition for criminality because of the close monitoring of behavior by external authority. Instead of crime, this style of control is more likely to produce problems related to mental illness, such as chronic depression. Pro-social behavior, such as the pursuit of an education or any activity that involves initiative or creativity, becomes highly problematic for such a person. But this control type can *under the right circumstances* lead to an explosion of violence if inner-directed anger is suddenly transformed into outer-directed rage (Katz 1988). The coercive behavioral modeling this control type provides may help form the impetus for such a violent outburst. If the nearly constant monitoring of behavior is lifted, inner-directed anger can be redirected outward since external constraints are not replaced by internal constraints. In fact, such a change would move the individual from a Type 3 toward a Type 4 pattern of control.

### *Type 4: Erratic, Coercive*

This control type involves a punitive reaction to misconduct that is highly inconsistent. Social support in this control relationship is weak to non-existent. The highly erratic nature of the coercion powerfully provokes a pointed recognition of a control deficit. This control type produces the following social-psychological outcomes:

> High levels of other-directed anger and defiance
> Low self-control
> External locus of control
> Low self-efficacy
> Very weak, negative, alienated social bond
> Strong coercive behavior modeling
> Strong perception of control deficit accompanied by feelings of
>    humiliation

And it produces the following behavioral outcomes:

> Defiant and hostile acts toward authority figures
> Coercion and intimidation of others
> Strong predisposition for chronic involvement in predatory street
>    crime

In this form of control, noncompliance is, on an erratic basis, either ignored or responded to with harsh punitive measures. At times serious noncompliance is ignored and minor noncompliance is severely punished. At other times, punitive responses may occur when no misconduct has taken place at all. On occasion, coercion takes the extreme form of retaliation, in which pain is inflicted well beyond the point of submission (Athens 1992). The schedule for such punitive interventions is thus erratic and arbitrary. Coercion that is inconsistent and seems arbitrary creates a strong sense of injustice and thus generates greater anger and defiance that are directed outward (Agnew 1992).

The erratic nature of the coercion also allows the individual to periodically escape control and, on random occasions, feel a sense of autonomy. Thus the experience of coercion (when it does happen) is highly provocative since greater feelings of debasement and humiliation accompany this rude reminder of a control deficit. An external locus of control is produced in which the individual feels at the mercy of events that are beyond his or her control; the inconsistency of coercion makes negative events appear to be random occurrences not the consequence of behavior. This pattern of inconsistency also produces low self-control. Lack of self-control means that few brakes are placed on the expression of anger that is directed outward. The social bond is highly negative, based on alienation and open hostility toward authority figures. Someone experiencing this type of control develops low self-efficacy since he or she has little confidence that *in the long run* his or her behavior will make any difference in removing negative consequences that seem to arise in circumstances beyond his or her control. But in the short run, coercion against others provides a sense of power that, at least temporarily, changes the individual's position in relation to coercive control.

For individuals emerging from a Type 4 pattern of control, crime tends to be impulsive with little rational calculation of costs or benefits of behavior; such consequences cannot be predicted but are seen as matters of luck and fate. (This is a major distinction between the criminal patterns of Type 4 and Type 2 since the latter involves a higher degree of rational calculation). Only short-term advantages often in the face of immediate coercive provocation are the anticipated outcomes of criminal behavior. This type of control produces a high predisposition for chronic criminality (the "life-course persistent" offenders [Moffitt 1997]). These offenders tend to start criminal behavior at an earlier age than do other offenders. While they engage in a wide variety of criminal behaviors, this group tends to engage more than other groups in predatory street crimes, including serious violent crimes (Elliott 1994). The coercive nature of these criminal acts is modeled by the coercive controls experienced by the individual. The patterns of control and crime under Type 4 (which accounts for the majority of street *crimes*) are most congruent with the strain theory explanation offered by Agnew (1992) because the individual is acting under the pressures of extreme negative stimuli.

## COERCION AND CHRONIC CRIMINALITY

It needs to be emphasized that under ordinary circumstances, coercion will tend to be more or less erratic. Extraordinary measures are usually required to consistently monitor behavior in order to deliver coercion on a consistent basis for rule violations. Snyder and Patterson (1987), in the context of parental discipline, discuss the enmeshed versus lax styles of disciplining. Enmeshed parents tend to be more coercive and do not ignore even trivial rule violations. But Snyder and Patterson explain that even enmeshed parents cannot punish each instance of misbehavior, so this style is often rendered inconsistent.

Since coercion does not produce an internalization of norms, self-monitoring in the absence of close supervision (as I predict for the Type 1 pattern) is not to be expected in the coercive forms of control. Under coercive conditions, self-monitoring of behavior can only be expected in the presence of fear of external coercion, which arises from consistent application. When that consistent application is lifted so is the self-monitoring, and a Type 3 control pattern can move toward a Type 4 control pattern. In some cases, an individual may move from a Type 3 coercive control pattern in childhood to a Type 4 coercive control pattern as parents monitor behavior less when the individual nears adolescence. A similar shift in control patterns could also accompany movement from a highly controlled, coercive workplace to a state of unemployment on the streets.

As mentioned earlier, this distinction between erratic and consistent control types has important implications for understanding gender differences in criminal behavior, since the degree of monitoring during childhood and adolescence appears to be much greater for females than it is for males (Chesney-Lind and Shelden 1998; Morash 1986; Rosenbaum 1987). This is a subject explored further in chapter 3.

While differential coercion theory explains a wide range of behavior and includes non-coercive relations, it is the impact of coercion on creating a predisposition for chronic predatory criminality that is the major focus of the next three chapters of this book. The control relations typical of Type 4 are most conducive for creating chronic predatory criminals. The other control types are important for purposes of comparison and for understanding other criminal and non-criminal behavior patterns. In chapter 5, where I connect the situational foreground of crime to the developmental backgrounds of individuals, I will come back to a discussion of these other control types and the criminal behavior patterns they produce.

I contend that coercive relations of control are conducive to chronic predatory criminality because they create a particular complex of emotions and personality traits: other-directed anger, low self-control, external locus of control, low self-efficacy, weak social bonding, coercive behavioral modeling, and perception of a control deficit that evokes debasement and humiliation. I label this complex set of emotions and traits *social-psychological deficits*. These social-psychological deficits include variables that have been related to criminal behavior and delinquency in the theories discussed earlier and in several research studies (Caspi et al. 1994; Grasmick et al. 1993; Peiser and Heaven 1996; Shaw and Scott 1991). But rather than viewing individuals as having hardwired personality traits (as Gottfredson and Hirschi [1990] do in their self-control theory), such traits are seen as arising out of coercive relations (initially in families [Patterson 1982]) and sustained by continuing coercive relations in a wide range of settings. The individuals who develop these social-psychological deficits have a high probability of eliciting coercive controls from authority figures and from peers. Thus there emerges a reciprocal relationship between these coercive controls and these social-psychological deficits that makes it more likely that the individual will be sustained in a path toward chronic criminality (Sampson and Laub 1993).

Together, these experiences of coercion and these social-psychological deficits contribute to the creation of *coercive ideation* in which an individual comes to view the world as an all-encompassing experience of coercion that can only be overcome through coercion. (Coercive ideation is similar to Athens's [1992] concept *belligerency,* discussed earlier.) Following insights from Tittle's control balance theory, the individual under Type 4 control, due to its erratic application of coercion, imagines that coercive attempts to overcome such an environment can be successful (at least in the short run). In contrast, an individual under Type 3 control, with its consistent application of coercion, will find it difficult to conceive such transcendent moments of deliverance. Only in a rare circumstance can such an individual muster the rage to organize their behavior into an attack, which is often futile, on the coercive source of their continual subjugation and humiliation (Katz 1988).

The theory I am developing should not be taken as a deterministic statement that predicts an inevitable outcome of chronic criminality. If relations change from highly coercive to non-coercive, an amelioration of social-psychological deficits may occur. Certain life events may create turning points that redirect the person away from criminal behavior (Sampson and Laub 1993). As I argue in this book, such turning points can involve a movement away from coercive to non-coercive relations and thus alter the social-psychological deficits that are conducive to criminal behavior. However, these are difficult turning points since these social-psychological deficits are not altered overnight. They may continue to elicit coercion and thus make the turning point a difficult juncture to maneuver.

Turning points such as these occur in an indeterminate fashion, depending on situational contingencies and chance encounters with individuals who make significant differences. For this reason, we must develop less deterministic theories that take into account unpredictable life changes (Henry and Milovanovic 1996). For instance, a boy from a coercive family environment may by sheer luck be assigned to a teacher who is especially skilled in working with "difficult children." She patiently works through his disruptive behavior; she uses consistent, non-coercive methods and slowly gains his trust and compliance. He begins to develop a strong social bond with her, gets a sense that he can control what happens to him, internalizes this into stronger self-control, reduces his anger, and begins modeling his behavior after her example. The encounter with this unusually patient and skilled teacher would stand as an important turning point for this child. Unfortunately, as is more likely to be the case, the child will encounter teachers who lack such skills and who view the "problem child" as a nuisance rather than a challenge. The child's behavior in this case is likely to elicit coercive responses from the teacher and the school, which only exacerbate the social-psychological deficits that propelled the child's behavior in the first place. For this child, continuity of behavior will be sustained through further coercive encounters with authorities in schools and other settings and with peers who often share the same coercive backgrounds. But, as I discuss in chapter 6, these tragic outcomes need not happen. We can, with better knowledge of what we are doing, create turning points for more individuals at earlier ages and thus take them off the trajectory leading toward chronic criminality. But in order to do this we must understand the connections between coercive controls, the social-psychological deficits these create, and chronic criminality.

Coercion can be direct, arising from an actual interpersonal relationship of control, or may be indirect, arising from impersonal forces beyond the individual's control. One such impersonal force is economic. Economic conditions may compel a person to stay in a coercive relationship (at work or in a family), to leave a job he or she likes, to move to a location to which he or she does not want to go, or to take a job when he or she does not want to. Changing conditions of unemployment may, on an erratic basis, repeatedly move a person back and forth from highly coercive workplaces to the streets where little direct control exists; thus an erratic schedule of coercive control may be produced by these larger impersonal economic forces. All of these can be experienced as erratic coercion and may have the same social-psychological impact on the individual as do direct interpersonal relations that involve inconsistent coercive control.

There is a tie between interpersonal coercive relations and these impersonal forms of coercion. A coercive interpersonal relationship may be more difficult to escape if impersonal forces do not allow access to legal escape routes. For instance, a person in a coercive relationship at work will find it difficult to escape if unemployment is high and alternative jobs are scarce. Such a situation also makes it easier to enforce a coercive control strategy at the workplace, since the threat of firing someone from the job has much greater impact if the person faces destitution as a result. Also in families, if control relations are highly coercive but the controller also holds economic power, it is much more difficult for spouses and children to escape if alternative forms of economic subsistence are truncated by larger economic conditions. These impersonal economic forces become coercive in and of themselves and they reinforce the interpersonal relations of coercion in various settings.

Coercive relations can appear in any number of settings, including workplaces, families, schools, among peers, and in state bureaucracies, such as welfare and criminal justice agencies. A person may pass through each of these settings in which various control relations are experienced. *To the extent that these settings create an accumulated experience of coercion, then the greater likelihood that the person will experience anger, weak social bonding, an external locus of control, low self-efficacy, coercive behavior modeling, and a perception of a control deficit.* Together, these controls and social-psychological deficits contribute to the development of coercive ideation. *To the extent coercion is erratic, then the perceived control deficit will provoke feelings of debasement and humiliation, the anger will be directed outward, self-control will diminish, and coercive ideation will include the thought that a coercive environment can be overcome through coercion.* These in turn produce a stronger predisposition for chronic predatory criminality.

The immediate contexts of work, family, school, peer relations, and welfare and criminal justice agencies are the locations in which the general theory of differential coercion operates. These specific contexts can in turn be shaped by larger cultural and economic forces, which will either exacerbate or reduce the degree of coercion experienced in these specific contexts. In chapter 3 we explore these specific contexts and in chapter 4 we look at the larger economic and cultural forces that affect coercion.

Can the propositions contained in the differential coercion theory help us interpret findings from criminological studies? The next three chapters look at a wide range of research findings from both quantitative and qualitative studies; this review of research provides a preliminary test of the propositions developed in this chapter. The review also helps us flesh out and refine the theory based on what is known about the causes of criminal behavior.

# Chapter 3

# The Immediate
# Contexts of Coercion ◉

The general propositions about the effects of differential coercion discussed in chapter 2 are here placed in various contexts in which coercion might be experienced. Immediate contexts include workplaces, families, schools, peer groups and gangs, and criminal justice and welfare agencies. It is from these social settings that studies of crime and delinquency most often develop measures of the variables that are believed to be antecedents to delinquent and criminal behavior. I contend that coercion to varying degrees is an important feature of these social settings. Yet coercion is a variable that is often overlooked in studies of crime and delinquency. It is a concept that may provide a richer explanation of the relationships between these social settings and the production of chronic criminality. This chapter and the two that follow examine evidence from a wide array of studies to determine, at least preliminarily, if the propositions contained in chapter 2 provide potentially robust explanations of empirical observations.

## WORKPLACES AND LABOR MARKETS

Various methods of workplace control have developed historically through the struggles between management and labor and through the imperatives of market competition. These larger historical trends will be discussed in the next chapter. For now, it is enough to note that these trends have produced differences in the way people are controlled at work and have created major fractions within the modern working class.

Richard Edwards (1979) presents a comprehensive analysis of major working class fractions, which he differentiates largely by the ways control is exercised in each. Fraction 1 is composed of workers who labor in more competitive industries and are involved in a "secondary labor market," which operates largely by the law of supply and demand for labor in setting the price of labor power. Thus, fraction 1 is most affected by, and includes a huge proportion of, the surplus population of unemployed persons, who through economic desperation and various state controls are compelled to compete for fraction 1 jobs. Fraction 1 jobs are "typically dead-end jobs, with few prospects for advancement and little reward for seniority in the form of either higher pay or a better job" (Edwards 1979: 167).[1] Employers in these jobs forcefully and successfully resist organizing efforts by workers.

Edwards defines the type of control used over fraction 1 workers as "simple control," which corresponds to Etzioni's (1970) "coercive compliance structure." This compliance structure rests predominately on coercive power, which is "the application or threat of application of physical sanctions" that include "controlling through force the satisfaction of needs." Threatened or actual dismissal from the job definitely involves the forced removal from the means for satisfying basic needs and thus is a coercive control mechanism. Such a threat hanging over the head of an employee allows an employer to treat employees in more punitive ways on the job. Of course the degree to which this type of workplace control can be effectively implemented is related to the size of the pool of unemployed people who are actively seeking work. If a person cannot be readily replaced or if the person can easily obtain another job, then the threat of job loss becomes less effective as a control tool. Thus the condition of the outside labor market affects control at the workplace, especially for workers in this fraction of the working class. There is a large turnover of employees in fraction 1, which undermines labor-organizing efforts and also reflects the predominate mechanism for worker control—threatened or actual dismissal from the job.

Because job turnover is high, a segment of people connected to this fraction of the working class will experience an erratic pattern of control, shifting from various coercively controlled workplaces, to no control at all, to control by state welfare and criminal justice bureaucracies. These erratic shifts are created by the whims of both employers and a changing economy. We should expect, then, that the surplus population connected to fraction 1 of the working class would be most likely to experience an erratic coercive experience that swings between no control and coercive controls at workplaces and state bureaucracies. As I discussed in chapter 2, coercive power, especially when it is experienced erratically, produces, among other attributes, an intensely negative bond to authority, other-directed anger, and low self-control. As these social-psychological attributes are created, we can expect that the person's involvement with workplaces will become increasingly erratic, leading to a vicious cycle. It is not only the coercion at work, but also the coercion of economic circumstances that makes one go to work against one's will that enhances the experience of coercion.

The other fractions of the working class involve less coercion. Fraction 2 is composed of organized workers who, through earlier struggles, gained wage and benefit concessions and protections from job competition through the establishment of industry-wide unions. According to Edwards, capitalists and their managers were forced to shift from the coercive "simple control" to a less coercive, more sophisticated "technical control" in response to organized worker resistance to the arbitrary and coercive discipline of simple control. Technical control is machine paced and impersonal and relies on the worker calculating his or her material self-interest for pay raises and job security based on seniority with the firm. Edwards identifies fraction 2 workers as being involved in a "subordinate primary labor market" that relies very little on the external pressure of job competition from the surplus population. Workers in this fraction are also protected by more generous, union-connected unemployment benefits. Job performance is usually routine and boring and holds little intrinsic interest for the worker. The main control is calculation of extrinsic rewards of material security through movement up a union pay ladder; this process produces a firm-specific "internal labor market" (Edwards 1979: 172). This form of control, which defines fraction 2, is non-coercive, similar to Etzioni's (1970: 109) "utilitarian compliance structure" that includes "remunerative power," involving the manipulation of material rewards. A "calculative involvement" of intermediate intensity on the part of the worker is produced in this type of control structure. It is a precarious ideological bond, depending on continual remuneration and advancement up the pay ladder and producing little loyalty on the part of the worker. Fraction 2, as I discuss in chapter 4 where we consider larger economic trends, has been most devastated by corporate restructuring and the global movement of capital since 1969. For many fraction 2 workers, this has meant movement to fraction 1 jobs or the loss of remunerative benefits as they precariously hold on to fraction 2 jobs. The drop in inflation-adjusted wage rates from the mid-1970s to the mid-1990s was largely the result of a decline in fraction 2 jobs and an increase in fraction 1 jobs. With global labor competition, fraction 2 jobs, which were formerly protected from competition of the surplus population, are now subject to competitive labor market pressures. This has made many fraction 2 jobs resemble more closely the coercive relations found in fraction 1 jobs. This is also reflected in the steep decline since the 1950s in the percent of workers who are union members.

Fraction 3 is defined by its involvement in an "independent primary labor market" composed of jobs that are likely "to require independent initiative or self-pacing" (Edwards 1979: 174). Occupations in fraction 3 are ruled by more universal standards of professional or craft guild conduct. This differs from the machine-paced and firm-specific standards of the "subordinate primary labor market" of fraction 2. This fraction, just as other working-class fractions, spans both blue-collar and white-collar occupations. What makes this fraction distinct is the self-pacing and relative autonomy that workers enjoy, which makes control of these workers much different than in the other two fractions. The surplus population plays virtually no role in controlling fraction 3 workers since higher professional and educational requirements or craft guild membership and high levels of skill prevent most workers from competing for these jobs. These factors make coercive controls untenable (unless high unemployment in a specific occupation allows for ready replacement of workers). The work tasks of fraction 3 occupations preclude the use of pure technical control, since these tasks cannot be easily routinized, requiring instead a certain degree of flexible response and initiative on the part of the worker. Thus, a noncoercive "bureaucratic control" (Edwards 1979: 131) is necessary to gain compliance from fraction 3 workers. Bureaucratic control involves an elaborate manipulation of symbols and statuses that elicits ideological commitments to the organization. (The Japanese auto corporations, which create a family-like bond of high loyalty with its workers, have perhaps come closest to perfecting this form of control.) The bureaucratic control structure "fosters occupational consciousness; that is, [it] provides the basis for jobholders to define their own identities in terms of their particular occupation" (Edwards 1979: 177). Thus, fraction 3 jobs hold more intrinsic meaning for these workers and foster self-control based on an internalized locus of control. While pay scales are commensurate with increases in job status, it is primarily the possibility of enhanced status and greater autonomy and self-pacing that compels worker compliance. Bureaucratic control corresponds to Etzioni's "normative compliance structure," which includes "normative power" that "rests on the allocation and manipulation of symbolic rewards" (Etzioni 1970: 104). This compliance structure elicits a "moral involvement," designating "a positive orientation of high intensity" on the part of the worker toward authority and the organization (Etzioni 1970: 107). While ultimate decisions about the organization are left to owners and top management, status among fraction 3 workers is based on the degree of autonomy and decision-making power allowed for each position. Status comparisons with peers provide a strong element of control. The job experience of fraction 3 workers, in which more complex tasks are encountered and greater autonomy and decision-making are exercised, conditions these workers' ideological orientation toward a more positive bond to their work, to authorities at the workplace, and to their organization.

The three fractions of the working class are based on the experiences that arise from the three primary structures of workplace control. These structures of control at the workplace are among the factors that help condition the extent (if any) to which an adult will possess social-psychological deficits. Coercive workplace environments contribute to higher anger levels, lower self-control, an external locus of control, lower self-efficacy, weaker social bonds, stronger coercive behavioral modeling, and a perceived control deficit that provokes feelings of debasement. The more coercive these structures of control at work, the greater the social-psychological deficits.

Since these workplace control structures correspond to labor market segments, we would expect that neighborhoods that contain greater secondary labor markets (those that operate directly through supply and demand of labor and are thus more inclined to be coercive) would have higher rates of crime. In fact, Robert D. Crutchfield (1989), basing his study on "dual labor market theory" (which distinguishes "good" primary labor market jobs from "bad" secondary labor market jobs), found that neighborhoods with higher levels of unemployed people, part-time workers, and those employed in secondary occupations have higher rates of violent crime. It is the unstable nature of employment in secondary ("bad") jobs that appears to be related to higher crime. Crutchfield argues that employment in secondary jobs, which have high turnover, offers limited opportunity to develop social bonds to a job, a workplace, or to co-workers, and thus contributes to a general weakening of social bonds and to a lower "stake in conformity." He also attributes the relationship between work instability and crime to "a situation of company" in which people not fully involved in the labor market spend significant time hanging out on the streets to become the personnel for street subcultures that encourage crime and deviance. Other studies of labor markets, bad jobs, and crime replicate Crutchfield's findings (Allan and Steffensmeier 1989; Crutchfield and Pitchford 1997).

I suggest a different interpretation of these findings than the one offered by Crutchfield. In the theory developed in this book unstable employment in secondary, fraction 1 jobs places these individuals under an erratic schedule of coercive control and thus contributes to the production of social-psychological deficits (including weak social bonding) that would make them more likely to engage in chronic criminality.

Such an interpretation may also help us understand the connection between teenagers' labor market participation and youth crime. Recent studies using samples of teenagers have uncovered a link between greater hours of working while in school and delinquency (Cullen, Williams, and Wright 1997; Williams, Cullen, and Wright 1996; Wright, Cullen, and Williams 1997). Francis T. Cullen and his co-researchers (1997: 129) interpret this finding by pointing to the structural context of the youth labor market: "From this perspective, the extensive employment of adolescents serves economic interests in two ways: as a pool of low-wage labor for jobs located in the secondary labor market, and as a pool of potential consumers to be enticed to desire goods and services." The demand for inexpensive, part-time labor has led to greater labor market participation for youth in just the types of labor markets (secondary) that, according to Edwards (1979), contain the most coercive relations of control. The part-time nature of this employment would render these controls erratic. Given that the United States employs more school-age adolescents than other advanced industrial societies, it is not surprising that we have a larger youth crime problem. While other interpretations of these findings are possible—work weakens the teenager's bond to school, work exposes teenagers to older, deviant individuals—it may also be the coercive nature of the types of jobs available to teenagers that creates the link between hours worked and crimes perpetrated. The specific processes involved here have not been researched, so we can only speculate that coercive work experiences of teenagers affect their social bonds and other social-psychological variables that lead to criminal behavior. For teenagers who already have accumulated social-psychological deficits, and are most at risk for criminal behavior, involvement in a coercive workplace (such as those available to teenagers) may add to these deficits and push them further along the path toward chronic delinquency (Wright, Cullen, and Williams 1997: 215). Presumably, high-quality jobs (involving less coercion and connections to meaningful adult roles and strengthened social bonds) would not have these effects, and in fact would tend to turn juveniles away from criminal involvement. So work per se may not be the key variable, but rather the *quality* of work available. Work quality is related to the coerciveness of relations at the workplace.

Given the weak social bond and reduced loyalty to the workplace produced by the coercive controls of secondary, fraction 1 jobs, it is also likely that these workplaces produce higher levels of workplace crime, including large-scale employee theft (Clark and Hollinger 1983; Coleman 1994; Greenberg 1990). It is likely, although research on this point is scant (Kraus 1987), that workplace violence, including that aimed at co-workers and supervisors, is also more likely to occur in occupations that generally are in secondary (fraction 1) jobs. Workers in fraction 3 jobs, which are least coercive and more likely to produce a high sense of loyalty to the organization, are more likely (when criminal) to engage in crimes that benefit the organization for which they work. The latter pattern of criminality is typical of governmental and corporate forms of white-collar crime (Coleman 1994).

For understanding the background to chronic involvement in street crime, the most important impact of workplace and labor market coercion is on the disciplinary styles parents use in their families. It is here that we see the beginning of a developmental process that can ultimately lead to chronic criminality.

## THE FAMILY

Families differ in the ways they carry out discipline. Research has tended to focus on four disciplinary styles: punitive, lenient, erratic, and "firm but fair" (Barkan 1997: 204–5; see also Loeber and Stouthamer-Loeber 1986; Wells and Rankin 1988). Punitive discipline involves very strict rules and frequent corporal punishment even for trivial offenses. Lenient discipline is lax or permissive involving few rules and allowing children to do just about anything they want. Erratic discipline inconsistently swings between punitive and lenient. In "firm but fair" discipline parents set clear and reasonable rules, give positive feedback, show affection, and use reason rather than physical punishment, which is only rarely if ever used. Research indicates that "firm but fair" discipline is the most effective in preventing delinquency (Loeber and Stouthamer-Loeber 1986; McCord 1991; Rankin and Wells 1990; Wells and Rankin 1988). Harsh, coercive discipline tends to increase crime and delinquency, as does erratic discipline (Loeber and Stouthamer-Loeber 1986; McCord 1991; Rankin and Wells 1990; Straus 1994; Straus et al. 1991).

If harsh punishment is taken to extremes, it becomes abusive. As Wauchope and Straus (1990: 147) argue, "Although most physical punishment does not turn into physical abuse, most physical abuse begins as ordinary physical punishment." Child physical abuse, the most extreme form of disciplinary coercion, has been linked to both juvenile delinquency and later adult criminality, especially to violent forms of these behaviors (Hotaling et al. 1990; Simons et al. 1994; Smith and Thornberry 1995; Straus 1994; Widom 1992, 1989). Joan Moore (1991: 92–95) reports in her study of east Los Angeles barrio gang members that over half of her sample expressed fear of parents based on their childhood experiences of physical abuse and punitive discipline. Mark S. Fleisher's (1995) ethnographic study of gang members and John Hagan and Bill McCarthy's (1997) study of homeless, delinquent street youth are replete with descriptions of abusive discipline in the backgrounds of these studies' subjects.

Snyder and Patterson (1987: 221) argue that inconsistent but frequent punitive discipline "sets up a coercive pattern of family interaction which elicits, maintains, and exacerbates the aggressive behavior of all family members." Aversive behavior by one family member engenders retaliatory actions by other family members. These aversive interchanges escalate until one of the participants yields. Since these coercive behaviors are often successful in temporarily stopping aversive actions of other family members, these interchanges encourage the use of this coercive style of control in future encounters with others. In this way, "highly aggressive children teach their parents to use high intensity, harsh discipline tactics, and the parents teach their child to persist in and to escalate their aversive behavior in the face of sibling, peer, and parental punishment of that behavior" (Snyder and Patterson 1987: 222). Thus coercive discipline in the home provides a training ground in coercive behavior for children.

Parents' coercive behavior toward their children is partly modeled on their experiences at work. Melvin Kohn (1977) found evidence that parents who experience greater external control at work impress upon their children conformity to external authority. In contrast, parents who experience a lower degree of external control and exercise greater decision-making power and autonomy at work come to view internalized self-control, initiative, and creativity as valued attributes that are impressed on their children. Kohn also found evidence that parents who work in more tightly controlled and routinized work situations (more typical of the fraction 1 jobs discussed earlier) use more punitive and physical disciplining practices and punish their children more for the consequences of their acts than for perceived intent of their behavior. Parents from more "self-directing" work situations (similar to the fraction 3 jobs discussed earlier) are less punitive, use reasoning more often than physical punishment, and ascertain the child's intent in determining whether or not to punish the child. An underlying message to the child in both instances is an ideological statement about the world: control of life circumstances and the determinants of one's behavior spring from either external compulsion or internal motivation. The child, in his or her everyday interactions with parents, learns that one acts toward authority either out of fear or calculation of external consequences or out of a sense of internalized respect or commitment. This is the same ideological message the parents receive from their experiences at work. Kohn's findings about workplace control and parental values and discipline have been replicated by several quantitative studies (Coburn and Edwards 1976; Erlanger 1974; Franklin and Scott 1970; Gecas 1979; Gecas and Nye 1974; Kohn 1976; Kohn and Schooler 1983, 1973; Kohn and Slomczynski 1990; Parcel and Menaghan 1994; Pearlin 1970; Wright and Wright 1976) and by two important qualitative studies on family and work (Komarovsky 1962; Rubin 1976). Kohn also reports findings of an inverse relationship between socioeconomic status (SES) and punitive discipline. However, the statistical associations, while significant, are fairly weak, and not as strong as the relationships he reports for workplace supervision and punitive discipline.

Other studies indicate a possible link between social class and coercive family discipline. Straus, Gelles, and Steinmetz (1980) in a national survey of self-reported family violence found significant inverse associations between class related variables (income and occupational prestige) and parental violence toward children, and a significant positive relationship between unemployment and parental violence toward children. These findings have been replicated using official data from child protective service agencies (Garbarino 1989: 234; Smith and Thornberry 1995). Other studies point to the greater likelihood of child abuse in poor families than in financially better off families (Greenland 1987; Kruttschnitt et al. 1994; Maguire and Pastore 1995: 278; Pelton 1981; Wauchope and Straus 1990).

Carolyn Smith and Terence P. Thornberry (1995) conducted perhaps the most sophisticated study into the issue of child maltreatment. Among their findings were substantial differences by social class, using underclass status as measured by either principle wage earner unemployed, family on welfare, or family income below official poverty line. (Other studies have used these same measures for defining members of the surplus population, who are presumed to be under the greatest coercion [Simpson and Elis 1994]). "Almost one fifth (19.5%) of the youngsters reared in underclass families were victims of maltreatment while 8.2% of the nonunderclass respondents were maltreated" (Smith and Thornberry 1995: 462–63). Drawing from official reports to child protective services, child maltreatment included direct physical abuse and sexual abuse as well as emotional maltreatment, physical neglect, and the failure to provide supervision and educational and moral support. This variety of maltreatment encompasses extreme forms of coercion, defined in chapter 2 as direct physical force and threats and/or the failure to provide (or the threatened removal of) material and emotional social supports. Smith and Thornberry (1995: 466–67), similar to other studies mentioned earlier, report significant relationships between child maltreatment and subsequent arrests and self-reported delinquency, including serious and violent delinquent acts. The more severe the maltreatment (those involving greater physical injury for instance) and the more frequent the maltreatment, the greater the likelihood of arrests and self-reported serious and violent delinquency. Minor forms of delinquency did not show any relationship to having been maltreated earlier in childhood. This latter finding may be related to differences between Type 4 and Type 2 patterns of control discussed in chapter 2. Type 4 (with its high level of coercion) is more likely to lead to serious predatory criminal behavior while Type 2 (which is not coercive but is permissive) will be more restricted to producing minor forms of criminal behavior.

Social class differences in the use of corporal punishment (spanking and hitting that may fall short of abuse) have been reported, with parents from lower classes using corporal punishment more often than parents from higher classes (Bronfenbrenner 1972; Giles-Sims et al. 1995). Erlanger (1974) found that these socioeconomic status (SES) differences were small. Overall, social class differences in the percentage of parents who use corporal punishment are not consistently reported. Part of this may reflect ages at which children are spanked. Corporal punishment decreases as children get older (nearly 90 percent of parents report spanking three-year-olds, but only 20 percent report corporal punishment of 17-year-olds) (Straus 1994: 23). With such high prevalence of corporal punishment, it is doubtful that prevalence rates (have you ever hit your child?) would consistently differ by social class. However, if we look at the age of the child and at incidence rates (how many times have you hit your child?), social class differences emerge. When looking at teenage children, social class differences in *prevalence* of corporal punishment show no linear relationship. In fact, a greater percentage of middle-class parents are more likely to report that they have ever hit their teenage children than are the percentages of lower- or upper-class parents (Straus 1994: 45). But the *incidence* of corporal punishment of adolescents shows an inverse relationship to social class, so that "the higher the social class, the less chronic the corporal punishment" of teenagers (Straus 1994: 46–47).

Samson and Laub (1993), using data from Sheldon and Eleanor Glueck's (1950) longitudinal study of blue-collar boys, measured family SES by average weekly income and reliance on outside assistance. They discerned three distinct conditions for these blue-collar families: "comfortable circumstances (having enough savings to cover four months of financial stress), marginal circumstances (little or no savings but only occasional dependence on outside aid), or dependent circumstances (continuous receipt of outside aid for support)" (Sampson and Laub 1993: 72). Sampson and Laub also developed a measure of parental discipline that combined three components: use of physical punishment, threatening and/or scolding behavior, and erratic and harsh discipline. The composite index measures "the degree to which parents used inconsistent disciplinary measures *in conjunction with* harsh, physical punishment and/or threatening and scolding behavior" (Sampson and Laub 1993: 73–74).[2] (I would interpret this measure as capturing a type of coercive discipline similar to the Type 4 pattern discussed in chapter 2.) They found significant inverse relationships between their measure of SES and both father's and mother's coercive discipline patterns (Sampson and Laub 1993: 79). (Besides SES, other variables that predict coercive discipline are larger family size, greater household crowding, foreign-born parent, and father's deviance. These variables point to other aspects of poverty and also to possible cultural influences on parenting styles.) Coercive discipline, in turn, was significantly related to parental rejection of the child and to weak attachment of the child to parents (Sampson and Laub 1993: 74). Coercive discipline was also negatively related to greater levels of "suitable supervision" of the child by the mother, which causes discipline to be more consistent. Sampson and Laub (1993: 81, 84) found that coercive discipline had direct effects on official measures as well as self-reported, parent-reported, and teacher-reported measures of delinquent behavior. Also related to all measures of delinquency are mother's supervision (in a negative direction), parental rejection (in a positive direction), and attachment to parents (in a negative direction). SES drops out as a direct predictor of delinquency, but clearly has indirect effects through its effect on coercive discipline, mother's supervision, parental rejection, and attachment to parents.

In a similar vein, Larzelere and Patterson (1990) argue that poor parental management (in the form of weak monitoring and coercive patterns of discipline) accounts for social class differences in early onset of delinquent behavior. That is, lower SES parents are more likely to use coercive discipline and erratically monitor their children's behavior. This in turn leads to higher rates of delinquency. In testing this hypothesis, SES was a strong predictor of parental management skills, which in turn predicted delinquency. When controlling for parental management skills, the initial significant statistical association between social class and delinquency disappeared.

Ronald L. Simons and his co-researchers (1994: 261) report similar findings. In their study, SES is related positively to effective parenting and negatively to a child's oppositional and defiant orientation. Parenting is designated as effective by these researchers when harsh disciplinary practices (being hit with belt, paddle, or something else) are infrequent, monitoring of children's activities is greater, discipline is more consistent, and behavioral standards are set through inductive reasoning with children. A child's oppositional and defiant orientation concerned "the extent to which adolescents demonstrated a coercive, noncompliant orientation in their interactions with others" (Simons et al. 1994: 257). Socioeconomic status was not related directly to delinquency, but "SES influences delinquency indirectly through its effect on quality of parenting and on development of an aggressive, noncompliant orientation" (Simons et al. 1994: 261). These latter two variables showed significant relationships to delinquency, especially for a group of juveniles who were identified in the study as "early starters" in delinquent activities. In fact, the key finding of this study was that two paths distinguish early and late starters in delinquency. Early starters are best explained by ineffective parenting (which is coercive and inconsistent), which creates a strong predisposition (in the form of a coercive, oppositional, defiant orientation) `for delinquency. For late starters, who are generally less chronic in their delinquency, the key variable is association with deviant peers, which is negatively related to effective parenting and thus indirectly related to SES. These juveniles do not develop the coercive, oppositional, and defiant orientation that predisposes early starters to delinquent behavior. Since early starters are more likely to become chronic offenders, their path to delinquency can best be described as similar to the Type 4 pattern discussed in chapter 2, while the late starters may be more consistent with the Type 2 pattern. It is difficult to determine what specific elements of these researchers' effective parenting scale are related to early versus late starters since only composite measures are reported. The discussion in chapter 2 would suggest that early starters would be more likely to score highest on the harsh discipline and inconsistency measures while late starters would score low on the monitoring and harsh discipline and high on the inconsistency measures; both would score low on parents' use of inductive reasoning. These differences in parenting (focusing primarily on the coerciveness of the discipline) may account for the key difference between early and late starters: the coercive, oppositional, defiant orientation that is produced by parenting practices for early starters but not for late starters.

Snyder and Patterson (1987: 236) also report on studies that link parental discipline patterns to delinquent outcomes. They draw a distinction between overt antisocial behavior (which includes aggression/assaults, aggressive conduct disorders, and person-oriented crimes) and covert antisocial behavior (which includes lying/stealing, nonaggressive conduct disorders, and property-oriented crimes). They argue that "children who engage in overt antisocial behavior come from families that are more punitive, harsh, and restrictive [and] . . . children who engage in covert antisocial behavior come from homes characterized by lax and permissive discipline." As discussed in chapter 2, these patterns also conform respectively to the Type 4 and Type 2 patterns of control, which correspond respectively to more predatory and less predatory forms of crime and delinquency.

Corporal punishment of children and adolescents has been related to future involvement in child abuse, problems of mental health, delinquency, and adult crime. Murray A. Straus (1994), who draws on data from the National Family Violence Survey conducted in 1975 and 1985, presents the most comprehensive analysis of the effects of corporal punishment. Straus

(1994: 84) argues "that the more parents were themselves hit as children, the more likely they are to be heavy users of corporal punishment on their own children, increasing the risk that it will escalate into physical abuse." He offers evidence that parents who experienced greater corporal punishment as children are more likely to physically abuse their children (Straus 1994: 93–94). The frequency of corporal punishment as an adolescent is also linked to greater depression among adults, especially for women, and to greater alienation (measured by a standard scale that taps feelings of powerlessness and "normlessness") for both genders (Straus 1994: 70, 143). Children whose parents use corporal punishment were more than twice as likely, while physically abused children were three or four times more likely, to violently attack siblings than children who did not receive corporal punishment (Straus 1994: 102). Teenagers who have received any corporal punishment from their parents are nearly twice as likely to steal something worth $50 or more and are over three times as likely to hit someone outside the family with an object than are teenagers who never receive corporal punishment (Straus 1994: 106). Greater frequency of corporal punishment increases the chance that a juvenile will be involved in a delinquent act, even when controlling for the degree of spousal violence in the home (Straus 1994: 108). Greater frequency of corporal punishment during adolescence subsequently leads to a much greater likelihood for both men and women that they will hit their spouses (Straus 1994: 93, 104). Adults who had experienced greater frequency of corporal punishment as adolescents have much greater frequency of assaulting someone outside the family; this pattern holds much more strongly for men than it does for women (Straus 1994: 110).

There is evidence that psychological factors mediate the relationship between parental discipline and illegal behavior. Shaw and Scott (1991), for example, found that punitive parenting was significantly associated with self-reported delinquency because it created an external locus of control. Newman and Murray (1983) found that coercive methods of parenting led to lower self-confidence (self-efficacy) and lower self-esteem among adolescents, along with externalized moral standards and greater susceptibility to peer pressure; these in turn would presumably lead to greater involvement in delinquency. Peiser and Heaven (1996) found strong positive associations among punitive discipline, external locus of control, and self-reported delinquency for both males and females. Punitive discipline was correlated with low self-esteem for girls, but not for boys. In their path analysis they found a strong direct effect of punitive discipline on self-reported delinquency among males, but unlike other studies this relationship was not mediated by locus of control or self-esteem. For females, punitive discipline did not have a direct effect on self-reported delinquency, but the parental use of inductive forms of discipline (using more open communication and appeals to reason) had a direct inhibiting effect on girl's delinquency.

As several of the above studies suggest, there are some differences in the effects of corporal punishment on males and females. One of the key differences may be the extent to which adults closely monitor each gender. Typically, daughters' behavior is more closely monitored than sons' behavior (Bursik et al. 1985; Morash 1986; Rosenbaum 1987). This is especially true for sexual behavior (Chesney-Lind and Shelden 1998: 111; Morash and Chesney-Lind 1991: 371). This double standard of closer supervision of girls may lead to a stronger bond among girls to conventional social institutions (Chesney-Lind and Shelden 1992: 89; Rosenbaum 1987). Jeanne H. Block (1984: 87–89) found clear evidence of differential socialization patterns by gender, which tended to diverge even more strongly in adolescent years. Comparing adolescent sons and daughters, she found that greater warmth and physical closeness characterized parent-daughter relationships. Parents expressed a greater reluctance to physically punish girls, but parents more closely supervised and placed more restrictions on their daughters than on their sons. On the other hand, while boys were encouraged to be independent, they were more likely to be subjected to more punitive discipline than were girls. Closer monitoring under conditions of coercive control could account for why women develop greater depression in relation to earlier corporal punishment while men have higher rates of aggression related to earlier corporal punishment (Straus 1994: 70, 110, 143). Drawing on the differential coercion theory developed in chapter 2, boys are more likely to experience the Type 4 pattern (erratic coercion) than are girls, who are more likely to experience the Type 3 pattern (consistent coercion) when control relations are coercive.

Several studies report that parents use corporal punishment more often on boys than on girls (Elder and Bowerman 1963; Maccoby and Jacklin 1974; MacDonald 1971; Straus 1994; Straus, Gelles, and Steinmetz 1980; Straus et al. 1991). Studies also indicate that boys are somewhat more likely to be physically (but not sexually) abused than are girls (American Humane Association 1986; Bryan and Freed 1982; Gil 1970; Straus, Gelles, and Steinmetz 1980). These differences in coercion "could reflect differences to the extent to which boys and girls may provoke parental anger" (Wauchope and Straus 1990: 134). These factors could partially account for the wide gender differences in rates of chronic predatory crime (Steffensmeier and Allan 1995; Tracy et al. 1990). They may also help us understand the findings of Cathy Spatz Widom (1989) who reports that physically abused boys, but not physically abused girls, were at high risk for arrests for violent crimes. When the abuse is sexual in nature, girls are much more likely to be the victims. In these cases, girls have a much higher risk of suffering from depression, running away from home, and, in order to survive as runaways, involvement in property crimes, drug use, and prostitution (Chesney-Lind and Shelden 1998: 33–43; Hagan and McCarthy 1997).

Simpson and Elis (1994) found some interesting gender/class interactions in their test of the Colvin-Pauly thesis. They provide some support for the theory in that fraction 1 youth had significantly higher frequencies of violent crime than fraction 3 youth. In sum they report that "a strict test of Colvin and Pauly's hypothesized relationships between social class, familial and school bonding, peer influences, and serious patterned delinquency shows consistent, although not robust, support for most of the theory's predictions" (Simpson and Elis 1994: 464). They extend the theory and analysis to include a wider range of class categories (surplus population is added) and by specifying gender differences in the processes postulated by the theory. First, they found that the greatest incidence of violence falls not in fraction 1, but in the surplus population (about which the Colvin-Pauly theory makes no specific predictions but includes as part of fraction 1). Second, they found that

> the influence of social class location on violent delinquency does not operate in a consistent manner for males and females. Being a member of the surplus population tends, for the most part, to produce greater gender similarities in violence. That is, marginalized males and females exhibit similar offending levels. On the other hand, while the data seem to show some support for the predicted directional effects of social class location on violence, in that most offending occurs within the lower reaches of the class system, apparently the inhibitory effect of positive bonds to authority (as expected in fraction 3) has a greater effect on females (Simpson and Elis 1994: 465).

Their data thus indicate that social class is a better predictor of female than male violence (Simpson and Elis 1994: 467). Messner and Krohn (1990) found similar class/gender relationships to delinquency in their analysis of the Colvin-Pauly theory. These findings indicate that while chronic male criminality is higher than that of females in all class levels, the gap between genders is closer as one moves down the social class ladder.

I postulate that the experience of coercion at the lowest class level may be more similar for boys and girls than it is in higher social classes. At lower social class levels, coercion may be more likely to create other-directed anger for both boys and girls (corresponding to the Type 4 pattern). In higher social classes, coercion may create other-directed anger for boys, but be more likely to create inner-directed anger for females (corresponding to the Type 3 pattern). Again, these may be related to gender differences in levels of behavioral monitoring by adults. At the lowest social class level (among the surplus population) behavioral monitoring may be less frequent for both boys and girls, leading to an erratic application of coercive controls for both sexes, and thus to higher other-directed anger. At higher social class levels, behavioral monitoring may increase to a much greater extent for girls than it does for boys. Thus, as indicated by the findings of Simpson and Elis (1994), gender differentials in violent crime may be greatest at the higher levels than at the lower levels of social class. Thus gender as a variable related to criminality might be accounted for by differentials in the degree of behavioral monitoring, which under conditions of coercive control create different sets of social-psychological deficits (self-directed versus other-directed anger being most important). This is clearly the implication of the differential coercion theory developed in chapter 2.

The family is the initial site in which social-psychological attributes are developed. If a child is subjected to erratic coercive discipline in the family, then the child develops social-psychological deficits (other-directed anger, low self-efficacy, a weak, alienated social bond, strong coercive behavioral modeling, a perceived control deficit with feelings of debasement, low self-control, and an external locus of control). The child brings these social-psychological deficits into other social settings. These social-psychological deficits contribute to child behavior that may elicit coercive controls in these other social settings, most importantly in the school.

## THE SCHOOL

Students experience differential treatment in schools. This differential treatment arises from two sources: tracking and the unequal distribution of resources among schools.

Tracking refers to the process by which students are divided into categories for assignment to various kinds of classes. Students are classified as fast, average, or slow learners and are placed into fast, average, or slow classes on the basis of their scores on achievement or ability tests. It has been demonstrated that such I.Q. tests are one way in which inequality is maintained from one generation to the next, with tracking as a major device for the reproduction of inequality (Fischer et al. 1996). I.Q. and aptitude tests may designate children with certain social-psychological deficits (such as low self-control and weak social bonding) for processing in lower-level tracks that are more regimented and coercive. It is not clear what aptitude tests actually measure; according to Christopher Jencks and his associates (1972: 55), the I.Q. test "probably measures a rather special kind of motivation." Since there is no extrinsic reward or punishment associated with giving right or wrong answers on these tests (and no feedback on how well one has done), those students who do not give random answers must be internally motivated to achieve. Thus a high I.Q. score denotes a positive internalized bond and strong self-control that was produced within the family. The I.Q. score is a primary mechanism for placement into educational tracks that contain differential structures of control (Menard and Morse 1984).

"However it is done, tracking, in essence, is sorting—a sorting of students that has certain predictable characteristics" (Oakes 1985: 3). In perhaps the most comprehensive study of school tracking, Jeannie Oakes (1985) analyzed data from 25 junior and senior high schools from all regions of the nation. The sample consisted of 299 classrooms and all the students and teachers in these classrooms. Researchers spent six weeks at each school interviewing principals and teachers, administering lengthy questionnaires to students, teachers and parents, and observing events in the classrooms. Tracking became a central concern of the study.

Oakes focused on differences in high and low track math and English classes. She found some important differences between the high and low tracks. First, students from high-track classes reported that "learning usually takes up most of their class time," while students in low-track classes reported that "getting students to behave" took up most of the class time (Oakes 1985: 103). Thus, in lower-track classes, a great amount of time is taken away from learning to deal with behavior problems and discipline. Second, in lower-track classes, there was a much higher level of teacher punitiveness, as measured by student and observers' reports of teachers making fun of or demeaning students, hurting students' feelings, making angry remarks to students, punishing unfairly, and creating fear in students. In lower-track classes, "punishment was relied upon to attempt to coerce students into compliance" (Oakes 1985: 131). In summary, Oakes (1985: 132) concluded,

A higher degree of punitiveness, a lower degree of trusting relationships, and less involvement in class activities are related to lower educational outcomes and are more associated with low-track classes. . . . [M]ore teacher time and energy were spent on getting students to behave in low-track classes. . . . Rather than participate cooperatively in what the teacher wanted them to do—as they would be likely to do if they viewed the teachers' directions as in their own best interest—low-track students tended to be noncompliant and apathetic. Apparently more of their time and energy was spent interfering with their teacher's plans.

These observations imply an interaction between coercive control and disruptive behavior. The children enter school with varying degrees of social-psychological deficits produced in the family. To the extent that these deficits are great, the child may give behavioral cues of being (in the teacher's perception) potentially disruptive. These behavioral cues are likely to elicit a labeling process that creates the "self-fulfilling prophecy" of a disruptive child who elicits still more coercive controls than before. The labeling process can be seen as a reciprocal relationship between individuals with varying degrees of social-psychological deficits and agents of control. The process of labeling in educational settings has been demonstrated experimentally (Leacock 1969; Rist 1970; Rosenthal 1973; Rosenthal and Jacobson 1968; Rubovits and Maehr 1971) although other researchers have been unable to replicate these findings (Barber et al. 1969; Gephart 1970).

The various tracking experiences in the school correspond to the social control requirements at workplaces (Bowles and Gintis 1976). The lower tracks emphasize strict discipline, regimentation, and conformity to external authority. The higher tracks emphasize initiative, creativity, internal control, and stronger affiliation with others. The generally more negative relationships and low levels of involvement in learning in lower educational tracks "socialize students in such a way that they are prepared to stay at the bottom levels of institutions, not only as teenagers in schools but in adult life as well" (Oakes 1985: 134). The relationships in these lower tracks promote acceptance of coercion and obedience to external authority. While most students resign themselves to this, a significant number of students actively (usually as individuals) resist. Such resistance leads to further coercive controls and ultimately to complete alienation from both the school and external authority in general. While the intended outcome of schools is to create compliant students, the latent outcome is the creation of a number of young people who become more marginalized with even greater social-psychological deficits.

Tracking not only takes place within schools, but between schools. This occurs because of the vast differences in financial resources of schools between lower-class and middle-class neighborhoods and communities (Kozol 1991; Lawrence 1998: 116–20). This difference in resource allocation springs largely from differential tax bases associated with geographic differences in income and property ownership. This circumstance creates differences in the availability of rewards and punishments for controlling children and adolescents in the school setting and often necessitates a greater reliance on coercive measures in lower-class schools. In fact, a recent book on inner city schools in low-income neighborhoods describes these educational institutions using the penal term "maximum security" (Devine 1996).

Richard Lawrence (1998: 152) discusses corporal punishment in schools in his book on schools and delinquency. The use of corporal punishment in schools is legal in 29 states in the United States. It is illegal in the other 21 states of the United States and the District of Columbia and in every continental European country as well as in Israel, Ireland, and Puerto Rico. Teachers and principals hit more than a million children each year with about 15,000 students receiving injuries that are serious enough for medical attention. Eighty percent of corporal punishments in school are of boys (who comprise 51 percent of students) and 37 percent are of African Americans (who comprise 25 percent of students). Support for corporal punishment is higher in regions of the United States that have lower expenditures per student, fewer school support personnel, and greater percentages of illiteracy and dropouts (McDowell and Friedman 1979). The 12 southern states accounted for about 80 percent of the corporal punishments administered in U.S. schools in the mid-1980s (Straus 1994: 111). This regional variation may partially account for Straus's (1994: 113) findings that states with less restrictions on schools' use of corporal punishment also have higher rates of assaults within schools by students and higher statewide homicide rates. Given that these are also the same states that tend to use the death penalty, these may point to wider cultural supports in some states for coercion, a topic I take up in chapter 4 where I discuss larger cultural forces. Only a couple of studies show no harmful side effects of school corporal punishment (Reardon and Reynolds 1979; Rose 1984). Most studies (cf., Bongiovanni 1979) do indicate harmful side-effects, including increases in deviance and delinquency (Straus et al. 1991), aggressive behavior in males (Welsh 1979), and memory and concentration loss and sleep disturbances (Hyman 1990).

Other research indicates that coercion at school and other related variables are associated with delinquency. A negative social bond to school, which I argue is one result of coercive controls, has been consistently associated with higher levels of delinquency (Cernkovich and Giordano 1992; Hindelang 1973; Hirschi 1969; Johnson 1979). Hirschi and Hindelang (1977) report that one of the most consistent relationships found in delinquency literature is the inverse association between I.Q. scores and delinquency. However, Menard and Morse (1984) conclude from their longitudinal data analysis that the differential treatment students receive in curriculum tracks explains the correlation between I.Q. and delinquency, which is rendered spurious by their findings. Lower educational track position has also been associated with delinquency in studies by Kelly (1977, 1974), Messner and Krohn (1990), Schaefer, Olexa and Polk (1972), and Simpson and Elis (1994), who also found that lower school resources are related to delinquency. Wiatrowski and his co-researchers (1982), using a sample of senior high school students, found a significant but very weak inverse relationship between curriculum track and delinquency. It may be, as Wiatrowski and his colleagues (1982: 158) argue, that tracking has a greater impact in junior high school than in senior high school. The sudden intensification of tracking that accompanies the shift from elementary to junior high school may be more crucial in explaining delinquency than are later tracking experiences in senior high school.

To understand sustained involvement in serious delinquency after junior high school, we must examine the growing influence of peer associations and the quality of these associations. The impact of peers begins to be seen in curriculum tracks, where peer groupings are partially shaped by schools' decisions concerning track placement. Oakes (1985: 126–27) found that

> students in low-track classes, far more than those in high tracks, told us that they felt other students in the class were unfriendly to them. Large differences were also found in the amount of angry and hostile interactions that were reported among students in class. Low-track students indicated considerably more arguing, yelling, and fighting with one another took place in their classes. Substantial differences were also found in the warm, helpful feelings students had about one another. High-track students far more often agreed that their classmates really liked one another and were willing to extend help. Low-track students told us that these kinds of things were much less a part of their classroom experience. . . . Clearly, the classes in the lowest track were considerably more hostile and unfriendly places. . . . Overtly hostile exchanges [among students] were certainly more frequent.

The lower tracks of schools thus present an unintended training ground for coercive relations among peers.

## PEER GROUPS, GANGS, AND DRUG MARKETS

It is likely that adolescents with similar social-psychological deficits (due to similar experiences of coercion in schools and families) will be in greater contact with each other and will be drawn to each other based on shared experiences. Specifically, students in higher educational tracks, in which positive social bonds and other reduced social-psychological deficits are produced, tend to form peer associations that are less coercive. Students in lower educational tracks, which tend to produce weak, alienated social bonds and other social-psychological deficits, tend to form more coercive relations among their peers. As Oakes's (1985) study on tracking indicates, the relations in the classroom among these low-track peers are more hostile and coercive. It is likely that their relations are coercive outside the classroom as well.

Studies strongly suggest that most delinquent behavior occurs in groups and that juveniles with delinquent peers tend to be delinquent themselves (Erickson and Empey 1965; Erickson and Jensen 1977; Short 1958; Short et al. 1965; Voss 1964). The key question is whether juveniles who already have delinquent propensities merely gather together to commit crime or if the group dynamics spur juveniles toward greater delinquency. Travis Hirschi (1969) argues that certain kinds of juveniles (those with weak social bonds and presumably with other social-psychological deficits) who are already delinquent merely hang out with other delinquent juveniles who engage in crime together. Learning theorists, such as Ronald L. Akers (1985), argue that the group creates an environment in which juveniles learn deviant values and behavior from each other, so that group learning processes are the cause of increased delinquency.

The theory that is developed in this book views both of these processes as important. Because of the types of controls that juveniles experience, they are likely to be placed in a position in which they interact with other juveniles who have similar positions in control relations and who have developed similar levels of social-psychological deficits. Those who have more coercive relations in their backgrounds will have greater social-psychological deficits and be more likely to be placed in interactions (through school and neighborhood associations) with juveniles who are similar. (This also is the result of rejection by and isolation from peers who do not share their coercive backgrounds or social-psychological deficits.) However, their interactions spur them toward greater delinquency, because these interactions are more likely to be coercive in nature and these coercive peer relations are likely to further increase the social-psychological deficits of the juvenile. The learning of deviant values or techniques of criminal behavior per se may not be the most important element that connects these peer groups to delinquency. (As Gottfredson and Hirschi [1990] argue, most criminal acts require little in the way of skills that must be learned from others.) It is more likely that the coercive relations that emerge in these groups have damaging social-psychological consequences that link them to chronic crime and delinquency. In terms of social learning theory, clearly one of those social-psychological deficits is coercive behavioral modeling. But the coercion within the group also weakens social bonds, enhances other-directed anger, lowers self-control, further externalizes the locus of control, and is a constant provocation with potential debasement and humiliation connected to recognition of a control deficit.

The most pertinent area of research related to the question of peer group influences on delinquency is gang studies. Two questions need to be addressed. First, does involvement in gangs increase delinquent behavior or are gangs merely collections of young people who would become delinquent anyway? Second, what is the nature of relations among gang members? Are they like close-knit families or do they lack cohesion? What role does coercion play in gang members' interactions?

Gang members are much more likely to become serious, violent chronic criminals than individuals who are not members of gangs (Covey, Menard, and Franzese 1992; Spergel 1995). Thornberry and his associates (1993) examined three alternative explanations for why gang members are more likely to engage in serious and violent crimes than non-gang individuals. The first explanatory model is derived from the arguments of Hirschi (1969) and Gottfredson and Hirschi (1990) who posit that delinquent-prone individuals (who engage in higher rates of delinquency) select gang membership; this is labeled the "selection" or "kind of person" model (Thornberry et al. 1993: 57). The second explanatory model, derived from social learning theory (Akers 1985), is labeled the "social facilitation" or "kind of group" model (Thornberry et al. 1993: 58). This model argues that gang members do not have a stronger inherent propensity for delinquency than non-gang members, but the normative structure of the gang propels them toward chronic criminality. The third explanatory model combines the other two models and is labeled the "enhancement model" because juveniles who already have delinquent propensities are drawn into gangs, which encourage greater involvement in delinquent behavior (Thornberry et al. 1993: 59). These researchers tested these models on a sample of 987 Rochester, New York, adolescents who were interviewed repeatedly over several years to track their involvement in gangs, delinquency, and drug use. Their analysis revealed the following:

> Results for transient members—those who were gang members for only one year and presumably less committed to the gang—are most consistent with the social facilitation model. Involvement in delinquency is particularly high when the boy is an active gang member but these boys are not consistently more delinquent than nongang members when they are not active in the gang. Results for stable gang members—those who remain as members at least 2 years and who are presumably more committed to the gang—are slightly more consistent with the enhancement model. In general, these boys exhibit the highest rates of general delinquency. But even for them, delinquent involvement is greatest during their years of active gang membership. None of these results are consistent with a pure selection model (Thornberry et al. 1993: 70–71).

When looking at specific criminal behavior patterns, rather than general delinquency, the findings supported the social facilitation model for violent crimes and for drug crimes. That is, both violent crime and drug crimes tend to be higher during periods of active gang membership than either before or after and differences in these specific crimes between gang boys and nongang boys only appear when gang boys are actively involved in gangs. Gang membership, however, showed little effect on property crimes.

The results of the Thornberry et al. (1993) study suggest that group processes among delinquent peers play a crucial role in producing chronic delinquency. These results (especially those related to violent crime) are "quite consistent with the group process perspective on gang behavior that argues that threats to status, cohesion, solidarity, and so forth are more apt to be responded to by aggressive, violent acts than by other forms of delinquency" (Thornberry et al. 1993: 81). Their study does not address the nature of these group dynamics. These researchers speculate

> that the gang is effective at communicating definitions and teaching techniques as Sutherland would argue. Or the causal processes might better be accounted for by referring to the reward structure of the group (as in Akers's arguments). Or the types of group processes described by Short and Strodbeck (1965) and others could be at play. What is evident from these results, however, is that in pursuing an explanation of why gang members have a higher rate of delinquency than nongang members, the structure and dynamics of the group context must be the central focus (Thornberry et al. 1993: 82).

The findings of this Rochester, New York study are similar to those from a study conducted in Denver, Colorado (Esbensen and Huizinga 1993) and to those from a Seattle, Washington study (Battin et al. 1998). These studies demonstrate that gang membership greatly enhanced the level of criminality. They reveal that individuals who joined gangs did have higher delinquency rates prior to gang membership, but their gang involvement led to greater delinquency, especially violent and drug-related crimes (as the Rochester study had found). The Seattle study controlled for the effect of having delinquent friends in testing the relationship between gang membership and increased delinquency. This study found that being in a gang had independent effects on delinquency beyond association with delinquent peers. This finding implies that more than differential association and learning from delinquent friends is occurring in the gang context. Group processes within gangs, not merely the bringing together of delinquent-prone individuals, have major effects on enhancing delinquency.

I suggest that one of the major group processes among delinquent peers, especially for gang members, is coercion. Coercion occurs both as an internal dynamic and an external force. Observational studies of gangs

(Decker and Van Winkle 1996; Fleisher 1995) report relations among gang members that are not particularly cohesive and that are punctuated, on an erratic basis, with violence and coercion. These are just the types of relationships (Type 4) that I believe create greater social-psychological deficits, enhanced coercive ideation, and chronic involvement in predatory crime.

Gang researchers make the distinction between core and fringe members of gangs (Klein 1995). A key difference is that core members have much greater involvement in criminal activities; by most measures they are chronically involved in criminal behavior (Covey, Menard, and Franzese 1992; Thornberry et al. 1993). The distinction between core and fringe gang members "seems to be based on psychological and social factors. Core members have more character deficits (e.g., lower measured I.Q., greater impulsiveness, and fewer social skills) and more need for group affiliations. That is, they are more dependent on their peers" (Klein 1995: 60). (These "character deficits" discussed by Klein are related to the social-psychological deficits I posit as important mediating variables between coercion and chronic criminality.)

Another issue is the degree to which gangs create a cohesive structure. The long-time gang observer Malcolm Klein (1995: 61) reports little evidence of gang cohesiveness: "I have seen enough internal fighting to wonder on occasion how these young people do manage to stay affiliated." Another long-time gang observer, James F. Short, Jr. (1998: 21), writes that "influences associated with close relationships depend in part on positive interpersonal experiences, but . . . antisocial friendships often are relationships of convenience [, which] resonates with observations from gang research, where status and dependency needs sometimes conflict amidst the rough and tumble of life on the street. Much gang behavior is characterized by verbal and physical aggression within gangs, as well as between gang members and others." Elsewhere, Short discusses Walter Miller's documentation of physical and verbal aggression by gang members in which "the great majority of these acts were directed toward other members of the gang" (Short 1996: 204). Gangs lack tight structures and are best described as "loose" and somewhat "fragmented" (Decker and Van Winkle 1996). Rarely do gang members describe their associates as "friends" and their networks "involve weak social ties" (Fleisher 1995: 122). Yet, core members form a commitment to the group and submerse their individual identities into that of the group. And cohesiveness within the gang can arise from external threats from rival gangs and from suppressive activities of the police (Decker and Van Winkle 1996; Hagedorn 1988; Klein 1995). The level of cohesiveness can be heightened if gang membership includes long-standing ties to families and neighborhoods, as in many Latino "barrio gangs" (Horowitz 1983; Moore 1991; Vigil 1988). External threats heighten the group's identity and force anti-social youth into closer ties, not based on affection, but on self-interest. Summarizing gang studies from the 1950s and 1960s, LaMar Empey (1967: 35) writes:

> The picture that is painted suggests that gang members, like inmates in prison, are held together, not by feelings of loyalty and solidarity, but by forces much less attractive. It is not that structure is lacking but that it is defensive and highly stylized, not supportive. Group members stay together simply because they feel they have more to lose than to gain by any breach in their solidarity. While they may appear to the outsider to be dogmatic, rigid, and unyielding in their loyalty to each other, the sources of this loyalty are not internal but external. Remove the pressure and you remove the cohesion.

While Lewis Yablonsky (1966) described authoritarian gang leaders who resort to coercion to keep gang members in line, most gang research downplays the role of leaders (cf., Klein 1995). This observation makes sense because it is doubtful that an ability to bow down to any authority figure, legitimate or illegitimate, would be part of the personality makeup of individuals who have spent their lives defying coercive authority figures. Thus most gang leaders (to the extent they exist at all) must carefully negotiate with gang members or risk losing their status.

Violence is a constant theme of gang culture. "That violence plays a significant role in the first gang activity (initiation) is no accident; violence, and its threat, plays an important symbolic role in gang life. Violence communicates a message to gang members and nongang members alike; violence is a regular part of gang life, and gang members are unafraid to use it or receive it. Violence also serves to reinforce the solidarity among gang members and accentuate the boundaries between gang and nongang members" (Decker and Van Winkle 1996: 16–17).

Most research depicts gangs as relatively unorganized, especially concerning control of members' behavior. Rules are rarely formal and, to the extent that there are any, arise out of common understandings among gang members. The internal use of coercive control within gangs arises on those occasions when group solidarity appears to be threatened (Decker and Van Winkle 1996). Violations of the informal rules of the gang are more likely to occur when the group experiences social discord and fragmentation, which impels greater use of internal coercive controls that may only fragment the group more. Since gangs have such fragile social structures, there is a need to have a constant external threat of violence to keep gangs together. So if such a threat does not actually exist, a group mythology can emerge that creates the perception of threat.

As I see it, this mythology feeds directly into the creation of *coercive ideation* in which the world is seen as a dangerous, violent jungle that must be responded to through coercive violence.[3] This mindset leads to proactive behavior by the gang, such as incursions into other youths' neighborhoods or striking poses that elicit in other youths a sense of dread (Decker and Van Winkle 1996; Katz 1988). These proactive gestures often create actual threats of violence in response, and thus strengthen the fragile group solidarity by creating the necessity for collective retaliation against these threats. Gang members initiate a cycle of violence, which then coerces them to repeatedly engage in violence. As Decker and Van Winkle (1996: 273) write, "Life in the gang is a life under threat of violence coupled with a willingness to use violence." Gang life creates an arena in which the force of coercion is most keenly felt.

These gang-generated external threats can be understood as coercion that, as in any setting, aggravates social-psychological deficits and contributes to coercive ideation, which are already somewhat pronounced before core members engage in gang activity. (This thesis fits with the "enhancement model," which the research on gangs, discussed earlier, supports). Combine these external threats with the occasions of verbal and physical aggression that are internal within gangs themselves and the gang experience can be seen as one of the most coercive experiences in existence. The constant fear of physical victimization from other gangs (and sometimes from the police) is the force that holds the gang together. Since this victimization is intermittent and unpredictable, it puts coercion on an extremely erratic schedule (as in the Type 4 pattern discussed in chapter 2). Thus it heightens, in core gang members especially, the other-directed anger, low self-control, externalized locus of control, low self-efficacy, weak social bonding, and strong coercive behavioral modeling that many had already acquired to some degree in coercive relations in families and schools. Gang life, in addition, contains constant threats of debasement and humiliation through coercion from others. Such provocations, which elicit a strong and immediate recognition of a control deficit, must be quickly responded to with violent coercive acts (even in the face of death) to fend off the certain loss of respect and status for a failure to act. In this sense, the mindset of core gang members represents one of the clearest examples of coercive ideation, which impels a violent response to a coercively conceived world. This ideation and the social-psychological deficits are reflected in the fatalistic attitudes often expressed by gang members, who see their impending deaths as an inevitable consequence of their gang activities (Bendau 1992; Decker and Van Winkle 1996; Miller 1958). So while gang members band together with much bravado in the group's self-defense, most express little confidence in avoiding, and in some cases express glory in, the prospect of being killed.

As some gang members began entering the crack trade in the mid-1980s, the coercion of gang life dramatically escalated. Not only did traditional gang rivalries become overlaid with drug markets to enhance violent threats but relations of control within crack-dealing organizations are also highly coercive. A *New York Times* report (Kolata 1989: 1) describes the crack business as "a modern, brutalized version of a nineteenth-century sweatshop." Employers dock their employees pay for not coming to work on time, and employees are subject to being shot or maimed if their employers perceive that they are trying to cheat them by holding back money earned from sales or by stealing drugs. The majority of workers in these organizations are at the bottom of the crack-selling pyramid, and they will most likely stay at the bottom. As street-level dealers and lookouts (who watch for police or rival drug dealers), they are exposed not only to the coercion of their employers, but are most vulnerable to attacks by rival drug organizations and to arrest by the police. Crack dealing is an unstable and risky activity in which "predatory arrangements thrive between actors at all levels" (Jacobs 1999: 43). Homicide victimization rates for these street-level dealers are among the highest of any group, as are their rates of arrest and incarceration (MacCoun and Reuter 1992: 484).

Despite the wads of cash they may flash to onlookers (the cash, by the way, has to be turned over to their employers), these street-level dealers actually make relatively modest wages from selling crack, "not the stuff from which Mercedes are purchased" (MacCoun and Reuter 1992: 488). At the very lowest levels, wages are quite meager. As the *New York Times* article (Kolata 1989: 42) reports:

> In East Harlem, said Dr. Phillippe Bourgois, who is an anthropologist . . . studying the Harlem crack business, lookouts make as little as $35 in a 12-hour shift, or $210 a week in six days. Dr. [Terry] Williams said that he knows lookouts in East Harlem who make only about $30 in a 12-hour shift. . . . In Chicago, Dr. Felix M. Padilla . . . spent months with a gang whose members control the selling of cocaine. He said drug sellers there make about $150 a week. For most people, said John Hagedorn, an anthropologist [who has extensively studied Milwaukee's gangs and drug organizations] drug selling is, indeed, "just another minimum-wage job."

The chances for these street-level workers to move up the drug-selling hierarchy, where exorbitant sums of money can indeed be made, are actually quite slim; for most it is a dead end job, resembling "an illegal extension of the 'secondary' youth-labor market" (Currie 1994: 301). The wages for most street-level crack dealers are thus inconsistent and much more modest than media reports would suggest. However, during the 1980s and early 1990s, many inner-city youth found crack selling to be a better source of income than the low-wage legal work available in inner cities (Fagan and Freeman 1999; MacCoun and Reuter 1992). Even though most street-level drug dealers hold low-wage legal jobs in secondary labor markets, they continue selling drugs because these (often sporadically available) legitimate jobs do not allow them to make money on a steady basis (Fagan and Freeman 1999). Also, these low-paying legal jobs are viewed by these youth as demeaning and humiliating. In comparison, the drug subculture provides a sense of status and a "hustler" image that are highly alluring to young people cut off from other sources of self-esteem (Currie 1994; Fagan and Freeman 1999). As they engage with this subculture many of them become addicted and are not able to hold legitimate jobs on any steady basis (Jacobs 1999). And many of these individuals become tied even more tightly to crack selling because they fall into debt to their employers in the drug trade (Jacobs 1999).

While many individuals who are also gang members become involved in selling crack, most gang researchers do not believe that gangs, as such, emerge as drug-selling organizations (Fagan 1989). Klein (1995: 119) argues that "street gangs are not in control of drug distribution and, in particular, not in control of crack distribution, as has often been alleged." The very nature of gang organization (which is relatively loose and fragmented) precludes the type of hierarchical relationships and tight networks necessary for a successful business enterprise (Decker and Van Winkle 1996). More likely, some individuals who associate with street gangs also work as street-level drug dealers for traditional drug-dealing organizations, which are not directly tied to any street gang and which hire as street-level dealers both gang members and those not associated with gangs. Thus drug selling is not a gang activity per se.

However, if a street dealer is a gang member and is attacked by a rival dealer, the gang might see this act as suitable for collective retaliation. If the rival dealer is also a member of a rival street gang, then the drug-market war between the two dealers might merge with a turf-war between opposing street gangs. In this fashion, the crack trade may be related to some inter-gang violence. This does not, however, make the street gang a drug gang. In fact, most drug-related homicides are not related to gangs, even in the notoriously gang-ravaged city of Los Angeles (Klein 1995: 126). But this possible overlay of the crack trade with gangs makes the environment of both gangs and drug selling all that much more coercive. Add to this the easy availability of semi-automatic weapons, which income from the crack trade allowed many gang members to obtain, coercion in the streets during the 1980s and early 1990s became more lethal than ever.

The crack trade, then, represents one of the most coercive workplace/criminal experiences an individual can endure. Following the theory developed in this book, I would expect the crack trade to be associated with extremes of chronic criminality because of the intense atmosphere of coercion it creates. In fact, some commentators connect the recent rise and fall of juvenile homicides (and violent crimes in general) to the rise and fall of the crack trade (Witkin 1998). From the perspective of this book, an immediate setting of coercion, which is represented by the crack trade, intensified the social-psychological deficits for a greater number of individuals. As the crack trade subsided, so did the intensity of its coercive relationships, both internal to the employer-employee relationship and external in the violent rivalries over markets and turf it created. Concomitant with a decline in crack during the 1990s was a lowering of the unemployment rate to a point (by 1999) not seen in thirty years. This context of low unemployment has made legitimate work not only more available but (as discussed earlier) less coercive, since replacement of workers as a coercive control strategy is greatly limited with the decline in unemployment. Thus highly coercive illegitimate work (in the crack trade) has been recently replaced for many by legitimate work that, owing to lower unemployment, is less coercive. The recent reduction in crime has thus occurred in a context in which coercion appears to have (at least temporarily) abated.

From the perspective of this book, coercion among peers, especially in the context of gangs or street-level crack markets, increases the social-psychological deficits and coercive ideation conducive to chronic criminality. While one is an active participant in these coercion-laden activities, social-psychological deficits are enhanced and criminal behavior increases. As one drops out of active gang membership or out of the crack trade, the experience of coercion recedes and the social-psychological deficits decrease along with the level of criminality. However, events may arise (such as arrest and incarceration) that enhance coercion and thus further heighten social-psychological deficits and coercive ideation, which freezes the individual for a longer period at chronic levels of criminality.

## STATE AGENCY CONTROLS: WELFARE AND INCARCERATION

Individuals can fall under the formal regulation of state agencies, particularly if they are poor. Welfare and criminal justice agencies provide varying degrees of incentives and sanctions to gain compliance from their clients.

To the extent that these controls are coercive, individual's social-psychological deficits will be heightened by these experiences.

Since the early 1980s, welfare clients have been subject to increasingly closer regulation that includes the constant threat of losing welfare benefits (Gans 1996; Katz 1997, 1990; Piven and Cloward 1997, 1993). Simpson and Elis (1994), in their test of the Colvin-Pauly thesis, argue that position within the surplus population, which is dependent on welfare, produces a coercive experience conducive to delinquency. In this case, the coercive control comes from an agency of the state. Welfare agencies have the power to intrude into the most intimate matters of family life to determine eligibility and changes in eligibility. Coercive control springs from the welfare agency's power to deny welfare benefits to families who refuse to cooperate with these intrusive investigations. The choice of going to work, for those who can actually make this choice, means finding a job at the lowest pay and under the most coercive workplace conditions. The loss of medical coverage and the need for transportation and child care services often makes this choice a losing proposition.[4] Shifting between a coercive workplace and a coercive welfare system, which is often the case for those mired in the impoverished condition of the surplus population, only heightens the inconsistency of coercion. The release from coercion only happens when one is released from both settings, which becomes financially untenable unless one can find an illegal alternative. As discussed in the last section, these illegal alternatives, such as selling drugs, contain their own coercive controls that may be even more extreme. For many poor people the escape from coercion becomes nearly impossible. The experience of being poor in the United States is the experience of being coerced on all sides (Kozol 1995, 1989).

Being placed in the "underclass" or "surplus population" (as measured by chronic unemployment and welfare status) has been associated in a number of studies with delinquency and criminality (Farnworth et al. 1994; Simpson and Elis 1994; Wilson 1987). One of the reasons that delinquency is associated with a family's receipt of welfare is that the family is placed in the uncertain condition of being at the mercy of a coercive welfare structure (Simpson and Elis 1994: 469). This condition of coercion can only heighten the social-psychological deficits for all family members who feel its force. Despite the popular image to the contrary, life on welfare is a life of constant hassle, financial uncertainty, fear, and hopelessness (Kozol 1995, 1989). Welfare recipients live under a coercive threat that on an erratic and arbitrary basis may be carried out at any time. The welfare system as it is currently operated in the United States is an extreme setting in which an individual is at the mercy of forces beyond his or her control. This becomes especially true during periods when the welfare system is under political attack and benefits and eligibility requirements become tighter year by year. Thus we would expect that families caught up in the welfare bureaucracy for an extended period of time would be more likely than even individuals in coercive workplaces to engender chronic crime and delinquency because this setting produces erratic coercive control.

The criminal justice system provides an even more coercive setting of control. Being locked up against one's will under force of guard is by definition coercive. While extremely coercive, especially in the United States, the criminal justice system is also erratic in its control of criminals. The certainty of punishment for any particular crime is quite low, although chronic offenders have an increased chance of being caught at some point in their criminal careers (Barkan 1997: 533–36; Currie 1994). After being arrested, the individual (especially if he or she is poor) is at the mercy of uncertain outcomes of plea bargains and decisions by prosecutors and judges. When convicted, the system in the United States is severe in its punishment compared to other nations (Donziger 1996; Kappeler et al. 1996) and in many ways may be more coercive today than it has been in its history (Colvin 1997). This criminal justice process creates an erratic coercive pattern of control, which I argue is most conducive to reinforcing social-psychological deficits and contributing to coercive ideation and chronic criminality.

When sent to prison, the individual is subjected to coercive formal state controls. But the degree of coercion can vary. My own study of a maximum-security prison (in Santa Fe, New Mexico) focused on the shift toward greater coercion by staff over inmates as a precursor to increased violence and prison disorder (Colvin 1992, 1982). This study first focused my attention on the relationship between coercive controls and violence and led directly to the Colvin and Pauly (1983) theory of delinquency.

The Penitentiary of New Mexico (PNM) shifted dramatically toward a coercive control structure in the late 1970s after an organized inmate strike in 1976 was violently suppressed. The inmates had been protesting the ending of an array of rehabilitation programs, which had created a control structure that Etzioni (1970) would describe as utilitarian (containing remunerative power used by the administration and a calculative involvement on the part of inmates). As programs and other amenities, which had provided incentive controls for good behavior, were cut, coercive punishments (including greater use of administrative lockup, coercing inmates to inform on other inmates, and beatings) increased. The greater use of coercion created greater alienation between inmates and staff and broke down the once strong sense of solidarity among inmates. As the social bonds between staff and inmates and among inmates themselves dissolved, the inmate society fragmented into small cliques, which banded together for self-protection. As the perception of external threat of coercion from both staff and inmates increased, several of these cliques began reacting through violent attacks on staff and on other inmates (similar to the processes observed in studies of street gangs discussed earlier). These violent attacks further fragmented the inmate society and created a process of competition for violent reputations among inmates that only heightened the coercive atmosphere of the prison.

It is important to point out that the coercion from both staff and inmate sources was delivered on an extremely erratic and arbitrary schedule. Neither staff members nor inmates knew when a violent inmate might attack them. Inmates were constantly kept off balance by an inconsistent disciplinary system, which might react to a minor incident with a severe punishment or a to major offense with a light sanction depending on which shift captain was on duty or on the mood of the guard who witnessed the violation. These processes of coercion, both in staff-inmate relations and among inmates themselves, culminated in 1980 in the most brutal prison riot in U.S. history. The 1980 riot was a disorganized and bloody affair, in which groups of inmates killed 33 of their fellow inmates and brutally injured some of the guards who were taken hostage (Colvin 1992).

The erratic coercive processes that led up to the riot are in stark contrast to two other periods in PNM's history. From 1968 to 1975, when the prison contained a number of incentive-based rehabilitation programs, individual inmates could predictably count on receiving rewards (better housing, access to educational and vocational programs, and early release on parole) in exchange for good behavior. The disciplinary lockdown unit was rarely used. Inmate alienation was lower, with many expressing optimism about programs, their chances for rehabilitation, and their ability to make positive changes in the prison environment. Violence was virtually unknown during this period. The elimination of these incentives in 1976 meant that inmates could no longer count on being rewarded for good behavior; they might, on an inconsistent basis, be punished for bad behavior. Prior to 1968, PNM had few incentive-based programs, but punishments were consistently delivered. Minor violations led to light punishments and major violations led to predictable periods of lockdown in the disciplinary unit. Inmates reported that the period prior to 1968 was "damned oppressive, but it was consistent" (Colvin 1992: 44–45). There was little violence in the prison during this period; inmates were extremely submissive but had little optimism about rehabilitation or their ability to change prison conditions.

In the typologies developed in chapter 2, we can see that the period from 1976 to the 1980 riot was increasingly characterized by the Type 4 pattern of control, which is inconsistently coercive. The period from 1968 to 1975 approaches (but is not purely, since it is unlikely many inmates developed strong moral bonds to the prison) the Type 1 pattern of control, which consistently gives rewards for good behavior and rarely uses coercion to gain compliance. The period prior to 1968 approximates the Type 3 pattern of control, which is consistently coercive and produces submission. (Similar patterns of change are reported in prison studies by James B. Jacobs [1977] and John Irwin [1980].)

A recent trend in American prisons is the development of super-maximum security prisons that increase the surveillance of inmates and the delivery of coercion to a level never before seen (King 1999). These so-called supermax prisons approach a pure Type 3 pattern of control. In some of these prisons, inmates are locked in individual cells 24 hours a day under the view of surveillance cameras. They might be allowed into an exercise pen for about 30 minutes a day in which they have no contact with other inmates. Under this very close monitoring, coercion is delivered consistently and with great certainty. Inmates become depressed; in fact, the greatest security problem in such settings is making certain that individual inmates do not obtain materials with which to commit suicide. Rehabilitation is out of the question under these circumstances. Anger is enhanced, but the only target is inward, toward the self. External locus of control is at the extreme. Social bonds are entirely eliminated. When the person is released from such a setting, and the constant monitoring of behavior is ended, self-directed anger may turn outward with even greater force than before.

Whether the coercion is consistent or inconsistent, the prison experience is likely to be related to recidivism. About 60 percent of prisoners have been in prison before (Greenfeld 1985). Studies that have tracked released prisoners show that most are re-arrested, with over 60 percent being re-arrested for crimes within three years of release (Beck and Shipley 1989, 1987; Sacks and Logan 1984). Released prisoners serving longer prison terms have higher rates of re-offending than those who served shorter terms for similar crimes (Austin 1986; Currie 1994; Gottfredson et al. 1973; Petersilia et al. 1978). And juveniles have been found to be *more* delinquent after being officially sanctioned through incarceration than before (Shannon 1982). Similarly, Sampson and Laub (1993) found in their longitudinal study that being incarcerated led to increases in criminal behavior. They argue that the relationship is due to the fact that incarceration prevents steady employment. This is part of the picture. The theory developed in this book sees incarceration as an extreme increase in coercion, which aggravates the social-psychological deficits and coercive ideation that make chronic offending more likely.

# LIFE AS A GENERALIZED
# COERCIVE EXPERIENCE

If an individual moves from one social setting to the next and experiences coercion in all of these settings, then his or her life becomes a generalized experience of coercion. It is likely that individuals moving toward chronic criminality perceive their lives this way. An individual who experiences a greater degree of coercion in a greater number of immediate social contexts is more likely to have social-psychological deficits sustained and reinforced over the course of his or her life. This individual develops coercive ideation that becomes a fixed view depicting a truly mean world. Through these social-psychological mediations, greater coercion creates a greater likelihood that an individual will become chronically involved in predatory street crime. Thus it is not the coercion experienced in one site per se (such as the family or workplace) but the overall mosaic of coercion one experiences that affects criminality. As one moves from a context in which coercion is a major feature, one is likely to behave in a way that elicits coercive responses in another context. The person is not merely a passive recipient of coercion but actively elicits this type of response because of the social-psychological deficits he or she brings into each new setting. In each setting, the reciprocal relationship between coercion and social-psychological deficits recurs. Unless chance interventions or events occur to create turning points for the individual, which remove the coercion in a particular setting and thus may begin to reduce social-psychological deficits, it is likely that these dynamics will be recreated across settings for the individual. These repeated social and psychological processes of coercion are likely to sustain an individual in a trajectory toward chronic criminality.

The effects of the immediate contexts of coercion are diagrammed in figure 3.1. Here an intergenerational, developmental theory of coercion and chronic criminality is sketched in which *social-psychological deficits* are created by and interact with *coercive controls*. These social-psychological deficits include high levels of other-directed anger, low self-control, an external locus of control, low self-efficacy, a weak, alienated social bond, strong coercive behavioral modeling, and a perceived control deficit accompanied by feelings of debasement or humiliation. These are the social-psychological outcomes related to the Type 4 pattern discussed in chapter 2.

Figure 3.1 represents the intergenerational reproduction of Type 4 control and its social-psychological and behavioral outcomes. A parent develops social-psychological deficits because of (1) coercive relations encountered at work and/or in state agencies of welfare and criminal justice and (2) coercive controls in the parent's background during his or her socialization in family, school, and peer associations. The social-psychological deficits of the

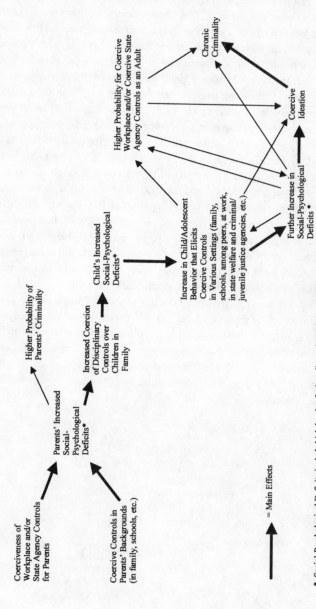

87

Figure 3.1   An Intergenerational, Develpomental Model of Coercion and Chronic Criminality

Coerciveness of Workplace and/or State Agency Controls for Parents

Higher Probability of Parents' Criminality

Parents' Increased Social-Psychological Deficits*

Coercive Controls in Parents' Backgrounds (in family, schools, etc.)

Increased Coercion of Disciplinary Controls over Children in Family

Child's Increased Social-Psychological Deficits*

Increase in Child/Adolescent Behavior that Elicits Coercive Controls in Various Settings (family, schools, among peers, at work, in state welfare and criminal/ juvenile justice agencies, etc.)

Higher Probability for Coercive Workplace and/or Coercive State Agency Controls as an Adult

Chronic Criminality

Coercive Ideation

Further Increase in Social-Psychological Deficits *

= Main Effects

* Social-Psychological Deficits include high levels of other-directed anger, low self-control, external locus of control, low self-efficacy, weak social bond (based on alienation), strong coercive behavioral modeling, and perceived control deficit with feelings of debasement.

parent contribute to the creation of coercive disciplinary controls over their children, who in turn begin to develop social-psychological deficits. These deficits begin to manifest themselves through behavior, such as aggression, noncompliance, and defiance, that elicits coercive controls from others, including parents, school authorities, peers, and state agencies. These coercive reactions further increase the social-psychological deficits, which propel the individual toward chronic misbehavior and delinquency. Unless the chain of causation is interrupted through deliberate intervention or chance encounters, the individual during late adolescence and young adulthood is likely to develop *coercive ideation* in which the world is conceived as an all-encompassing experience of coercion that can only be overcome through coercion. As in the Type 4 pattern of control, discussed in chapter 2, the erratic coercion experienced by the individual allows him or her to periodically imagine that this coercive environment can be overcome through coercion. Such a mindset is an immediate precursor to chronic criminality and is reflected in the predatory nature of the crimes committed. (It is this mindset that most immediately connects the background of criminality with the foreground of crime, as I discuss in chapter 5.) As a young adult, the individual is likely to be involved erratically with coercive controls at work and in state agencies of welfare and criminal justice, which only serve to sustain social-psychological deficits, coercive ideation, and chronic criminality.

This developmental theory grows out of the discussion of the immediate contexts of coercion and is supported empirically by the research cited in this chapter. In the next chapter, I add to this diagram by including larger economic and cultural forces that affect the levels of coercion in these immediate social contexts and thus the development of chronic criminality. (See the Appendix for a guide to literature on measurement of variables contained in figure 3.1.)

# Chapter 4

# The Larger Contexts of Coercion: Economics and Culture ◉

The immediate social contexts (of work, family, schools, peer groups, and state agencies) through which an individual passes during socialization are affected by larger social and historical trends that can influence the degree to which coercion will be present in individuals' lives. The variables we consider in this chapter typically are ignored in criminological studies of differences in individuals' criminal behavior because they do not, in a statistical sense, account for very much of the "variance explained." This statistical term, related to the R-square in regression analysis, is interpreted too literally in its use of the term "explained." The macro-level variables focused on in this chapter are more typically used in understanding variations in aggregate rates of crime; and this is clearly an important issue, which is addressed in this chapter. Macro-level background variables rarely show much statistical association in studies of individual criminal behavior when controlling for the variables that reflect the micro-level processes arising from the immediate contexts discussed in chapter 3. But even if they are not statistically substantial, these macro-level variables and trends are nonetheless profoundly important in understanding the larger patterning of forces that shape the immediate contexts in which criminality is produced. Without these larger forces, the immediate contexts (from which the variables that show substantial associations to crime and delinquency arise) would be tangibly altered. Larger economic and cultural background forces profoundly shape the immediate social processes that produce criminality. Leaving these out of the discussion is like a physicist explaining the motion of electrons without any reference to the magnetic fields that influence their movement.

# ECONOMIC CONDITIONS, DEMOGRAPHICS, AND COMMUNITY

Strong economic conditions, with low unemployment and opportunities for good, stable jobs, create the foundation for a society that can offer strong social supports for individuals and their families (Cullen 1994; Currie 1998, 1994, 1985). These same conditions create the building blocks for cohesive neighborhoods and communities, which provide networks of social support outside the family. Governmental and non-governmental agencies, under strong economic conditions, have more resources to expend on social support activities, which are more likely to be demanded when communities and neighborhoods are cohesive, stable, politically active, and organized. These structural conditions create an environment in which fewer individuals experience coercion; predatory street crime, as a consequence, is less likely to occur.

Poor economic conditions are the basis for a coercive society. When unemployment is high, the workforce is less stable, and good quality jobs are less available, working conditions generally become more coercive. Under these economic conditions, unions have greater difficulty organizing workers, alleviating poor working conditions, and successfully pressuring government for social support expenditures and activities affecting workers and the unemployed. Workers have fewer options under these conditions. They cannot readily leave an aversive workplace. They cannot risk resisting bosses' demands. They have little bargaining power because the "reserve army" of unemployed people can easily replace them. The competitive struggle among workers (both employed and unemployed) undermines cohesion and undercuts their ability to organize for community and political purposes. And the experience of being unemployed is more or less desperate depending on the general state of the economy (whether unemployment is merely "frictional" or "structural") and on the strength of governmental social supports for the unemployed (Carlson and Michalowski 1997). To the extent that these unemployed people are forced to compete for jobs by restrictive welfare provisions, severe criminal justice policies, and the desperation of economic necessity, life becomes a generalized coercive experience, contributing to high rates of predatory street crime.

Since economic conditions tend to change in relatively long cyclical patterns, pressures arising from the economy are historically situated. For the United States from 1929 to 1999, sustained periods of economic decline have been followed by long waves of economic growth. These long swings of economic growth and decline correspond to long-term fluctuations in crime rates because the experience of work and unemployment is different in periods of growth than in periods of decline. A positive correlation between annual unemployment rates and annual crime rates in the United States has been reported in various studies (cf., Chiricos 1987; Fagan and Freeman 1999; Freeman 1995; Walker 1989).[1] But depending on the years used in these time series, the unemployment rate may or may not demonstrate a significant relationship to the crime rate.

Susan M. Carlson and Raymond J. Michalowski (1997: 235) provide a possible answer to this apparent puzzle: Their time-series analyses indicate that "unemployment is associated more closely with burglary, robbery, assault, and homicide during periods when the social structure of accumulation generates structural unemployment than when it results in frictional unemployment." Social structures of accumulation are "the specific institutional environment within which the capitalist accumulation process is organized" (Gordon, Edwards, and Reich 1982: 9). This external environment in which business pursues profits includes the institutional arrangements between labor and capital and the government policies affecting factors like the money supply, credit, business regulation, union activities, welfare, and unemployment benefits. The social structure of accumulation is determined by the relative strengths of labor and capital. In some periods labor is strong enough to push successfully for compromise arrangements in industry and government that are favorable to workers and the unemployed while still allowing for robust business profitability. A favorable global economic climate allows for the consolidation of these institutional arrangements, which are effective, at least for a time, in promoting the accumulation of capital. Thus a long wave of economic expansion ensues. During these expansionary periods, like the one from 1948 to 1966, unemployment tends to be *frictional* in that it is largely temporary and new workers and the unemployed have good chances of finding jobs. Real (inflation-adjusted) wages during these periods tend to be higher. And relatively generous unemployment benefits cushion the experience of being unemployed. Unemployment thus lacks the sense of desperation and hopelessness, which would otherwise create a highly coercive social experience for the unemployed, and partially as a result the experience of work is less coercive.

But the institutional arrangements that make up this particular social structure of accumulation contain potential limitations for the growth of profitability, so they eventually decay. Global economic shifts may put pressure on profits encouraging business and government elites to undo the institutional arrangements that had represented a compromise between capital and labor and to weaken governmental policies favorable to workers and the unemployed. As the social structure of accumulation decays under the stress of global economic shifts and renewed warfare against the rights and privileges of labor and the poor, a long wave of economic decline ensues.

For a long period, new ways of operating the economy, government, and industry are explored with erratic success as industry and government attempt to build an entirely new social structure of accumulation that might reverse the economic decline. During such periods of decay and exploration, like in the 1930s and in the 1970s through early 1990s, unemployment becomes *structural* as a large surplus population is increasingly cut off from any realistic expectations for stable employment. Under these conditions, the social experiences of work (especially low-wage work) and unemployment are filled with coercion, which seems to radiate into every aspect of life.

Carlson and Michalowski (1997) demonstrate in their analysis that the relationship between unemployment rates and crime rates is historically contingent. The meaning and social experience of unemployment differs depending on the configuration of labor-management relations and governmental policies that constitute a social structure of accumulation. I argue that the key difference in these historical periods, which show differential strength in the unemployment-crime relationship, is the relative presence or absence of coercion in the lives of the unemployed and the working poor.

Given the historical contingency of these larger coercive forces, it is instructive to review what has taken place in the United States during the post - World War II period in which both economic changes and shifts in the crime rate have been dramatic (LaFree 1998a). The period from 1948 to 1966 saw some of the lowest average unemployment rates along with historically low crime rates, which only began increasing toward the end of this period (Bureau of Labor Statistics 1999; LaFree 1998a). Unemployment tended to be frictional rather than structural, although as early as 1960 some inner city areas of large cities began experiencing structural unemployment as jobs increasingly moved to suburban areas and discrimination and residential segregation blocked minorities from job opportunities (Bursik and Grasmick 1993; Patterson 1996: 74–76, 380–84; Sugrue 1996). This nascent structural unemployment (and its geographically uneven development) may in part account for the beginnings of the rise in crime rates during the early 1960s, which was concentrated primarily in these inner city areas (Bursik and Grasmick 1993; Sugrue 1996: 205, 217). (In addition, the early 1960s saw the first cohort of baby boomers, which I discuss later, entering their late teens, when risk for criminal involvement is at its highest [LaFree 1998a: 44; Patterson 1996: 77–81]. And the rapid growth of suburbs in the late 1950s and early 1960s according to Marcus Felson [1998], whom I discuss in chapter 5, enhanced opportunities for crime.) Overall, national unemployment statistics remained low, as did crime rates.

From 1948 to1966 the engine of growth had been a strong unionized manufacturing sector that provided stable, good-paying blue-collar jobs to millions of Americans. These jobs created, next to the factories, stable urban neighborhoods where workers gathered in union halls, local taverns, ball fields, and backyards to discuss common problems, mediate disputes, entertain themselves, and organize for political actions. The unionized workplace was a facilitator of neighborhood and community networking, which included connections to good blue-collar jobs for young people (Sullivan 1989). While factory work was boring and routine, unions' pay scales (with annual cost of living adjustments) and promotion ladders created a remunerative system of control and allowed many workers to achieve middle-class status. During this period, union contracts protected workers from competition, so management could not effectively use the coercive tactic of bringing in replacement workers.

With unions at their strongest levels in U.S. history, a booming economy that produced tight labor markets, and government social supports that cushioned the experience of unemployment, the workplace during this period was generally less coercive for more workers than it has been before or since. These non-coercive, unionized workplaces and the stable neighborhoods built around them contributed to the lowest crime rates witnessed in the twentieth century during the 1950s and early 1960s.

Then from 1967 to 1992, the economy generally eroded as inflation increased, corporate profitability decreased, average unemployment (which became more structural in nature) rose, unions and real wages declined, economic inequality widened, and governmental social supports for the working poor and the unemployed were generally curtailed (Michalowski and Carlson 1999). This period saw a dramatic overall increase and then leveling off at historically high levels in the rates of assault, robbery, rape, homicide, burglary, larceny, and motor vehicle theft reported annually in the Federal Bureau of Investigation's *Uniform Crime Reports* (LaFree 1998a).[2]

Before the late 1960s, American manufacturers had enjoyed a virtual monopoly in many industrial activities such as production of steel, autos, energy, and rubber. This monopoly position allowed them to accede to organized labor's demands for pay increases by passing these costs on to consumers. This non-competitive market situation allowed for the establishment and maintenance of the remunerative system of control over these industries' workers. Suddenly in the late 1960s, these industries began to feel the effects of growing competition from rising European and Japanese industries and from a consortium of oil producing nations that banded together to raise worldwide oil prices. As this global economic competition emerged, American-manufacturing industries became more subject to setting their prices according to market supply and demand. And rising oil prices and other sources of inflation increased their costs of doing business. In 1966, a long period of decline in U.S. corporate profitability began (Harrison and Bluestone 1988: 8). With rising costs and stronger downward pressure on their selling prices, these industries could no longer pass labor costs on to consumers without further cutting into their already declining profits.[3] At this point, American industry began to accelerate a process aimed at undercutting the power of manufacturing unions and thus reducing the cost of labor. In the process, they made the workplace more coercive, and they destroyed the basis for the stable blue-collar neighborhoods in U.S. cities.

American manufacturing industries had already been slowly undercutting the power of unions through technological innovation (Zieger 1986). During the 1950s and 1960s union workers traded individual job security (protected by seniority) for a toleration of automation that gradually replaced human labor. As older union workers retired, younger workers did not replace them. This slow process of attrition reduced the proportion of the work force that was unionized from 36 percent in 1944 to 27 percent in 1970. Some manufacturing industries began moving factories away from unionized states to non-union states after passage of the Taft-Hartley Act in 1947, which allowed states to pass "right to work" legislation that outlawed union shops. The southern states of the United States had long been a source of cheap unskilled labor, by the 1950s industries that had to deal with unions in northern states began to relocate to these southern states.

After the oil crisis and foreign competition of the early 1970s placed new economic pressures on unionized manufacturing industries, the process of undercutting unions accelerated. Increasingly, manufacturing plants were closed in unionized northern states as production was shifted to new foreign factories that used abundantly available cheap labor in nations where the ruling classes were violently hostile to unions. For the first time in decades, unionized workers were faced with job competition that undermined their bargaining position. Striking unions were increasingly faced with replacement by non-union workers, a tactic that was perfected in President Ronald Reagan's permanent replacement of unionized air traffic controllers in 1981, a move that dramatically signaled to American industry that war on unions was official. By 1988, unionized workers comprised only 17 percent of the workforce, dropping to 15 percent in 1996.

The busting of unions was facilitated by a series of recessions beginning in the early 1970s. Unemployment rates reached levels in 1974 and 1975 not seen since the Great Depression. Government fiscal policy accelerated this recessionary trend, as the Federal Reserve raised interest rates to protect investors and banks made vulnerable by the slowing economy and rising inflation. These recessions swelled the ranks of the unemployed that competed directly for work and contributed to the growth of a (semi) permanent underclass who were increasingly cut off from the mainstream economy in the 1980s and early 1990s. This rise in structural unemployment occurred at the same time that government social supports for the poor and the unemployed were slashed (Currie 1998, 1994, 1985). These factors provided the basis for a multiplication of coercive workplaces. Workers under non-coercive remunerative control declined significantly as the unionized manufacturing sector shrank. And those who were directly affected by growing structural unemployment faced an increasingly harsh and coercive social environment.

During the 1980s, economic growth returned for a few years, but blue-collar and low-wage workers did not benefit from this growth in GNP. While manufacturing jobs in the primary labor market continued to decline because of disinvestment, the secondary labor market, with low-paying, dead-end jobs, showed astonishing growth. These are the "bad jobs" that Crutchfield (1989) and others (Allan and Steffensmeier 1989; Crutchfield and Pitchford 1997) have related to higher violent crime rates. These jobs operate primarily through coercive control, which was enhanced during the 1980s and early 1990s by high levels of structural unemployment. (Official unemployment rates, which often do not capture large segments of those affected by structural unemployment [see Michalowski and Carlson 1999: 231–32], remained historically high [hovering above 5.5 percent] even during the so-called boom years of the mid-1980s).

Unlike the unionized manufacturing jobs of the 1950s and 1960s, turnover and job instability are extremely high in these secondary labor market jobs. While the neighborhoods surrounding unionized factories were stable and cohesive, owing to a strong economic base and powerful networks of interaction arising from work and union activities, secondary labor market jobs contribute to instability of community relations as workers move frequently from place to place in search of work. Such neighborhoods lack the crucial networks that connect young people to stable jobs (Sullivan 1989). And increasingly after 1966, work was moving from inner cities to suburban areas, which cut masses of unemployed inner city youth off from the legitimate job market. (Isolation from these suburban job markets was exacerbated by a declining public transportation infrastructure in metropolitan areas.) The growth of secondary labor markets contributed to the falling inflation-adjusted wage rate for workers (Freeman 1994) and to a widening gap between rich and poor, which began to emerge in 1966, accelerated in the 1970s, and peaked in the 1980s and early 1990s (Weinberg 1996). The declining rate of real wages during this period is connected to the period's growing crime rates (Gould, Weinberg, and Mustard 1999), as is the increasing level of economic inequality (LaFree 1998a: 124). These economic trends provide the structural background for the high levels of crime in the 1970s, 1980s, and early 1990s, when work (and life in general) became a more coercive experience for a greater number of people.

The economic expansion that started in 1993 (and continues to surge ahead as of the writing of this book) has steadily lowered the unemployment rate in the United States to a point not seen since the late 1960s (Bureau of Labor Statistics 1999). This drop in unemployment coincided with a steady reduction in crime rates in the late 1990s (LaFree 1998b; *Washington Post* 1999a). It is possible that in the late 1990s a long wave of economic expansion was commencing (based on consolidation of what might be a new social structure of accumulation created by technologies that have enhanced labor productivity, which keeps inflation low despite low unemployment and pressures toward rising wage rates). Unemployment thus began in the late 1990s to shift from structural to frictional unemployment, which is associated with lower crime rates (Carlson and Michalowski 1997). These recent economic trends have begun to give workers greater power to resist coercive control since they have more choices in jobs; and employers in many areas are desperate to hire and retain workers. Under these conditions, even secondary labor market jobs must become less coercive or risk losing workers. Work and life in general are less coercive during such economic upturns in which unemployment is lower and workers feel greater power.

Young African American males, who accounted for a disproportionate amount of urban crime from the early 1960s through the early 1990s, were drawn into the late 1990s' booming job market, which has been linked to their falling crime rates (Nasar and Mitchell 1999). An analysis by Richard B. Freeman and William M. Rodgers III (1999) of low-wage young men in 322 metropolitan areas in the United States reveals that lower unemployment is directly related to lower crime rates. This finding holds when controlling for the rate of incarceration. Of particular significance, those metropolitan areas that showed the greatest drop in unemployment rates from 1992 to 1997 had the greatest drop in crime rates. The analysis shows that employment gains during this period for young African American males uniformly outstripped the more modest gains for all young males. This trend is far different than the mid-1980s economic "boom" when many young black males were left out of the growth in jobs, which occurred overwhelming in white suburban areas. During the late 1990s, entry level pay, which had been declining by 25 percent in real (inflation-adjusted) dollars since the early 1970s, improved to the point that legitimate work was perceived by many young men as more rewarding than gains from the underground economy. Between 1992 and 1997, in the metropolitan areas with the tightest job markets, real hourly pay increased 15 percent for young, less-educated black males, a complete reversal of the trends from the previous two decades (Freeman and Rodgers 1999). Increasingly for these young men in metropolitan areas with tight labor markets, frictional unemployment was replacing structural unemployment. This improving economic picture has thus particularly affected a group that was economically marginal from the early 1960s to the early 1990s and had accounted for a disproportionate amount of predatory street crime during that period. The most important fact of the late 1990s is that, unlike previous economic expansions, young, less-educated African American males were beginning to enjoy some benefits from an economic boom (*Washington Post* 2000b). As their job prospects improved in this booming economy (and because of these very tight labor markets these jobs are less coercive), many see their lives as a less coercive experience, which alters the processes, discussed in chapter 3, that produce chronic predatory street crime.

Demographic changes cannot be ignored as a factor shaping these economic and crime trends. The impact of the baby boom (persons born between 1946 and 1964) has been enormous during the second half of the twentieth century in the United States (Marvell and Moody 1991; Patterson 1996). During childhood, the baby boom was partially responsible for the growing economy of the 1950s and 1960s, as parents bought houses, cars, and educational opportunities to create the suburban "good life" for their children. By the early 1960s, the first cohort of the baby boom was entering two important phases of life: labor market participation and explorations in deviance. By the 1970s the baby boom swelled the proportion of the population who were in their late teens and early twenties and began entering the labor market just as a series of economic recessions began. Their movement into the labor market (at entry levels) accelerated an already expanding pool of unemployed, contributing to lower pay and coercion of the work world. Near this same period, the baby boom generation entered the highest risk years for involvement in street crime (late teens and early twenties). Thus they entered their crime-prone years at the very time that heightened economic pressures were already conducive to crime. This conjuncture contributed strongly to the surging crime rates of the 1970s, which remained high until the early 1990s. By the mid-1990s, the baby boom generation was entering middle age, a time when employment stability and income tend to be at their highest levels. The economic boom of the late 1990s can partially be explained by the enormous buying power that the baby boom generation possesses during its prime income-producing years. Greater consumer spending and a rising stock market are among the engines of recent economic growth in the United States, and these are primarily due to the economic activities of the baby boom generation. Contributing to lower unemployment and lower crime during this period of high consumer spending is the relatively small proportion of the population that in the 1990s were in their late teens and early twenties. And these young people were entering a much improving job market in the 1990s.

To the extent that lower unemployment has been created by these demographic trends, work in the late 1990s became less coercive and the desperation of the unemployed was reduced, thus curtailing the economic pressures that help foster coercive ideation. With the greater availability of legitimate work that was now less coercive, many young people moved from coercive illegitimate work, which is reflected in the decline of the crack trade during the 1990s, to these less coercive work situations. In the process, crime rates steadily declined during the late 1990s (*Washington Post* 1999a).

Thus historically situated economic pressures can affect the degree to which an individual experiences coercion both at the workplace and in other areas of life. The combination of low unemployment, strong unions, higher real wages, and greater levels of governmental social support contribute to a less coercive society, as was the case from about 1948 to 1966 when crime rates were at their historic lows. With higher unemployment, weaker unions, lower real wages, declining governmental social supports, and rising economic inequality (as from the late 1960s to the mid-1990s) society generally becomes more coercive and crime rates are higher. The recent dramatic lowering of the unemployment rate has been an important factor in producing a less coercive economy. Structural unemployment declined in the late 1990s, which means that the experience of unemployment was not as coercive a social experience as it had been just ten years earlier. Unions remained historically weak but showed some organizing and political strength in the late 1990s. Governmental social supports also remain weak, but the strong job market has reduced the number of people who need the safety net these supports provide. Weak unions, weak governmental social supports, and continued economic inequality may be some of the reasons that, while certainly lower than in the late 1980s and early 1990s, rates of violent crime still remained considerably higher in the late 1990s than they had been in the late 1960s (*Washington Post* 1999b).[4]

In Merton's classic strain theory, the economic pressures discussed in this section are directly related to crime because of the strain they cause. I understand the strain arising from economic pressure as coercion. This coercion can be interpersonal, experienced as direct control by others, or impersonal, experienced as desperation brought on by economic necessity. These forms of coercion contribute to the development of social-psychological deficits in older teenagers and adults who directly interact with workplaces and the labor market. They indirectly affect children and younger teenagers through their effects on parents' social-psychological deficits and coercive family processes (Conger et al. 1994). (See chapter 3 for a detailed discussion of the latter point.)

Since economic conditions are not uniformly distributed throughout a nation like the United States and long waves of economic decline hit some areas well before they impact the nation as a whole, some geographic locations are affected to a greater extent by poor economic conditions. In the twentieth century, it was usually the inner city areas of major metropolitan regions that were most severely affected by economic downturns (Hagan 1994). It is these areas where the "truly disadvantaged" (Wilson 1987) reside in conditions of "social disorganization" (Shaw and McKay 1942). The movement of financial and physical capital during the twentieth century in response to global economic change produced concentrations of poverty located primarily in inner cities that became segregated from the mainstream economy and society (Hagan 1994; Sullivan 1989). These areas in the United States were affected even earlier by the structural unemployment that marked the long wave of economic decline from 1966 to 1992. Many of these areas had already become economically marginal by 1960 as jobs began to migrate to the suburbs, which helps us understand the start of the upward trend in crime rates that began in the early 1960s (Bursik and Grasmick 1993; Sugrue 1996).

Along with the loss of legitimate jobs in these areas came a reduction in social capital, which John Hagan (1994: 67–69) defines as the social networks within families and communities that are vital for the transmission of productive and social skills, as well as job connections, to children (see also Sullivan 1989). The absence of financial, physical, and social capital gives rise to cultural adaptations that "involve the cultivation of attitudes and actions that diverge from, or are in actual opposition to, more routine and conforming societal norms and values. However, they are often also the only or best life choices available, and these adaptations can become powerful influences on later life outcomes" (Hagan 1994: 70). Thus capital disinvestment includes not only the loss of financial and physical capital but also the loss of social and cultural capital for a geographical area.

In Francis T. Cullen's (1994) social support theory such disinvestment entails the loss of both instrumental and expressive social supports. It is this economic background (the loss of financial and physical capital) that creates the impoverished social and cultural environment. Such an environment creates the basis for coercive ideation that affects families and individuals through both economic pressures and cultural codes of the streets that promote violent responses to adversity and conflict.

Hagan pinpoints the economic sources of social disorganization, which Clifford Shaw and Henry McKay (1942) describe as a breakdown in social ties within a community. As with Hagan's discussion, Shaw and McKay argue that the vacuum created by social disorganization in inner city areas gives rise to the "cultural transmission" of deviant values and lifestyles. This type of social environment fosters and sustains a street culture that is both a product and a producer of coercion. It is tied to larger economic forces of coercion and to cultural forces that encourage coercive ideation.

## CULTURAL INFLUENCES ON COERCION

In addition to economic pressures, various elements of culture in the United States contribute to a coercive society. Among these cultural influences is a culture of violence that has roots in the southern code of honor and is reflected in a violent code of the streets in many inner city areas. In addition, coercion is promoted by a culture of hyper-individualism, competitiveness, and materialism that is rooted in the mass consumerism of advanced capitalism.

### From Southern Honor to the Code of the Streets

A cultural code that focuses on the demands of honor remains a strong tradition in the United States. This code has its roots in the Scotch-Irish immigration to America during the eighteenth century. A violent cultural tradition was fostered by continual warfare along the borders of Scotland and England from the fourteenth through the eighteenth centuries (Butterfield 1995; Wyatt-Brown 1982). Many of the Scotch-Irish, who had been caught up in this violence for generations, were forced by economic and political circumstances to migrate first to Northern Ireland and then to the American colonies. "When they came to America, they brought with them a penchant for family feuds, a love of whiskey, and a warrior ethic that demanded vengeance" (Butterfield 1995: 10). In the frontier areas of the American South, where most of them settled, the violent tradition was further reinforced by warfare with Native Americans who resisted these settlers' intrusions into their traditional lands. This long experience of violence and warfare nurtured a culture of fierce independence in which males were expected to respond violently to any attacks upon or insults to their sense of personal honor. Under this code of honor, a male's identity was entirely dependent upon the reputation he gained from others (Lane 1999: 221). This reputation was based on his demonstrated ability to exact retribution for personal slights or threats to himself or his family. Southern families relied on male brawn and courage for security and protection. Avenging fathers and brothers not the law (which was very weak in the South before the Civil War) secured retribution for offenses against family members. Thus upholding the sense of honor laid beneath the dueling, vigilante justice, blood feuds, and other forms of violence that were more common in the South than in other regions of America (Ayers 1984). In fact, the southern states today generally continue to have the highest homicide and assault rates in the United States, partially because of this cultural tradition (Messner and Stark 1999).

Child-rearing practices used in southern homes nurtured the code of honor in male children. The disciplining of children swung erratically between indulgent permissiveness and brutal coercion. Boys, especially, were encouraged to "run free" and "be aggressive, even ferocious" (Wyatt-Brown 1982: 138, 142). Their wild behavior included fighting, starting fires, and destroying property. Much of their destructive behavior was overlooked, and at times even praised by bemused adults. At other times, however, defiance of paternal authority quickly produced a violent reaction. Such defiance, which could include a failure to carry out a command from the father or perceived disrespectfulness toward the mother, was seen as an affront to the father's honor. Such defiance demanded an immediate, unrestrained physical reprisal from the father, who felt no need to offer any explanation for the attack. Parental disciplinary patterns were thus highly erratic and coercive (as in the Type 4 pattern discussed in chapter 2, which is most conducive to producing chronic violent behavior). This style of discipline engendered low self-restraint and aggression that stayed with individuals into their adult years. "The lack of self-restraint in southern adults' behavior owed much to the ambivalences and inconsistencies of parental discipline" (Wyatt-Brown 1982: 152). This type of inconsistent corporal punishment was common throughout the South. It differed from nineteenth-century parental disciplining patterns in the North where use of the rod was a last resort against unruly behavior and was accompanied by lectures on the meanings of wickedness and punishment, aimed at instilling internalized self-control in the child (Wyatt-Brown 1982: 149). (By 1850, northern states were being strongly affected by successful anti-corporal punishment campaigns, which had no influence in the South [Glenn 1984].) In southern families, wild behavior was often ignored and sometimes encouraged, but defiance of a father's right to rule (an important part of his sense of honor) was immediately met with an unreasoning violent explosion; no verbal lesson on the meaning of the punishment was given. The southern family thus became an important training ground for the code of honor and for unrestrained violence and coercive methods of dealing with conflict.

The southern institutions of slavery and enforced segregation also engendered violence because of their highly coercive patterns of control. No group in American history has been subjected to coercive control for as long a period as have African Americans. From slavery, through violently enforced segregation, to structural unemployment in inner cities, African American history has been one of struggle against coercive forces. Slave compliance was exacted through a brutal system of coercion which included whips, chains, mutilation, branding, forced removal from family members through sale, and even rape and murder. Yet slave plantations were by no means total institutions (Kolchin 1993). Slaves could and did resist, defying overseers' orders, sabotaging production, and frequently running away (Franklin and Schweninger 1999). And slave masters and overseers varied in their efficacy at slave control. Overall, the coercive system on slave plantations was rendered erratic because of defiance by many slaves and the constant dilemmas of control, which demanded frequent use of violent measures that never seemed to solve the problems inherent in forced labor for very long.

After slavery was abolished, African Americans in the South still suffered under coercive controls, but these were even less consistent and more arbitrary and impersonal than the coercive controls of slave plantations. Sharecropping and its accompanying debt peonage, chain gangs, and convict leasing replaced slavery in an attempt to control black labor; and vigilante violence, Klan terrorism, and lynching became tools of intimidation over blacks (Ayers 1992, 1984; Colvin 1997). While brutal and highly repressive, these operations were not particularly efficient in controlling people. (Escapes were very common from leasing camps and chain gangs.) And these methods were administered in a highly arbitrary and inconsistent fashion. At the same time, many young black males who had never experienced the controls of plantation slavery enjoyed a new sense of freedom, dodging chain gangs and lynch mobs while moving from town to town in search of work and adventure. In the process, they adopted from the white community the code of honor that had long propelled violence in the South. By the 1890s, the murder rate among blacks outpaced that of whites in the South (Ayers 1984: 231). The combination of the traditional southern code of honor along with the brutal but inconsistent coercive control that emerged after the end of Reconstruction fostered chronic violent behavior among an increasing number of young black males. The enormous poverty in the South, especially for blacks, only enhanced the coercive nature of life and fed the growth of coercive ideation among southerners, both blacks and whites.

The violence and forceful attempts at subordination by whites against blacks placed within the black community a cultural stamp of honor on black men who resisted these attempts at humiliation. Resisting blacks were labeled as bad by whites. Soon this designation of being "bad" was taken as a badge of honor among young blacks who developed a sub-culture that celebrated the rebellious "hard-man" who would not bend to the will of others, especially to the will of whites (Levine 1977; Silberman 1978). In the process the traditional code of honor was transformed into a new idea among young southern blacks of receiving respect (Butterfield 1995). The notion that the world was a coercive place that could only be overcome through coercion was instilled in growing numbers of young black males as it became clear that attempts to maintain respect were met with white violence. Violence had to be used to gain respect. This affected not only relations with whites but also relations among blacks who demanded respect from each other. This new cultural demand for "respect" enhanced the cultural support for coercion and violence among black males. It should be no surprise then, given the history of brutal but erratic coercion and the coercive ideation represented by this transformed code of honor, that "black rates of homicide have exceeded white rates at least since 1910, and probably longer" (Hagan 1994: 26; see also Lane 1999: 221).

This culture of violence did not remain uniquely southern. After the Civil War, many southern whites migrated to western states and territories and brought the code of honor with them. Thus western states began to rival southern states in levels of violent crime. During the twentieth century, waves of migration of southern blacks to northern and western cities brought the culture of violence to inner city areas, where blacks were isolated by segregation and discrimination. This culture of violence was further reinforced by the coercion experienced in workplaces, the continual poverty and structural unemployment for those who could not escape the inner city, white racism, and (often violent) confrontations with the white-dominated criminal justice system. In this new setting, the southern culture of violence was transformed into a violent code of the streets.

Elijah Anderson (1994: 82), who studied the street culture of Philadelphia in the early 1990s, describes the code of the streets as

a set of informal rules governing interpersonal public behavior, including violence. The rules prescribe both a proper comportment and a proper way to respond if challenged. . . . At the heart of the code is the issue of respect—loosely defined as being treated "right," or granted the deference one deserves. . . . [Importantly] respect is viewed as almost an external entity that is hard-won but easily lost.

The connection between this concept of "respect" and the old southern notion of "honor" is apparent (Lane 1999: 222). Both promote an atmosphere in which violent retaliation becomes an expected response to perceived insults, or, in the language of the streets, a response to being "dissed."

While much of the content of the code of the streets stems from traditions brought with black migration from the South to northern cities, Anderson argues that this violent code is also rooted in the desperate poverty, structural unemployment, and social isolation that shape the circumstances of contemporary inner city life. Coercive relations in the street and in the family perpetuate this code as well. "Simply living in such an environment places young people at special risk of falling victim to aggressive behavior," even for those inner city children who come from "decent" homes (Anderson 1994: 81). All children must learn to handle themselves in the street, which means that they must become familiar with, and adhere to, the code of the streets.

For some children, these lessons in coercion come early, in the home. As Anderson (1994: 83) explains,

> The need both to exercise a measure of control and to lash out at somebody is often reflected in the adults' relations with their children. At the very least, the frustrations of persistent poverty shorten the fuse in such people. . . . In these circumstances a woman—or a man, although men are less consistently present in children's lives—can be quite aggressive with children, yelling at and striking them for the least little infraction of the rules she has set down. Often little if any serious explanation follows the verbal and physical punishment. This response teaches children a particular lesson. They learn that to solve any kind of interpersonal problem one must quickly resort to hitting or other violent behavior.

The inconsistent, coercive pattern of discipline in these inner city families, described by Anderson, is remarkably similar to that of nineteenth-century white southern families, described by Bertram Wyatt-Brown (1982), which nurtured the South's code of honor and its high levels of violence.

Since many inner city women in these impoverished circumstances become street-oriented mothers, who hustle for food and money, they also become sporadic mothers. Many of their children become street-oriented as a result, growing up hard with little supervision, running free in the streets, and learning the lessons of coercion from short-tempered adults. "The children observe these goings-on, learning the lesson that might makes right. They quickly learn to hit those who cross them, and the dog-eat-dog mentality prevails" (Anderson 1994: 83). Thus coercive ideation springs from highly inconsistent and highly coercive controls encountered by many inner city youth (the Type 4 pattern of control discussed in chapter 2). In turn, coercive ideation feeds the cultural reproduction of the violent code of the streets.

Gaining respect (and oftentimes a sense of protection) in these circumstances depends on the reputation for violence one can acquire. The code of the streets is thus reproduced through these violent interchanges in the family and on the streets of the inner city. It is a cultural adaptation to a violent situation that is nurtured by the economic and social isolation of the inner city. Some of the content of the code of the streets has been handed down from the old southern code of honor, transmitted by repeated waves of migration from the American South, and transformed by the realities of inner city life.

The culture of honor and the violence it promotes is not an exclusive phenomenon of the American South. Similar codes of honor existed in Ireland and southern European countries such as Spain, Italy, and Sicily that contained near-feudal relations as recently as the early twentieth century. These particular codes of honor were also relayed to American inner cities in the nineteenth and twentieth centuries through immigration from Ireland, Sicily, Italy, and Mexico (Lane 1999). These immigrants were typically isolated in inner city areas where they worked in highly coercive work environments and suffered under the coercive constraints of poverty. Cultural importation of notions of honor along with these coercive conditions created a violent ethos that is similar to the code of the streets discussed by Anderson. But these codes of the street and other violent cultural traditions are not the only influences on coercive ideation. Cultural changes accompanying the rise of mass consumerism also affected crime and coercion.

## The Impact of Mass Consumer Culture on American Values

Beyond subcultures of violence, the larger culture of the United States has experienced enormous change with the advancement of capitalism that has also contributed to coercive ideation. During the nineteenth century, a Protestant-based Victorian middle-class culture represented the triumph of what Norbert Elias (1982 [1939], 1978 [1939]) calls the "civilizing process." According to Elias, the advancement of Western civilization from about the sixteenth century onward entailed the growth of inhibitions on violence, aggression, and open displays of sexual and other basic desires. An important aspect of Elias's argument is that "distasteful" behaviors are not necessarily eliminated by the civilizing process, but are pushed out of public view and not discussed in polite conversation. In other words, they, in a Freudian sense, are repressed through self-control. During the nineteenth century, America underwent a dramatic cultural change based in evangelical Puritan traditions that promoted the values of self-discipline, self-control, and denial of personal pleasure (Sellers 1991). The temperance movement was one of the more visible manifestations of this cultural change, with Prohibition representing the ultimate triumph (and last gasp) of Victorian cultural dominance. This value system, with its emphasis on self-disciplined effort and denial of pleasure contributed to rapid industrialization in the late nineteenth and early twentieth centuries.

Elias wrote his treatise in the 1930s when this Victorian culture still had a strong influence on American (and European) culture. But during the 1920s, America for a brief period saw the first glimpse of a consumer-based culture that over the next 70 years would erode Victorian values. After productive capacity reached then-historic heights during World War I, American manufacturers increasingly relied on mass advertising through radio and magazines to promote the sale of products, which were abundantly overproduced during the 1920s. Images of the "good life" and the "American Dream" of rapid financial success were broadcast to the masses. People enjoying luxurious pleasure were presented in advertising, magazines, and movies. The "flapper" who was playful and ready for pleasure rivaled the dominant ideal image of woman as restrained and asexual. People were encouraged to try new fads. Instead of hard work and saving, people were enticed into spending on consumer items through indebtedness. Unfortunately, many Americans were caught up in the fad of buying stocks with money they did not have, through buying "on margin." For awhile, this became a channel for cash that could be used to participate in the new consumerism. But the nascent consumer culture soon hit a limit. Overproduced goods could not possibly be bought by the mass of the population who still worked for low wages or on farms that increasingly returned lower prices for crops. The stock market crash in 1929 dried up a major source for consumer spending and the ensuing Great Depression brought consumerism to a halt. Businesses could not sell their products and workers were continually laid off. The dual contradiction of overproduction and under-consumption hit American capitalism. It would not be solved until Americans had the financial capacity along with a culturally induced desire to spend.

After the end of World War II, which boosted productive capacity enormously and increased pent-up demand for consumer products, consumer culture emerged stronger than ever before. With rising wages due to union contracts and veterans' benefits that provided government assistance for education and home buying, the financial basis for consumer culture came into being. Advertising became a major industry, which scientifically studied the best inducements for getting people, including teenagers who now represented a growing market, to spend their money (Gilbert 1986; Halberstam 1993; Patterson 1996). As Yale social historian David Potter wrote in the 1950s, "Advertising now compares with such long-standing institutions as the school and the church in the magnitude of its social influence. It dominates the media, it has vast power in the shaping of popular standards and it is really one of the very limited groups of institutions which exercise social control" (quoted in Halberstam 1993: 502). These new elements changed the nature of capitalism. As David Halberstam (1993: 506) writes in his history of America in the 1950s,

> For this was not simple old prewar capitalism, this was something new—capitalism that was driven by ferocious consumerism, where the impulse was not so much about what people *needed* in their lives but what they needed to consume in order to keep up with their neighbors and, of course, to drive the GNP endlessly upward. "Capitalism is dead—consumerism is king," said the president of the National Sales Executives, defining the difference between prewar America and the new America orchestrated by Madison Avenue. The people surging into the middle class were the target market, and they were supposed to buy any way they could—if necessary, indeed preferably, on credit. This was an important new development . . . the new consumerism depended not merely on mercantile seduction but on credit as well, and ordinary buyers were extended levels of credit never enjoyed by such people before. . . . As that happened, the old puritanism was dramatically weakened.

Soon, society's "civilized sensibilities," based on the old Victorian culture of self-denial and self-control, were increasingly undermined by media images in movies, magazines, and television that promoted the immediate gratification of desires. Motivational research experts who worked for major advertising firms sought to overcome the restraints imposed by Puritan and Victorian traditions. "The job for the advertiser . . . was therefore not so much to just sell the product 'as to give moral permission to have fun without guilt.' This was . . . a major psychological crisis in American life: the conflict between puritanism and appetites whetted by the new consumerism. . . . Each year seemed to take the country further from its old puritan restraints; each year it was a little easier to sell than in the past" (Halberstam 1993: 507).

The cultural basis for self-control was thus undermined as adults struggled to "keep up" with their neighbors in the accumulation of material possessions. Their children, facing the newly invented "teen" years, anxiously sought the items that would provide the symbols of an independent, precocious adulthood, which were highly prized in the new peer culture that emerged with the rise of consumerism (Gilbert 1986; Palladino 1996). "This new independence of adolescents marked a further social evolution of the American family. It also marked a further step of its junior members into the commercial nexus, where they joined adults as equals. . . . Mass [consumer] culture broke into the traditional ties of family and community, creating an intervening peer group that responded to national market trends" (Gilbert 1986: 205). The advance of capitalism from a production-based to a consumer-based economy thus had a profound impact on American culture.

Some commentators have labeled this cultural upheaval "the Great Disruption" (Fukuyama 1999). Traditional bonds of kinship were disrupted with the rapid movement of jobs and population from rural areas, small towns, and central cities to suburbs. The cultural center moved from localized family and community-based structures to a nebulous realm accessed through mass media. Conservatives, such as former Education Secretary William J. Bennett, view this change as simply a breakdown in moral values, citing rising divorce rates and out-of-wedlock births, the ready availability of explicit sexual and violent material in the media, drug use, and crime as the indicators (Bennett et al. 1996). Clearly these do represent a lowering of the threshold of what became acceptable images to the public, and do reflect a decline of traditional moral constraints. And many changes in the structure and institution of the family are indeed related to rising crime rates in the post–World War II period (LaFree 1998a). However, these cultural disruptions are deeply rooted in the rising consumer culture produced by businesses and corporations that increasingly used sexual titillation and violent images to attract viewers and to sell products. This consumer culture and the economic pressures it induces also produced many of the changes in family relations related to higher crime, as family members increasingly spent time away from home and away from each other as they engaged in market activities (LaFree 1998a). In other words, these cultural disruptions are the product of the same free enterprise system (in its search for a solution to the problem of under-consumption) that is celebrated by many of the same conservatives who decry the moral decline it has produced.

The American culture that has been produced by this dramatic change has certain unique features that are conducive to criminal behavior. Steven F. Messner and Richard Rosenfeld (1997) delineate criminogenic elements of American culture and discuss why these have such an impact on producing in the United States the highest serious and violent crime rates among industrial democracies.[5] According to Messner and Rosenfeld (1997) American culture emphasizes achievement, individualism, universalism, and materialism. This combination of values in which individual achievement is measured by material acquisition, which is presumably open to everyone, produces an impetus toward crime when social institutions of the family, education, and government are weak. The economic needs and prerogatives of the business sector take precedence over and undermine the strength of these social institutions, which when strong effectively socialize, guide, and constrain individuals. Economic imperatives dominate in the United States to such an extent that the activities of these other social institutions are devalued and undermined and must accommodate themselves to these economic imperatives. Therefore, compared to other industrial democracies, governmental social supports for families and education (such as paid family leave, health insurance, and virtually free higher education and vocational training) are weak because of demands from the business sector to keep taxes low and employee benefits to a minimum. At the same time parents struggle to keep money coming in by working long hours, while they and their children, who are less supervised in the process, are induced by mass advertising to keep spending and spending. Self-control and the ideal of deferred gratification have a difficult time surviving in this economic and cultural environment. As a result, young people have less social support during the socialization process and are more likely to end up in marginal positions in the economy and society. In essence, they are left to fend for themselves but at the same time are induced to pursue the American dream of success by any means necessary. The inducements come from many sources including family, friends, and others who are also caught up in the market society. But ultimately it is the media, which is also dominated by economic interests, that is the source of these inducements.

David Matza and Gresham Sykes (1961) discuss how the larger culture promotes a set of "subterranean values" that appear to contradict prevailing values. But in fact, there are important convergences between the values in delinquent subcultures and the dominant values of society. For example, the norms of the business sector and the highly praised culture of free enterprise in America promote risk-taking, excitement, and the desire for getting rich quick that are adopted by delinquents. The society also promotes violence "since fantasies of violence in books, magazines, movies, and television are everywhere at hand. The delinquent simply translates into behavior those values the majority are usually too timid to express" but who nonetheless enjoy vicariously (Matza and Sykes 1961: 716). (The media violence to which Matza and Sykes referred in 1961 was quite tame compared to that appearing after 1970.)

The apparent contradiction between so-called dominant values and these subterranean values can be historically situated in the conflict between a declining (but still influential) Victorian culture, which promotes inhibition and self-control, and the rising consumer culture, which promotes immediate gratification and deviant thrills. This consumer culture especially affects adolescents who may drift toward delinquency as they explore the enticing pleasures of deviance whose images become ubiquitous in the media. In fact, beginning in the 1950s and 1960s teenagers became the focus of much media advertising as a new youth-oriented culture, which celebrated immediate gratification, began to spread through the mass media (Palladino 1996).

Those adolescents under Type 2 control, discussed in chapter 2 as involving permissive, lenient, and inconsistent discipline, are most likely to follow such inducements toward immediate gratification, since the constraints of self-control are weaker than for those adolescents under Type 1 control, who learn self-control through consistent, non-coercive discipline. Nonetheless, adolescents under Type 1 control, who have strong social bonds to legitimate authority, can follow these inducements to the extent that they can neutralize the guilt that would otherwise hold them back from such experimentation (Sykes and Matza 1957). Such "neutralizations" (which spring from various sets of rationalizations that allow juveniles to neutralize the effect of guilt) are available in both the mass media and the peer cultures that have risen with consumerism. Thus it would seem that the vast majority of minor delinquency, which is the bulk of all delinquent behaviors, could be explained by the inducements to pleasure offered by the consumer culture, which has emerged powerfully since the 1950s.

A culture that produces fierce individual striving and competition undercuts the commitments to family and community that for some seem to get in the way of achieving individual material success and status (Bellah et al. 1985). The individual becomes obsessed with his own pursuits and image as he or she "looks out for number one" and learns to "win through intimidation," to paraphrase the titles of two important best-selling advice books of the 1980s. In the 1970s as concern about the community's health was replaced by a search for "personal fulfillment," even religion and spirituality became commodities to be consumed and hawked through the mass media. Increasingly, the consumer culture evolved in the 1980s into a "culture of narcissism" in which the focus on the self became extreme and "self-image" became a marketable commodity (Lasch 1991).

During the 1980s consumer culture took a dramatic turn in which previous limits on violent imagery seemed to be lifted. At the same time, a brutal dog-eat-dog mentality, nurtured by hyper-competitiveness, exploded on the scene and gave new license to coercion in government policies, among businesses, and in personal relations. The mean-spirited edge to American culture in the 1980s and 1990s was reflected in government policies that cut social supports to the poor (just as the economy was rapidly reducing job opportunities for the less educated) and replaced rehabilitation with a coercive effort to "get tough" on criminals. It was also reflected in a virulent business ethic of cutthroat competition in which "hostile takeovers" became the norm for American business. This same viciousness was reflected in the illegal cocaine trade, which became one of the few substitutes for economic opportunity in inner city areas, and in a street gang lifestyle broadcast in the media and copied by adolescents in towns that had never had gang problems before. In short, American culture by the mid-1980s became much meaner and generally contributed to coercive ideation throughout society. With the lowering of inhibitions and self-control that accompanied the decline of Victorian culture, open expressions of violence were more likely in this new culture that celebrated coercion.

Popular media are, of course, only one influence on coercive ideation and are very much in the background. Wide audiences view movies, television shows, and video games that depict violence, but only a small minority of them ever engage in violent crime. Here is where the nexus between the immediate and larger backgrounds comes into play. Media provide the raw materials to construct fantasies; but real life creates the context in which these fantasies are actually constructed and gives direction for transforming these fantasies into action (Jenkins 1999). Thus a child who views violent material but otherwise lives in a non-coercive environment may find the fantasies entertaining but not relevant to his or her life. Conversely, for a child who experiences coercive relationships in his life, media violence enhances the construction of coercive ideation as the imagination applies media images to personal experience. Thus we have instances in which the connections between media depictions of violence and actual violence appear. For instance, fights and shootings that followed the viewing of "gang movies" occurred in some areas where gang violence was already prevalent but not in areas that lacked gang violence. And two teenagers who were heavily involved with violent video games and fantasies of fame and glory, but who were also rejected, ridiculed, humiliated, and physically assaulted at school by bigger teenagers and members of popular cliques, committed the 1999 shootings at Columbine High School in Littleton, Colorado (*Time* 1999). In both cases, the violence of the movies or video games fed the imagination, but the coercive relations with others transformed these otherwise benign fantasies into lethal action. Actual coercive relations create the immediate experience from which coercive ideation emerges; popular culture's celebration of narcissism and violence and its promotion of a coercive ethic enhance this coercive ideation for those already involved in coercive relations.

Inner city areas have been especially hard-hit by a coercive ethic. Elias (1982 [1939]) argues that wars, economic depressions, and natural disasters can derail the progression toward civilized sensibilities. By the 1980s, many inner city areas became zones of war, economic depression, and *un*natural disasters. More than anywhere else in the United States, the hold of civilized sensibilities dramatically weakened in the inner city as its economy and community structure declined. At the same time, these areas were affected by the rising consumer culture, which helped foster a "hypermaterialist" ethic in drug-ravaged inner cities (Currie 1998: 32; Fagan and Freeman 1999: 264). As the larger culture turned mean in the 1980s, humanitarian concern for those caught up in these hellish ghettos declined. And the larger culture's promotion of a coercive ethic combined in the 1980s and early 1990s with a re-energized "code of the streets" to create an especially virulent culture of violence in the inner city. The economic upturn that began in 1993 has to some extent produced a counterweight to this inner city cultural code as young people increasingly enter a less coercive work world. But many still remain mired in both the economic and cultural poverty of inner city areas.

### Economic and Cultural Background and the Processes of Socialization

The economic and cultural factors discussed in this chapter affect the developmental processes that produce chronic criminality. Figure 4.1 adds these larger background factors to the immediate contexts of coercion discussed in chapter 3.

Historically- and geographically-situated economic pressures affect adults' social-psychological deficits both directly and indirectly. These economic pressures are directly coercive to the extent that they create desperate feelings of being forced by impersonal external economic circumstances. The pressures from the economy are also indirect in that they contribute to the coercion experienced at the workplace, which varies with the rate of unemployment, as discussed earlier in this chapter. These economic forces affect both adults who socialize their children and adolescents and young adults as they enter the job market. These economic pressures vary over time and space, and partially account for temporal and spatial variations in crime rates. They act through the developmental processes, discussed in chapter 3, and help shape the nature of these processes and thus indirectly contribute to the production of chronic criminality.

Cultural forces also shape these socialization processes by promoting beliefs, values, and emotions that are conducive to coercion. Sentiments

Figure 4.1  Expanded Model of Coercion and Chronic Criminality

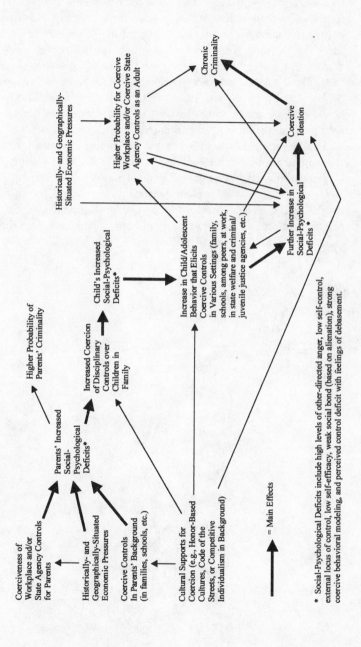

* Social-Psychological Deficits include high levels of other-directed anger, low self-control, external locus of control, low self-efficacy, weak social bond (based on alienation), strong coercive behavioral modeling, and perceived control deficit with feelings of debasement.

= Main Effects

contained in the code of honor, the code of the streets, and the hyperma-terialism and dog-eat-dog competition promoted by post-industrial con-sumer culture all influence the production of coercive ideation. The decline of cultural traditions that emphasize self-control and constraint in the wake of rising consumerism, which actively encourages immediate gratification, places fewer limitations on the direct expression of coercive ideas. These cultural influences occur directly for individuals exposed to these cultural messages and indirectly through the effects these have on family relations and the other contexts of socialization. (See the Appendix for a guide to literature on measurement of variables in figure 4.1.)

Thus the immediate contexts that shape chronic criminality are them-selves influenced by larger economic and cultural forces. The propensity for crime (criminality) that these larger and immediate background factors create cannot adequately explain specific acts of crime. They only create the potential that such acts might occur. The foreground of criminal events must be explored in order to understand how a propensity for crime can be transformed into an actual criminal act. The foreground of crime is the focus of the next chapter.

# Chapter 5

# Coercion in the Foreground of Crime ◉

To this point our discussion has focused on the background factors that play a role in producing criminality. The propensity for chronic criminal behavior springs from a developmental process during socialization that is punctuated on an erratic schedule with coercion. This developmental process, as discussed in chapter 3, is shaped by the immediate social contexts of family, school, peer associations, and state agencies, including those of the juvenile and criminal justice systems. To the extent that these contexts contain coercive relations, an individual interacting with them is more likely to develop coercive ideation and thus a greater propensity for chronic criminal behavior. In turn, as discussed in chapter 4, this developmental process is influenced by wider economic and cultural trends that to varying degrees over time and space promote coercive relations and coercive ideation. Taken together, these are the immediate and larger social contexts that promote coercion. These contexts, along with the individual's experience of coercion, form the background from which criminal behavior arises. The more coercive this background, the more likely the individual will engage in criminal behavior, especially predatory and violent criminal behavior.

But now we face some problems. First, not all, or even most, individuals from a coercive background become chronically engaged in criminal behavior, although they have a higher probability than other people do. Second, even those who do become chronically involved in criminal behavior spend the vast majority of their time in non-criminal activities. It is only at certain points in time and space that they engage in crime. So it is one thing to develop a theory that explains criminality (the propensity to engage in crime) but entirely another to explain crime itself. The situation in which a crime occurs is shaped by several factors, only one of which is the presence of an individual who is motivated because of past experience (which I argue is shaped by coercion) to commit a crime. Other factors that must be considered lie in the foreground of the criminal event. These factors include the actual and perceived opportunity to commit a crime. These opportunities change over time as a society's economy and culture alter the patterns of people's "routine activities" (Felson 1998) that make opportunities for crime more or less available. The foreground also includes the mental state of the individual at the time of the criminal event, including his or her calculations of success in the criminal endeavor (Cornish and Clark 1986), and the emotional state of the individual, which may propel or retard the action (Katz 1988). These mental and emotional states are affected by past experience (the background) and by situations and events more immediately coterminous with the criminal event.

In exploring the foreground of crime, we will look for evidence of coercion as a motivating force during and immediately preceding acts of crime. This coercion can be interpersonal, arising from a threat or actual act of violence from others, or it may be impersonal, felt as a desperate economic or other need arising from circumstances that seem beyond the person's control and that require immediate action (Hagan and McCarthy 1997). That these coercive elements in the foreground, which motivate a criminal act, are in part the creation of the individual is an insight not often recognized by the person caught up in these foreground dynamics. He or she feels compelled toward the act by forces that seem beyond his or her individual control. In fact, many criminal acts can be seen as attempts to overcome these coercive forces. This is a theme I develop in this chapter where we explore the experiences of committing a variety of crimes as reported in several qualitative studies.

It is important to keep in mind that types of crime do not necessarily translate into types of criminals since over time an offender may engage in a variety of crimes. Some offenders escalate their involvement toward more serious violent crime but at the same time continue to engage in less serious offenses (Elliott 1994).

## THE STRUCTURE OF CRIMINAL OPPORTUNITIES

Marcus Felson (1998: 53) discusses the three essential elements that must be present for a crime to occur: a motivated offender, a suitable target, and the absence of capable guardians. The motivated offender is someone who is willing to break the law. Felson does not deal very much with the factors that create a motivated offender suggesting only that low self-control, following the theory of Gottfredson and Hirschi (1990), plays a role but also arguing that virtually anyone in the right circumstances can be tempted to commit a crime. The right circumstance for crime is an abundant availability of suitable targets (both property and vulnerable individuals) at times and places in which people who could potentially intervene to prevent a crime are absent. These capable guardians include not just the police (who in fact play a relatively minor role in crime control) but private citizens going about their daily routines who (whether they know it or not) send out reminders to potential criminals that someone is watching. Thus three elements provide the basic structure of all criminal events: motivated offender(s), suitable targets, and absence of capable guardians.[1]

These elements change over time and space. Felson's (1998) most important insights concern the ecological patterns of crime. Some spatial arrangements (for example, houses with large shrubs covering their windows located next to busy commercial areas with a lot of traffic) are more conducive to crime because they are more likely to provide suitable targets and be devoid of capable guardians. Strangers walking in the area are little noticed since these commercial areas have a lot of traffic. The houses offer quick and easy access and regress but also contain areas hidden from public view. Potential offenders who happen into these spaces (and for the most part they seem to "happen into them" since few crimes are carefully planned) find crime to be a relatively easy (if not compelling) choice to make.

These spatial arrangements are clear when considering property crimes, such as burglary. But some spatial arrangements are also conducive to violent behavior. For instance, a large barroom with a mostly male clientele in their early twenties provides a suitable environment for violence, both in the bar and in the surrounding area. Since young males are more likely to engage in and be victims of violence this site brings motivated offenders together with suitable targets, and older people, who are more likely to intervene to prevent violence, are not present in this situation. Such a site can contain the elements that allow a violent interaction to proceed unimpeded.

David F. Luckenbill (1977) was one of the first criminologists to discuss the situational dynamics of homicide, which can also be applied to assaults since many of these violent acts fall just short of being homicides. Individuals in these situations come into conflict, which escalates as neither party backs down. The absence of capable guardians in these circumstances is apparent since in Luckenbill's study the audiences in these events did not intervene and in fact usually encouraged the violent interactions. The violence may be aimed at controlling the behavior of the other combatant, and in fact one party giving an order to the other party, who then refuses to accede to the demand, may initiate the interaction. Both parties in the interaction attempt to maintain favorable self-images and want, above all

else, to save face and avoid humiliation. With both parties deeply committed to a self-image of someone who will not back down, the violence escalates until one of the combatants (most often the one who initiated the
interaction) is killed. Felson (1998) points out that such an interaction can
only occur in specific settings that, first, bring the two parties together and,
second, allow for the unimpeded flow of a social interaction that leads to
a violent outcome.

Over time, the supplies of suitable targets and capable guardians
change. Felson (1998) argues that increases in crime in the post–World
War II era occurred because of fundamental changes in the patterns of
daily life wrought largely by the widespread use of automobiles and the
mass production of highly portable consumer items. The automobile,
which itself became a growing target of crime, allowed for the dispersal
of the population to suburbs, which was also facilitated by the interstate
highway system. This movement eventually changed the center of daily
activities of work and leisure from central cities to widely dispersed areas
throughout the increasing sprawl of metropolitan regions. This social
change had enormous impact on the availability of suitable targets and capable guardians. The trip between work and home, for instance, took
more time, which meant that people were away from their homes, as were
their neighbors, for much of the day. And neighbors in this highly mobile
environment did not know each other as well as they did in the "urban
villages" of central cities or small towns in rural areas. This meant that
many more places lacked capable guardians for longer time periods during typical twenty-four hour periods, especially as suburban housewives
entered the labor market. Empty homes during the day in an area that
looks vacant become tempting targets for burglary. They became even
more tempting as they contained an increasing number of small, portable
electronic appliances that can be easily lifted and sold in the underground
economy. And individuals were more vulnerable as crime targets as they
regularly traveled to areas in which they interacted with strangers and tra-
versed suburban landscapes (such as huge parking lots) that contain places
conducive to crime.

As suburbs grew, central cities lost population and lost the crucial social interactions that come with daily work and leisure activities. While
this social interaction had increased potential targets of crime, it more importantly increased the capable guardians who could prevent crime. As
these capable guardians decreased, inner city crime increased. This adds an
important criminal opportunity element to our understanding of growing inner city crime, which (as argued in chapter 4) was motivated, in
part, by growing structural unemployment in inner cities between 1960
and 1990.

But crime in general, in cities, suburbs, and rural areas, increased as people's routine activities took them further from home, reduced their ongoing social interactions with others, placed them (and their cars) in circumstances more vulnerable to criminal victimization, and provided them with an array of easy-to-steal consumer items. In short, the changes in people's routine activities enhanced the opportunities for crime because of an increase in suitable targets and a decrease in capable guardians. Felson argues that crime would have increased during the post–World War II era even if the number of motivated offenders had remained constant.

The shifts in routine activities that Felson (1998) discusses are rooted in the larger economic and cultural changes I discussed in chapter 4. Greater opportunities for crime increased with the rise of the hyper-materialist consumer culture and the changes in patterns of work that followed investment decisions of businessmen, which moved homes and work sites away from central city areas to housing tracts, industrial parks, and shopping centers dispersed throughout suburban areas. These economic and cultural changes, which increased opportunities for crime, are related to shifts toward a more coercive society, as discussed in chapter 4, which helped to produce individuals more motivated to commit crime.

While Felson is clearly correct about the importance of criminal opportunities and the forces that shape these, he pays little attention to the forces that produce individuals who are highly motivated to commit crime. If an opportunity for criminal gain is readily available, will individuals usually take it? Felson (1998: 48) seems to endorse the notion that "opportunity makes the crime," which downplays the role of the motivated offender. Felson does mention self-control as an important factor, which I believe is one of the elements in an individual's social-psychological makeup that would prevent him or her from taking advantage of even a clear opportunity for criminal gain (see chapter 2). But we have to look at the background of the individual entering the situation to see if the opportunity is particularly compelling to the potential criminal. As I argue in chapter 2, certain sets of social-psychological characteristics emerge from different sets of control relations through which individuals are socialized. Some of these characteristics make it more likely that an individual will find a criminal opportunity highly compelling, while others make it unlikely that the individual would contemplate breaking the law even if faced with a clear opportunity to get away with it. Later, I will relate these social-psychological characteristics, formed in the background, to the dynamics of the foreground, which include the opportunities present at the time of a potential criminal event. For now, it is enough to acknowledge that the opportunity structure discussed by Felson is indeed a crucial element of crime, but the presence of a motivated offender in the situation is more problematic than Felson acknowledges. The motivated offender springs from forces that Felson downplays in his analysis. The background factors discussed in chapters 3 and 4 produce the supply of motivated of- fenders. But the right circumstances must be present to transform the po- tential for crime these individuals represent into criminal acts. The opportunity must clearly be present in the foreground. But also, the po- tential offender must be in the right mental and emotional state to be se- duced into a criminal act by the opportunity.

## MENTAL AND EMOTIONAL STATES COTERMINOUS WITH CRIMINAL ACTS

Opportunities for criminal behavior are abundant. But even people chron- ically involved in crime do not always seek them out or take them when they are clearly available. A person's mental and emotional state has to be at a certain point to make a criminal opportunity compelling, and these states vary from individual to individual and over time for a specific individual.

There is some debate over exactly what individuals are experiencing when they commit a crime. Some commentators view crime as rational, goal-oriented, instrumental behavior (Cornish and Clark 1986). The crim- inal event is seen to result from a rational choice on the part of the of- fender who has weighed the anticipated benefits and potential costs of committing the act. This does not necessarily mean that careful planning has been involved in the decision, only that the offender has at least rudi- mentarily analyzed the immediate situation before he or she acts. In this sense, the situation presents the potential offender with a set of potential rewards and punishments, which are weighed in the course of deciding to commit a crime. That is why rational choice theorists focus on the crime more so than the criminal's background. They are interested in the field in which decisions are made. Some situations create a field more conducive to criminal calculations of rewards and punishments than do others. Many of the factors discussed in Felson's (1998) "routine activities theory" make these rewards and punishments more or less available in any particular sit- uation. The "reasoning criminal" decides to commit a crime based on his or her understanding of the costs and benefits presented by the immediate situation, an understanding that may of course be a faulty reading of the situation. As one becomes more experienced in particular crimes, skills and knowledge may improve that refine the ability to calculate risks and judge benefits. These calculations may vary by type of crime, such as a burglar dealing with a different set of contingencies than say a robber or a savings and loan swindler, but in each case some degree of rational calculation is made before the crime proceeds.

Jack Katz (1988) has challenged this view of the reasoning criminal. In his discussions of petty property offenses, murder, gang violence, and robbery, Katz argues that many non-rational elements are in play during criminal events. Crime is much more wild, spontaneous, and expressive than the image of the reasoning criminal suggests. Rather than being driven by a desire for material gain, Katz argues that non-material motives are the primary contributors to crime. Individuals are seduced toward crime by the excitement and thrill of breaking the law, by the sense that honor must be defended, by the feelings of power, domination and control, and by the boost to self-image that comes with demonstrations that one's will predominates no matter what the cost. Many of these motives defy rational calculation; they are, as Katz says, beyond reason.

While rational choice theorists focus on the intellectual or mental calculations of the criminal, Katz focuses on the emotional experiences involved in committing a crime. At the base of these emotions is an overriding fear of humiliation, which Katz relates to (but does not discuss in much detail) the background of individuals who become attracted to crime. Humiliation can occur when one is dominated by others or "shown up" as someone who does not really act according to the self-image he or she portrays. These threats of humiliation lie in the immediate background of the criminal event and make the dynamics of the foreground all that much more seductive to the individual.

This is clearly seen in the case of "righteously enraged" homicides in which the killer perceives the victim as attacking the killer's self-worth and senses that there is no escape from this state of "eternal" humiliation (Katz 1988). This sense of humiliation is transformed into rage. The subsequent attack on the victim may or may not lead to a homicide depending on the ability of the attacker to organize his or her behavior for the assault. The potential for humiliation also plays a role in gang violence; the failure to demonstrate "heart" (an insistence on receiving respect no matter what the consequences may be) may lead to a loss of status and humiliation for the individual gang member or the gang itself. Similar emotions are at play for persistent robbers whose constant pursuit of action creates lives of personal and financial turmoil and a constant threat of humiliation in the street culture in which they avidly participate and from which they receive their sense of identity. And cold-blooded killers are faced with potential humiliation for failure to prove their oft-repeated claims to be "awesome" deviants when challenged by others to act on these claims.

Katz focuses our attention on the emotional and expressive dynamics that may be at play in the foreground of crime. Rational theorists such as Derek B. Cornish and Ronald V. Clark (1986) focus on the mental calculations and instrumental elements contained in the criminal event. Several recent qualitative studies of both incarcerated and non-incarcerated criminals shed light on the degree to which these various dynamics influence criminal decision-making.

## QUALITATIVE STUDIES OF CRIMINAL DECISION-MAKING

Qualitative studies, which use in-depth interviewing and observational techniques, provide rich accounts of the experiences and thought processes of criminals that could never be obtained with survey research and quantitative methods. While the results of these qualitative studies cannot be readily generalized, enough ethnographies of criminal decision-making now exist to apply the logic of replication to identify some common themes emerging from several studies. It is possible to draw some preliminary conclusions about the motivations and thought processes that go into the commission of a variety of crimes. But since ethnographic research of crime is still in its infancy, more qualitative explorations into a broader array of crimes and in different locations and circumstances are needed to obtain a more complete picture of the processes at play in the foreground of crime. With that proviso in mind, we examine the thought processes and circumstances of crimes as reported in a number of studies.

The review begins with violent crimes and then works its way to property crimes and white-collar crimes. We will examine what is known about the motives and decision-making for each of these crime categories.

Homicides and aggravated assaults are treated together since the dynamics of these crimes are quite similar. As David F. Luckenbill (1984: 25) explains, "many murders and assaults involve similar participants, interacting in similar ways, for similar reasons, in similar settings." Luckenbill's (1977) pioneering study of homicide situations, mentioned earlier, demonstrated that violent confrontations emerge from a dynamic interchange between opponents. Conflict is escalated as both parties try to save face and refuse to back down. Whether the aggression stops at an assault or escalates to a homicide depends on the aggression of the victim during the interchange (which spurs on the aggression of the attacker), the ready availability of firearms, and the quality and availability of medical treatment.

The triggering event for most homicides and assaults is some form of interpersonal dispute that escalates into violence. "Fights initiated by verbal conflict over money, infidelity, ownership of property, courage and masculinity, status or moral character, and entitlements are clear examples of interpersonal disputes" (Miethe and McCorkle 1998: 39). Donald Black (1984) argues that most homicides and assaults are acts of informal social control in that they are responses to perceived violations of behavioral norms by the victim. In a similar vein, Katz (1988) argues that enraged violent attacks are responses to what the attacker perceives as an assault by the victim on some sacred moral value. These "righteous slaughters" become comprehensible when these attacks on "eternal values" become identified in the killer's mind with a simultaneous attack on his or her self-worth. Thus the cheating wife simultaneously attacks the sanctity of marriage as well as the self-esteem of the husband who kills her. It is the righteous element, Katz explains, that turns the individual's sense of humiliation into a murderous rage.

Marvin Wolfgang (1958) was the first criminologist to suggest the importance of "victim precipitation" in many violent crimes. Homicide and assault victims are often caught up in a conflict that they help provoke. In these cases, a dynamic, coercive interaction is in the immediate foreground of the criminal event. A stressful situation of conflict threatens an individual with loss of control over his actions and moral self-image. Instead of caving in to this threat through submission (and consequent humiliation) the individual resorts to coercive violence. This violence may end the conflict at an assault or if the victim counters with coercion, the violence may escalate to a homicide. Thus in the most common forms of homicide and assault interpersonal coercion is an immediate provocation to criminal action.

These forms of homicide and assault do not generally evoke the image of the reasoning criminal. Individuals are caught up in rage, which blinds them to future consequences. Katz's focus on the emotional dynamics seems to be clearly correct with respect to these forms of homicide and assault. It is possible that the reasoning person learns how to avoid situations in which they may get caught up in these dynamics or is able to defuse the situation before it gets out of hand, thus avoiding violence. But in those cases where assaults or homicides occur, reason apparently has quit the scene. One could argue that the offender is calculating throughout the event the best course of action to take in order to prevail, for instance, in those cases where one party seems to be giving up, leaves the scene, only to return with a lethal weapon that allows him to prevail. In these cases it is an open question as to whether reason or raw emotion is at play. But given the fact that attackers in these situations are easily identified (and often arrested at the scene) one is tempted to believe that it is the emotions that are the predominant element in these situations. Rational thinking is limited to only the immediate contingencies of the situation, not to the potential consequences following the event. And the key emotion at play is anger, an anger that is controlled only enough to organize behavior for a successful assault.

Clearly some people are more susceptible than are others to being provoked to anger when encountering similar situations. Here the background, which I discussed in chapters 3 and 4 and will take up again later in this chapter, plays a role in determining how the dynamics of the foreground will be interpreted and acted upon by the individual. Those with much coercion in their backgrounds will perceive this foreground differently than those who have little coercion in their backgrounds. And if being a victim of crime can be understood as being subjected to coercion, then the immediate background of many violent offenders is coercive: violent criminals have higher rates of violent crime victimization than do other individuals (Fagan et al. 1986; Lauritsen et al. 1991; Wright and Decker 1997). Entering the foreground, these individuals are more likely to be on guard against both physical and psychic threats to self and to be on a hair trigger of explosive anger to any coercive provocation.

Similar dynamics are in play in violence among gangs. As discussed in chapter 3, gang membership tends to escalate an individual's criminal involvement, especially in violent crimes. Gang interactions place an individual in repeated situations in which coercive provocation arises. In perhaps the best ethnography to date of urban street gangs, Scott H. Decker and Barrik Van Winkle (1996: 185) write, "Starting with threats inside and outside the neighborhood creating the need for protection and culminating in endless repetitions of revenge and retaliation, violence permeates the lives of our subjects." Gangs can easily become caught up in deadly feedback loops "where each killing requires a new killing" (Decker and Van Winkle 1996: 186). In gang violence we can see the creation of tragic cycles in which an individual gang member is actively involved in creating the situational dynamics that lead to his or her use of violence. While coercive provocations to which the gang member responds are external, these provocations are often the partial products of the gang member's own actions. Thus gang members' retaliations to external threats contribute to the regeneration of the foreground dynamics that make violence more inevitable. As the individual gang member and the gang seek protection from real or perceived physical threats, they develop a "bad ass" image that broadcasts to the world their readiness to use violence no matter what the cost (Katz 1988). This very image is a provocation to other groups who (because of their fears of physical threats) are intent on developing the same image. The inevitable conflict among these "bad ass" groups creates the foregrounds for violence as each group provokes the other. The increase in real violence only validates the groups' fears while also enhancing feelings of respect among "warriors," who in the face of violence showed "heart." As the social environment becomes more violent as a result of these repeated interactions, the perceived physical threat is further enhanced. Coercive ideation peaks as "it's a jungle out there" becomes a widespread perception and as a truly violent world, which one helps to create but which now must be responded to, becomes a compelling coercive force that requires an enhanced "bad ass" image and greater violence. The escalating production of these foreground situations, which contain coercive provocation, propels violence that becomes a further provocation creating the next foreground situation. Those caught up in this cycle of violence feel pushed by forces beyond their control, even though they are the co-authors of these forces of interpersonal coercion.

Thus the majority of homicides and assaults in both gang and non-gang situations appear to be provoked by interpersonal dynamics that involve coercion. Individuals who become chronically involved in violent crime are repeatedly caught up in foreground situations in which interpersonal coercion is experienced as a provocation. Those with coercive experiences in their backgrounds are more likely to be attracted to and seduced by these situational dynamics that lead them to violent crimes. And each foreground event, once completed, becomes a new experience added to the person's background, reinforcing coercive ideation that is carried into the next foreground situation in which coercive provocation may either pop up or be elicited by the individual. As this cycle repeats itself, chronic violent behavior becomes more likely. The cycle of gang violence is the clearest example of this process, but is likely to be a common characteristic of many homicides and assaults.

While engaged in this cycle of gang violence, core members of gangs further cut themselves off from the legitimate world of work and education. Thus in addition to the interpersonal coercion that arises from gang interactions, coercive ideation is enhanced by the impersonal coercion created by unemployment, poverty, and economic desperation. What John Hagan and Bill McCarthy (1997: 82) refer to as the "foreground circumstances of desperation and destitution," which, they argue, form the immediate adverse conditions of class, can be understood as impersonal coercion in the foreground of crime. These impersonal coercive forces make leaving the gang, and the repeated cycles of violence, all that much more difficult. Thus during the long wave of economic decline from the late 1960s to the early 1990s, the "aging out" process in which gang members moved into legitimate work and marriage appeared to be postponed from the late teens (in the 1960s) to the late twenties or even early thirties (by the 1980s) (Hagedorn 1988; Moore 1991). The escape from coercive forces was made more difficult during these years by growing structural unemployment in inner city areas.

Impersonal coercion also forms the motivational dynamics of robberies. Wright and Decker (1997), in their ethnography of persistent robbers, found that robberies emerge from a situation in which offenders feel an overriding pressure to get cash fast. "By and large, the offenders do not view themselves as having the luxury of freedom of choice in committing stickups. Rather, they typically see their decisions to offend as emanating from a desperate financial need that cannot easily be met through more conventional means. In a sense, the pressure of their immediate situation attenuates the perceptual link between offending and the risk of incurring sanctions; they enter a state of 'encapsulation' in which all that matters is dealing with the present crisis" (Wright and Decker 1997: 129). The present crisis that compels robbery results from forces beyond the individual's control and from forces of the individual's own making. The larger structure of society has placed most armed robbers at birth or early in life in circumstances of social and financial impoverishment that frame their personal backgrounds. The impersonal and interpersonal coercion that shapes their view of the world and their social-psychological makeup is part of this background. The resulting weak links to conventional society allow these individuals to drift toward a street culture in which the desperate pursuit of immediate pleasure and "action" is a strong normative expectation. "The offenders are easily seduced by street culture at least in part because they view their future prospects as bleak and see little point in long-range planning" (Wright and Decker 1997: 37). As they get caught up in the "desperate partying" of the streets, their lives become more chaotic and their money quickly disappears. Cash is needed quickly to get back into the game. Thus the immediate crisis emerges and repeatedly reemerges as they pursue action through gambling, womanizing, drug use, and alcohol consumption. Clearly, this is a cycle that they help to create and perpetuate, but it nonetheless produces a coercive power over them, which shapes the immediate foreground of their crimes. "Their motivation to commit a stickup emerged during a period of intense self-indulgence and from a growing sense of frustration and anger because they felt themselves locked into a cycle of events that was leading nowhere" (Wright and Decker 1997: 36). Robbery is a desperate, and usually ill-fated, attempt to break out of this cycle. During robbery one gains cash and, for a brief moment, complete control over a situation, alluring attractions for someone whose life is out of control and who is in desperate need of cash (Katz 1988). The coercive control exercised during a robbery also allows the offender to reverse the equation of interpersonal coercion that is often in the distant and immediate background of the offender. It is thus a moment of short-term transcendence, as Katz (1988) would say. A successful robbery, however, usually leads to an intensified pursuit of action, which only brings on the social and financial pressures that lead to the next crisis. The freedom from coercive forces that seems to be experienced during the robbery is in fact fleeting. Captured in a pattern of hedonism, low self-control, frustration, and anger, the persistent robber keeps recreating the conditions that make robbery more likely.

Caught up in the immediate pressures of the moment, little heed is given by the robber to long-term consequences. Targets are chosen on the basis of convenience and likelihood of obtaining quick cash. Robbery offers the quickest avenue to cash and requires the least amount of time away from the desperate partying prized by the street culture in which these individuals are both ensconced and willing participants. Many times the most convenient targets are other criminals: drug dealers are especially good targets since they are readily available in the robber's neighborhood and have a lot of cash (and drugs). Many of these drug dealers engage in conspicuous displays of wealth as they pursue action and build their street images. Such displays are personal affronts to those who want desperately to pursue action but whose current lack the cash prevents them from doing so. These personal affronts "should not go unpunished. Often the punishment of choice is armed robbery" (Wright and Decker 1997: 37). The conspicuous consumption that the robber subsequently engages in creates personal affronts for others; thus many robbers themselves become the victims of robbery (Wright and Decker 1997: 62). This cycle of mutual victimization contributes to a coercive environment immediately surrounding the foreground of these criminal events.

Robbers seem little deterred by the potential of violence that could explode during a robbery; in fact one prerequisite of robbery is being able to stomach the violence inherent in this offense. The fact that drug dealers, who would have few qualms about violent retaliation, are often chosen as targets shows that consideration of consequences is not high on the robbers' radar screens. If these immediate consequences of retaliation do little to deter the offense, it is unlikely that the more abstract and distant punishment offered by the criminal justice system would have much effect. Robbers do not neatly fit the image of the reasoning criminal. They do very little if any planning; instead, at a moment of desperation, brought on by partially self-created impersonal coercive forces, they take quick advantage of convenient opportunities for fast and easy gain. Calculation is usually rudimentary; they quickly size up the convenience of the target and the potential that money may be available in the immediate situation. As they commit more robberies, their assessments of opportunities become routine and fast, as they learn the cues that signal good targets. They can then rob with little thought. These impulsive criminals give no consideration to long-term consequences or to the possibility of being arrested; they are responding more to the imperatives and pressures that arise from their involvement in street culture. Several studies of robbers and persistent property offenders draw this same picture (Feeney 1986; Jacobs and Wright 1999; Katz 1991; Shover 1996; Shover and Honaker 1992; Tunnell 1999).

Although to a much lesser extent than men, women also engage in robbery. Their motivations for robbery are much the same as men's. Jody Miller's (1998: 47) study of men and women robbers found that for both men and women "motivations to commit robbery are primarily economic—to get money, jewelry, and other status-conferring goods, but they also include elements of thrill seeking, attempting to overcome boredom, and revenge." As with the studies cited earlier of male robbers, financial pressures to rob are placed upon women because of their involvement in street culture. But given the strong masculine bias of this culture, women are less likely to participate in it as fully as are men, thus the lower involvement of women in robbery. Miller found that while the motives for robbery are similar, women's enactment of robbery diverges from men's. This difference is structured by a background of gender stratification in which "men are perceived as strong and women are perceived as weak," a notion that is even more exaggerated in the culture of the streets (Miller 1998: 61). Because of this, women who rob tend to target other females or use their own presumed weakness and apparent sexual availability to lure men into circumstances that make them easy robbery victims. Thus the way in which robbery is carried out, and the choice of targets, is structured by gender. But for both men and women, the impersonal coercion created by participation in street culture forms the motivational dynamics of robbery.

In another ethnography, Wright and Decker (1994) studied the decision-making involved in burglary. Similar forces as in robbery are at work in the motivational dynamics of this property offense. The decision to commit a residential burglary is made in response to a pressing need for money or other items that promote status and self-esteem in the street culture. The pressure of these immediate needs creates a sense of desperation that drives individuals toward burglary. "These offenders were not motivated by a desire for money for its own sake. By and large, they were not accumulating the capital needed to achieve a long-range goal. Rather, they regarded money as providing them with the means to solve an immediate problem. In their view, burglary was a matter of day-to-day survival" (Wright and Decker 1994: 36–37). In some cases, the survival needs included basic necessities. When money was sufficient, burglary would not be considered. In most cases, however, the financial pressure came from imperatives involved in participation in the street culture. Money was needed to engage in desperate partying that continually recreated the desperate need for more money. "Their offending is not a result of a thoughtful, carefully reasoned process. Instead, it emerges as part of the natural flow of events, seemingly coming out of nowhere. In other words, it is not so much that these actors consciously choose to commit crimes as that they elect to get involved in situations that drive them toward lawbreaking" (Wright and Decker 1994: 40). As with robbery, these situations contain partially self-created impersonal coercive forces that compel a criminal solution to an immediate crisis that appears to be beyond individual control. It becomes a criminal solution because these individuals are cut off from most legitimate avenues for quick money, and their continued engagement with street culture virtually ensures that they will remain cut off from legitimate opportunities. Their choice of burglary "represented what they perceived to be the most proximate and performable crime available to them" (Wright and Decker 1994: 53).

These offenders did not necessarily specialize in burglary; many were also involved at various times in shoplifting, car theft, street corner drug sales, and robbery. But at times, these other crime choices seemed either physically or psychically unavailable or too risky compared to a burglary. (One has to be in the right frame of mind to pull off a robbery in which the victim is directly confronted; the whole point of burglary is to avoid contact with the victim.) Thus some offenders tended toward burglary as their crime of choice and spent much of their time as they partied or engaged in daily routines casually being on the lookout for potential targets that might be returned to in a time of immediate need. This was not calculated planning. Indeed, as Wright and Decker (1994: 60–61) report:

> This often seemed to happen almost automatically, the crime occurring with minimal calculation as part of a more general path of action (e.g., partying). To the extent that the offense ameliorated their distress, it nurtured a tendency for them to view burglary as a reliable means of dealing with similar pressures in the future. In this way, a foundation was laid for the continuation of their present lifestyle which, by and large, revolved around the street culture. The self-indulgent activities supported by this culture, in turn, precipitated new pressures; and thus a vicious cycle developed.

Again, as with robbery and gang violence, we see offenders caught up in a cycle that is partly their own creation and that contains coercive pressures that repeatedly compel them into making criminal choices. Similar foreground patterns in which impersonal coercion (self-created and not) plays a role in the motivation of crime have been reported in studies of selling drugs on the streets (Hagedorn 1994; Jacobs 1999), shoplifting (Ray and Briar 1999), and theft, prostitution, robbery, and violence by homeless street youth (Hagan and McCarthy 1997).

While not all crimes fit these patterns, the bulk of crimes engaged in by chronic street offenders appear to involve responses to interpersonal and/or impersonal coercion. Whether these coercive forces are partially self-created by the offenders or not, they create pressure in the immediate foreground that makes a criminal act more likely. When these coercive forces are not present in the foreground, crime is a path generally not considered. It is usually only in the face of coercive pressure and provocation that the criminal decision-making process is activated. And careful calculations of long-term consequences are not often part of this process as the offender moves quickly to remove the immediate source of distress.

It is unclear whether this same pattern affects other crimes. It is doubtful that the foreground of rape, for instance, fits the pattern, although clearly rape is primarily motivated by a need to dominate, control, and humiliate another human being (Miethe and McCorkle 1998: 65). The foreground of rape, however, does not seem to involve a coercive provocation. The background of rapists, however, may involve coercive relations including, for some, sexual assault victimization and high levels of exposure to depictions of violence toward women contained in pornography and other media, which helps to produce coercive ideation that revolves especially around women (Miethe and McCorkle 1998: 62). In a similar vein, serial killers do not appear to be responding to any coercive forces in the situational foreground, unless internal psychological compulsion (the "force" as convicted serial killer Ted Bundy labeled it) can be considered coercion (Holmes and De Burger 1988: 136). But this may be carrying the concept of coercion too far beyond the social and situational dynamics I focus on in this book. But, again, many serial killers appear to have had coercive relations in their backgrounds, which contributed to the formation of violent fantasies (a form of coercive ideation) that preceded their involvement in killing (Hickey 1991). As with rapists, we still do not know very much about the situational dynamics involved in the foreground of serial killings. It is not clear to what extent, if any, coercive forces play a role in the commission of these crimes.

White-collar crimes have long plagued criminological theories because they presumably do not involve the same structural or cultural forces propounded by theories that focus largely on the crimes committed by poor people. Does the concept of coercion help us understand white-collar crime? The short answer for why people engage in white-collar crime is usually formulated as good old-fashioned greed coming together with an easy opportunity for a fast buck. James William Coleman (1994: 195) acknowledges that "although the desire to get rich quick is certainly a motivating factor in many white-collar crimes, other kinds of financial motivations are often equally important. Many white-collar offenders are driven by the fear that they will lose what they already have rather than the desire for more." This fear derives directly from the coercive force of competition. Competitive forces emerge from a culture that promotes the ideal of winning at all cost and from a structure of economic (and political) struggle that compels certain actions. These competitive forces can be understood as creating impersonal forms of coercion. Like the hustler in the underground economy of the street culture, business people and politicians can never relax for fear of losing out to the competition.

Competitive pressures are seen in several case studies of white-collar crimes, which offer hints that coercive forces may play a role in forming the motivation for some white-collar crimes. The infamous Ford Pinto case involved the sale of a defective automobile (a gas tank that exploded in low-speed rear-end collisions) and a subsequent cover up by Ford Motor Company of the problem (Cullen et al. 1987). At least 50 people died in fiery Ford Pinto crashes directly involving gas-tank ruptures (Coleman 1994). Ford was indicted for reckless homicide, but not convicted; and hundreds of civil suits forced Ford to pay out millions of dollars in wrongful death settlements. The Ford Pinto was rushed into production in the early 1970s in response to competitive pressure from Japanese and European automakers who were successfully gaining market shares by flooding the United States with low cost, fuel efficient small cars. This economic pressure caused Ford executives to put pressure on their engineers and car designers to come up with a cheap, low weight car. The hasty design and quick manufacture led to the defects in the car. The later discovery of these defects and the subsequent cover-up occurred in an atmosphere in which fear of losing out in the market competition was overriding. This market competition created a coercive force that impelled Ford to make hasty decisions. It also contributed to a coercive environment within the organization that put pressure on middle management to conform to the expectations of top management. This is a pattern seen in many corporate crimes. As John Braithwaite (1995: 129) reports, "middle managers are frequently reported as squeezed by a choice between failing to achieve targets set by top management and attaining the targets illegally. In other words, while it is middle management who perpetrate the criminal acts, it is top management which set the expectations, the tone, the corporate culture that determines the incidence of corporate crime." Top management is responding to the coercive pressures of market competition; in turn, they create coercion within their organizations by "squeezing" their employees to meet the threat presented by the external pressures. As Coleman (1995: 369) reports, "One of the most powerful techniques to win conformity with organizational expectations is the threat of dismissal," a powerful tool of coercion.

Monopoly sector firms, like Ford Motor Company, are motivated toward criminal involvement when their monopoly position is threatened.

Competitive sector firms, however, may be even more vulnerable to criminal involvement because their relatively precarious economic position makes market competition an even more coercive force. "Industries in this sector find it more difficult to pass on every increase in wages, taxes, or regulatory costs to consumers as easily as businesses in the oligopolistic sector. . . . Thus, competitive-sector industries frequently operate on a narrow margin of profitability" (Aulette and Michalowski 1995: 172). Thus, as Coleman (1995: 375) reports, it is not surprising that "a very considerable body of research shows firms with declining profitability are more likely than others to break the law." These companies are under greater competitive pressures.

This became apparent in the deadly fire, which killed 25 workers, that occurred at Imperial Foods chicken processing plant in Hamlet, North Carolina, in 1991. "By the late 1980s Imperial Foods was under considerable pressure because of the general economic decline and because of specific fiscal problems with the corporation. Even before the fire in Hamlet, it appears that Emmett Roe, the owner of Imperial Foods, was facing financial difficulty. . . . The financial difficulty which Roe faced may have increased the likelihood of decisions that placed profitability ahead of the health or safety costs to workers" (Aulette and Michalowski 1995: 177). Preventable safety violations led to both the fire and the trapping of workers in the burning building. The trapped workers could not open a fire door, which was deliberately kept locked by the company. The pressure accruing from economic difficulties motivated the poor working conditions and safety violations that led to felony manslaughter charges against the owner. The opportunity to engage in such practices was enhanced by the absence of capable guardians because of a very lax regulatory environment in North Carolina. This lax regulatory environment was itself created by impersonal economic forces in which poor states like North Carolina are forced to compete with other states for industries by offering low taxes, restrictions on unions, and virtually no regulations of health and safety practices. This coercive economic atmosphere creates both the motive and opportunity for corporate crimes like the one that occurred at the Imperial chicken processing plant.

While taking different forms, and arising from different cultural settings, the coercive forces that motivate many street crimes also seem to be a part of the motivational dynamics of at least some white-collar crimes. Further research into the dynamics of white-collar crimes are clearly needed to pin down the extent to which these crimes are motivated by structural and organizational coercive pressures.

These pressures may lead to a process in which ethical constraints are neutralized, which facilitates the commission of these crimes (Coleman

1994). This is clear in Donald Cressey's (1953) classic study of embezzlers, who act under the force of a pressing financial problem they cannot share with others. With ready access to money through their job, they have the means to overcome this pressure. They are able to take advantage of their position by rationalizing their stealing of funds as "borrowing." Other white-collar crimes may fit this same pattern, with coercion (largely from impersonal forces and competition) playing a role in motivating both the crime and the need to rationalize the illegal behavior.

Competitive pressures (between countries or political parties) may also motivate some political crimes. For instance, the Watergate scandal was precipitated by political competition in which President Richard M. Nixon and his operatives went after political enemies and broke into Democratic Party headquarters to get "dirt" on its party chairman and to discover if he knew of information damaging to Nixon (Kutler 1990). And many of the violations of civil liberties and state-sponsored terrorism promoted by U.S. intelligence agencies were done in the context of superpower competition during the Cold War (Bushnell 1991). To the extent that coercive pressure from these forms of competition is a real or merely rationalized force in these cases is open to serious question. It is likely that it is a little of both. At this point, coercion seems to be a potentially useful concept for guiding inquiries into this area of criminal activity.

## COERCION AND CONTROL:
## TYING THE FOREGROUND TO THE BACKGROUND

Coercion appears to be a salient factor in the foreground of many crimes. Homicides and assaults are often directly provoked by interpersonal coercion. Robbery, burglary, and street dealing of drugs appear to emerge from the coercive pressures unleashed by active involvement in street culture. Coercive forces also appear to play a role in some white-collar crimes in the form of impersonal economic pressures arising from competition and interpersonal organizational pressures placed on middle managers by top management.

These coercive processes in the foreground would seem to affect the crimes most often engaged in by chronic offenders, both those in the streets and those in the suites. Since chronic criminals commit most of the serious *offenses* in our society, this is a significant point (Elliott 1994; Wolfgang et al. 1972). It is not clear that individuals who engage in exploratory offending (the vast majority of criminal *offenders*) are reacting to these same coercive pressures when they engage in crime. Here the background, discussed in chapters 2, 3 and 4, must be considered. Why do some foreground dynamics induce criminal decision-making for some people while these same dynamics do not provoke criminal choices for other people? Foreground dynamics must encounter an individual with particular background experiences to motivate criminal behavior. The differential coercion theory developed in this book posits that background experiences are shaped by variations in impersonal and interpersonal coercion. These variations, as discussed in chapter 2, form four ideal types of control relations, which produce different sets of social-psychological characteristics, some more responsive to the foreground dynamics that induce criminal behavior than others.

In chapter 2, two of the four ideal types of control relations were hypothesized to be more conducive to criminality. In the Type 2 pattern, the individual experienced lenient and erratic controls, which were largely non-coercive. This individual develops low self-control, but learns that manipulation of events and people is very much within his or her power. Thus, this individual approaches a criminal opportunity with confidence that the contingencies of the crime can be correctly calculated. Little holds this individual back from seizing upon a criminal opportunity except the rational calculations involved in weighing costs and benefits. With great confidence, this individual is more likely to explore the potential pleasures of criminal involvement if these outweigh the potential risks of apprehension. This individual is less likely to be responding to a coercive provocation than to an enticing invitation to pleasure and instant reward offered by a criminal opportunity calculated to involve little risk. Type 2 fits most closely with the reasoning criminal postulated in rational choice theory. They approach crime from a calculating spirit nurtured by a background in which they learned to manipulate authority that was overly lenient, erratic, and non-coercive. They are not driven by anger, which means their criminal activities tend to be non-violent. Depending on the type of criminal opportunities available to them, they can engage in property-related street crimes or white-collar crimes. They tend to explore deviant pleasures (such as drug use) available to them in the immediate foreground, but remove themselves from situations that are perceived to cause pain.

For this reason, these individuals may live for a time on the edges of street culture, enticed by the pleasures and "action" of the streets. Their engagement with street culture can lead to an important turning point for some of them. Given their propensity toward low-self control, an overindulgence in the pleasures of street culture may elicit the impersonal coercive force of a financial crisis, which will either drive them deeper into street culture or shock them into a rational reconsideration of the costs of participating in street-culture activities. In the latter case, as costs to personal freedom, health, and safety mount, they tend to desist from criminal behavior based on the rational principle of maximization of pleasure and avoidance of pain, which has guided them in the past. If, however, they are driven deeper into street culture as a response to financial crisis, they begin to experience a shift in control patterns, as greater coercion is experienced on an erratic basis in both its impersonal and interpersonal forms. As this occurs, they fall into a pattern more typical of Type 4, and their exploratory involvement in criminal behavior turns toward more chronic involvement. What has changed is their experience of coercion, which alters their so-cial-psychological characteristics and their propensity for crime. They begin to resemble the characteristics more typical of someone under Type 4 control.

Under a background more typical of a Type 4 pattern, the individual experienced an erratic form of control that was highly coercive. This indi-vidual develops not only low self-control (which is also true for the Type 2 control pattern) but also a fatalistic attitude about directing events. In ad-dition, a strong sense of anger colors interactions with others. Criminal op-portunities do not evoke a calculating spirit; they are more likely to be seized upon with little regard for consequences. For these individuals, a criminal opportunity offers an outlet for anger and a chance to turn the tables on people and a society that has coerced them.

Street culture offers even greater enticement to individuals emerging from a Type 4 background than it does to those from a Type 2 background. While both are attracted to the material pleasures of the street, the culture of the street offers something that is especially salient for someone coming out of a longer background of coercion. The "conspicuous display of in-dependence" (Shover and Honaker 1992: 284), which is the hallmark of street culture, is overwhelmingly seductive to individuals who come out of backgrounds filled with interpersonal and impersonal coercion. These background experiences on a frequent but erratic basis remind them just how much "under the thumb" of other people or external forces they ac-tually are. (How great their "control deficit" actually is, using Charles Tit-tle's [1995] terminology.) As they are seduced into street culture, they enter a world in which the illusion of independence and autonomy can tem-porarily be realized through criminal activities and high living in pursuit of action. But interpersonal and impersonal forces of coercion, which emerge from these activities, repeatedly threaten this false sense of auton-omy. Yet, for these individuals who are increasingly cut off from legitimate paths to independence, street culture offers the only apparent avenue of es-cape from coercive forces. So they pursue with great desperation and a strong sense of fatalism the action in the streets, which affirms their much-prized sense of independence. The exaggerated need for independence grows out of a background in which it is constantly threatened by coer-cive forces. And this exaggerated need for independence is heightened by a subculture, which is also shaped by these same coercive forces, that emphasizes and gives status to those who can appear to be autonomous. Those from a Type 4 pattern of control find this subculture most seductive because it at once reflects their own background and seems to offer an instant escape from this background. The coercion in the background has rendered an individual with a set of social-psychological characteristics that perfectly match (and are sustained by) the life in the streets.

The street culture and the foreground dynamics it creates become especially important for understanding the production of chronic offenders who engage in predatory street crime. Unlike individuals emerging from a Type 2 pattern, engagement in street culture for those emerging from a Type 4 control pattern does not represent a potential turning point so much as it does an affirmation of life's general experience of coercion. Street culture accelerates and concentrates the coercive processes that have shaped the lives of such individuals. Street culture both pulls and pushes them toward chronic criminal involvement. The subculture is the embodiment of coercive ideation that is both suggestive of independence from the control of others (through coercive action) and fatalistic about ever experiencing this beyond fleeting moments.

The other patterns of control, Type 1 and Type 3, are least conducive to seduction from criminal opportunities. An individual from a Type 1 background who has predominately experienced consistent, non-coercive control will tend to have the type of social-psychological makeup that will shield him or her from even beginning to calculate potential rewards when faced with even a clear opportunity for illegal gain or illicit pleasure. The strong social bond, based on a moral attachment to others, provides a major constraint on behavior. The enticements that may be present in a foreground conducive to crime will not be sufficiently attractive to induce any serious consideration of committing a crime. Only if this individual can muster up the necessary rationalizations (with possible assistance from others in his or her peer group or corporate organization) can the moral constraints be temporarily neutralized to allow this person to contemplate taking advantage of a criminal opportunity in the foreground. A coercive provocation can be walked away from or avoided because the background provides this person with enough positive experiences so that this foreground situation does not become a "last stand" for self-worth. Such coercive provocation does not recall, as it would for someone from a Type 4 background, painful humiliation from the past. Thus it is highly unlikely that criminal foreground dynamics will induce a person with a background that is primarily shaped by Type 1 control relations into committing a crime.

An individual from a Type 3 background, who has been subject to consistent coercive control, will face a criminal opportunity with the fear that he or she will almost certainly be caught and severely punished. Experience has consistently taught this lesson, which will tend to preclude the criminal act, if not its contemplation. This fear can only be overcome if the foreground situation can successfully induce a normally self-directed anger to explode outward. Then in a moment of rage, the individual may attack the long-standing source of coercion and its accompanying humiliation. But this may only occur at moments when the individual can begin to visualize an existence outside the coercive relationship. This can be seen in Katz's (1988: 14) discussion of the famous Francine Hughes case, in which a wife who had been beaten and abused for years by her husband finally killed him by dousing him with gasoline and setting him on fire while he slept in his bed. Francine had suffered physical abuse and humiliation for at least a dozen years. It was only in the immediate background context of beginning her education and seeing a possible life independent of her husband that his abusive behavior provoked a violent, anger-driven response. And the immediate provocation was not another beating but the husband's burning of her schoolbooks, which symbolized her imagined path out of the long-term coercive relationship. This violence represented a sudden transformation of Francine's usual self-directed anger into an outwardly directed rage, a transformation induced by just the right foreground and immediate background dynamics. This was behavior that had never occurred before and that would in all likelihood never occur again. When all avenues of escape from coercive control seemed shut, crime was not an option. It was only when an escape could be imagined that crime, in the form of an enraged killing, became possible.

## COERCION IN THE BACKGROUND AND FOREGROUND OF CHRONIC CRIMINALS

The foreground is the meeting place of the cultural and economic factors discussed in chapter 4, the individuals' past experiences with coercion discussed in chapter 3, and the criminal opportunities and individual states of mind discussed in this chapter. The foreground brings a motivated individual, whose background has been shaped by interpersonal and impersonal forms of coercion, together with an opportunity or a provocation to commit a crime. Since we are primarily interested in the forces that produce chronic involvement in street crime, the dynamics that produce Type 4 patterns of control in both the background and foreground are especially important.

What was operating in the background to produce criminality, is also operating in the foreground to produce crime: coercion. The individual is not merely a passive recipient of coercive forces; in both the background and foreground, the individual is an active (although usually unwitting) participant in the creation of coercive forces that reinforce his or her social-psychological deficits and that compel and motivate behavior.[2] This behavior in turn eventually elicits additional coercive forces. The individual becomes caught up in a coercive cycle; crime represents a desperate and usually ill-fated attempt to break out of this cycle. On an erratic schedule, crime allows individuals to escape, at least temporarily, the desperation brought on by coercive forces. But crime more often than not merely perpetuates the cycle of coercion. It either elicits direct retaliation from others or becomes the gateway to intense involvement in street culture, which quickly sucks away the person's finances and further undermines his or her social capital. Coercive forces quickly reemerge and coercive ideation is fortified by this repeated experience.

Chronic criminals, who are responsible for the majority of street crimes, are intensely caught up in this vicious cycle of coercion. They are the products of past coercion. Based on this background experience, they act in ways that continually recreate the coercive forces that repeatedly compel them toward crime. The street culture, which is the primary arena in which chronic offenders operate, is a product of larger economic and cultural forces, discussed in chapter 4, that subject entire neighborhoods and groups of people to intense yet erratic coercion. Street culture thrives in this general coercive environment because it offers the illusion of quick (and possibly the only) escape from coercive forces. The key enticement in the foreground of crime is the possibility of a quick end to the experience of coercion. That the foreground experience may only give temporary reprieve from coercive forces spawns both the hope that the next foreground experience will be a release from coercion and the fatalistic attitude that in the long run this can never be.

For chronic offenders, then, coercion is the key concept in understanding both the background that creates their propensity for criminal behavior and the foreground in which their crimes actually take place. Our efforts at controlling and preventing criminal behavior need to be informed by an understanding of the coercive dynamics that shape the lives and actions of chronic criminals. In the next chapter, I propose a set of policy recommendations aimed at reducing the coercive forces that drive chronic criminal behavior.

# Chapter 6

# A Theory-Driven Response to Crime: Toward a Non-Coercive Society

C oercion is an important component in the etiology of chronic crime and criminality. In both its interpersonal and impersonal forms, coercion is present in both the background and foreground of crime and at both the micro and macro levels of explanation. Coercion experienced on an erratic schedule is most conducive for chronic involvement in predatory street crime. This pattern of coercion, labeled Type 4, creates a set of social-psychological deficits (other-directed anger, low self-control, an external locus of control, low self-efficacy, a weak alienated social bond, strong coercive behavioral modeling, and a perceived control deficit with feelings of debasement and humiliation). In turn, these social-psychological deficits lead to behaviors that elicit or create further experiences of interpersonal and/or impersonal coercion, which sustain the individual in a vicious cycle that deepens social-psychological deficits and opens the individual to chronic involvement in predatory street crime. Public policies aimed at reducing chronic criminality must intervene in and prevent this vicious cycle. Unfortunately, our current reactions to crime involve interventions that often exacerbate this vicious cycle of coercion. This chapter lays out a theory-driven response to crime that seeks to reduce the coercion that leads to chronic criminality.

## TOWARD AN INTEGRATED THEORY OF CRIME AND CRIMINALITY

The differential coercion theory developed in this book draws on several existing theories of crime and criminality, bringing them together in a new, integrated theory that focuses on the theme of coercion. The theory has clear implications for understanding the production of chronic involvement in predatory street crime. This aspect of the theory (the Type 4 pattern) is connected most closely to the strain theory tradition, especially Robert Agnew's (1992, 1985) re-conceptualization of strain as negative stimuli that create anger. Coercion is a prevalent negative stimulus experienced by many in several social settings across the socialization process.

In addition to anger, other emotional and cognitive states and psychological traits grow out of and are sustained by the experience of being coerced. Following and expanding upon Gerald Patterson's (1982, 1995) insights, I maintain that coercion is an unmeasured variable in most studies that connect childhood propensities to later social relations and psychological states that more immediately affect criminality. Thus the theory developed in this book integrates social causation and social selection perspectives in criminology (Wright et al. 1999). The social causation perspective argues that social relationships (such as social bonds developed in work, families, schools, and among peers) promote or prevent criminal behavior. The social selection perspective argues that preexisting (childhood) characteristics, such as low self-control, influence the development of both social relationships and criminal behavior, thus rendering spurious the correlations drawn from the social causation perspective. A recent longitudinal study (Wright et al. 1999) put these competing perspectives to empirical test and found that variables drawn from both influence the development of adult criminal behavior. Childhood self-control affects self-control in adolescence and directly influences social bonds, involvement with delinquent peers, and adolescent delinquency. In turn these adolescent-stage variables directly, and independently, affect young adult criminal behavior, which is no longer related to childhood self-control when these adolescent-stage variables are considered. (A similar pattern of findings are reported by Sampson and Laub [1993].) Thus social causation variables partially mediate the relationship between social selection variables and criminal behavior. The Wright et al. (1999) study presents a major breakthrough in our understanding of crime causation suggesting reciprocal effects between psychological propensities and social relations. However, it does not measure the social processes that explain the initial development of childhood traits, like low self-control, and how these childhood traits elicit certain social relationships that weaken social bonds and produce and sustain other social-psychological deficits that are implicated in crime causation.

Coercion in these social processes, I maintain, is the missing variable that connects social selection variables with social causation variables. These processes create and sustain the coercive vicious cycle that is key to understanding the etiology of chronic predatory street crime. The cycle emerges from the highly negative stimuli involved in the erratic application and experience of coercion.

Differential coercion theory also has implications for other patterns of criminality that emerge from non-coercive, erratic control (labeled Type 2). Both exploratory offending and white-collar crime involve elements of rational calculation of gain or pleasure that emerge from permissive, lenient patterns of control in which coercion is virtually absent. Strain theory explanations of these patterns of criminality are problematic since they lack coercive negative stimuli in the background. For these patterns of criminality, differential coercion theory draws on the control theory tradition, which focuses on social bonds, self-control, and, most recently, control surpluses. Individuals engage in these criminal behaviors to the extent that they feel free from constraint, a perception that has been nurtured by the experience of erratic, non-coercive control in which their only calculations involve the maximization of pleasure or gain.

Hence, the theory developed in this book can best be understood as a theory of *differential* coercion in that it posits variance in both the strength of coercion and the consistency to which it is experienced. Depending on the relative strength and consistency of coercion, different criminal and non-criminal outcomes are predicted by the theory. Chronic involvement in predatory street crime emerges from an erratic, coercive pattern (Type 4). Exploratory offending and most white-collar crimes emerge from an erratic, non-coercive pattern (Type 2). Non-criminal outcomes that involve a high propensity for pro-social behavior emerge from a consistent, non-coercive pattern (Type 1). Outcomes that are primarily non-criminal but involve low levels of pro-social behavior and a high propensity for mental health problems (such as depression) emerge from a consistent, coercive pattern (Type 3).

The theory also makes a distinction between the background from which a general propensity for criminal involvement (criminality) emerges and the foreground of crime in which situational pressures converge at specific points in time and space with opportunities to commit crime. Predatory street crime appears to involve both interpersonal and impersonal coercive pressures in the foreground and the immediate background of the criminal event. Even some white-collar crimes can be seen to involve similar coercive pressures in the foreground that influence the rational calculations that lead to the decisions involved in this criminal behavior pattern.

Differential levels of coercion and consistency appear in micro processes of social control and at the macro level involving larger economic and cultural forces of society. Predatory street criminals emerge from an experience of erratic coercion during socialization processes in families, schools, among peers, in workplaces, and in the bureaucracies of welfare and criminal justice agencies. Both cultural norms and economic conditions influence the levels of coercion in these sites.

The theory developed in this book implies that coercion must be reduced in both the immediate and larger backgrounds in order to prevent chronic predatory criminality. In addition, consistent messages of disapproval of all types of criminal behavior are necessary for more effective crime reduction. Current criminal justice policies tend to ignore background factors, and in many ways these policies perpetuate and reproduce the same type of erratic, coercive controls that, in the first place, led to chronic predatory criminality. Inconsistent and at times overly lenient official reactions to white-collar criminals (and to some extent exploratory offenders) reproduces the erratic, non-coercive pattern that may form the etiological background of these offenders (the Type 2 pattern). This inconsistent and lenient reaction reduces the likelihood that these offenders will take responsibility for or alter their behavior.

A theory-driven response to crime and criminality must be articulated. Such a response must focus on the reduction of coercive relations and forces that induce chronic criminality, and provide consistent, although not necessarily harsh, sanctions for criminal conduct. The main focus of discussion in this chapter is on the appropriate response to chronic, predatory street criminals. But I also focus on exploratory offenders and white-collar criminals who emerge from different experiences than do chronic predatory street criminals. Appropriate intervention and prevention strategies must be developed for all three types of criminal behavior.

## A THEORY-DRIVEN RESPONSE
## TO CRIME AND CRIMINALITY

Jeffrey Reiman (1995) offers an instructive thought experiment that tells us much about our current criminal justice practices. Instead of thinking of how we might design a criminal justice system aimed at reducing crime, he proposes that we imagine designing a system whose aim is to encourage the creation and maintenance of a sizable group of chronic criminals in our society. Among other features, the system would offer highly inconsistent, arbitrary outcomes by allowing wide discretion in arrests, prosecution, and sentencing. Wealthy offenders, especially those involved in white-collar crime, would be able to take advantage of numerous legal loopholes that allow them to escape punishment or receive much more lenient treatment even if their behavior caused much more harm than poorer criminals who receive harsher sentences. This inconsistency would ensure that those caught up in the system (who know of others who were "let off" or made bargains for leniency) will feel a strong sense of injustice, defiance, and rage, instead of remorse (Sherman 1993). The system should also include a process by which offenders (on an arbitrary basis) are brutalized and humiliated through constant threats of assault and rape while incarcerated. We would also want to undermine offenders' capacities for self-control by placing them in an enforced dependency in which for a period of years all decisions are made for them. In addition, we would want to completely sever the social bond to conventional society by cutting off all ties to the community of law-abiding, conventional people. Instead we would want to completely immerse them in a violent criminal subculture through forced confinement with other criminals with whom they must interact twenty-four hours a day over many, many years. We certainly would not want to give them viable job skills through training and education. But at the same time we should blame them for their failure to rehabilitate themselves. Then with no preparation for the transition, we should send them back to a hostile community with a long-lasting stigma that reduces their economic opportunities and continually subjects them to the whims of police and parole officers who at anytime can send them back into the system. In short, to increase crime we should develop a system that enforces an intense coercive experience delivered on a highly erratic schedule. Of course, no rational society would wish to deliberately design a system that encourages crime. But in the United States and increasingly in Great Britain and other countries (Weiss and South 1998) this is precisely the type of criminal justice system we have developed. It is one that is highly inconsistent and coercive. Is it any wonder that we have high rates of recidivism?

Our criminal justice practices reproduce the vicious cycle of coercion that creates chronic predatory street crime. As a mere reaction to crime, it does not affect the social processes that criminological theories and research have implicated in crime causation. It merely exacerbates these processes. Our responses to crime need to be both proactive and reactive. At present, we put the bulk of our resources into reacting to street crime after it occurs. And this reaction generally reproduces the same pattern of inconsistent coercion that produced criminal behavior in the first place. A deliberate policy of crime prevention needs to be the cornerstone of an effective crime-reduction effort. Prevention must take place at both individual and societal levels and must affect the dynamics of coercion to be effective.[1]

## A Comprehensive Plan for Effective Crime Prevention

The problem of street crime is connected to the processes of social reproduction (Colvin and Pauly 1983). Social reproduction involves the institutions of socialization that prepare young people for productive roles in society. Rising crime rates in the United States from the 1960s through the early 1990s were the by-product of a fractured process of social reproduction that did not mesh with our society's productive needs in an increasingly global economy. With technical and problem-solving skills at a premium for successful labor market participation, our society has failed to prepare young people for these new economic realities, leaving them instead to the vagaries of the market economy. As a result, growing numbers of young people from 1970 to the mid-1990s were unable to create social bonds with legitimate avenues to adulthood; many became marginal to our nation's economic and social institutions. Through some fortuitous circumstances, economic expansion in the late 1990s brought increasing numbers of young people into the economic mainstream, which aided in a decrease in crime. But a fundamental gap between our social institutions that are supposed to prepare young people for the future and the realities of a global economy continues to widen as we fail to make the types of social investments needed to ensure a viable economic future. A sudden downturn in economic fortunes could quickly undo the progress in job creation and lower crime we witnessed in the late 1990s.

Our continued failure to invest in human development, human capital, and the institutions of social reproduction represents an enormous gamble. The failure to make these investments now leaves us highly vulnerable to growing crime and economic disruptions as the number of young people in their crime-prone years is forecast to grow dramatically in the United States in the first decade of the twenty-first century (Fox 1996; LaFree 1998a; Steffensmeier and Harer 1991). Of course, the mere factor of growing numbers of youth in no way makes rising crime inevitable (Zimring 1998); the key determinate is not the size of this cohort but its experience as it passes through childhood and adolescence. And these experiences, whether positive or negative, are shaped by the relative health of our economy and of our institutions of social reproduction.

Many current proactive crime-prevention programs focus almost exclusively on the individual's immediate situation without addressing the larger context that shapes that person's socialization. These programs have limited effects, often showing greatest success when the economy is booming, thus reinforcing program effects through fortuitous circumstance instead of through planned policy implementation. These become sporadic efforts when they are not linked to a comprehensive program of crime prevention. These programs often lack public commitment and financing because they are seen as helping specific groups (i.e., the poor) at the expense of middle-class taxpayers who receive no direct benefits from these programs.

For a crime-reduction program to have permanent impact (not just temporary success when economic conditions are good), it must deal with the underlying sources of crime through comprehensive, proactive measures. To receive wide public support, the program must be aimed not directly at crime or the poor but rather at broader economic and human development problems (related to crime and poverty) that directly affect large segments of the population. Crime-reduction would thus be a byproduct of a comprehensive program dealing with sustained economic growth and human development, which affects the mass of the population. In the process, both interpersonal and impersonal forms of coercion, which are at the heart of crime production, can be dramatically reduced in our society.

Nations that invest in human capital (the skills and productive capacities of a nation's workforce) and infrastructure (the physical assets that allow for the smooth and rapid flow of commerce and greater labor productivity) are in the best position to compete in the global economy. They become the beneficiaries of a virtuous cycle set in motion by their public investments. As economist and former U.S. Labor Secretary Robert B. Reich (1991: 43) explains:

> A work force possessing a good basic education, which can efficiently bring the fruits of its labors to the global economy, can attract global capital for its performance of moderately complex tasks. The experience gained by performing these tasks generates additional on-the-job training and experience, which serve to lure global capital for more complex activities. As skills build and experience accumulates, the nation's citizens receive more and more from the rest of the world in exchange for their services—which permits them to invest in better schools, transportation, research, and communications systems. . . . [T]heir links with the world steadily improve, their income rises.

These nations create a permanent basis for a non-coercive society that is more protected against the vagaries and uncertainties of global economic change. They are on a better footing to respond and adapt to changing economic circumstances and labor force needs.

Nations that fail to make these public investments in human capital and infrastructure fall into a "vicious cycle in which global money and technology are lured only by low wages and low taxes" (Reich 1991: 43). With these enticements to global capital, the financing of education and infrastructure becomes more problematic as the tax base erodes, and training and experience in more complex, higher-paying jobs are not provided. This vicious cycle "can continue to push wages downward until citizens of the nation (or region, or city) have a standard of living like that typical of the Third World" (Reich 1991: 43). This vicious economic cycle forms the basis for a coercive society in which citizens feel the constant threat of impersonal forces overtaking their lives as they struggle in this uncertain economy. From the late 1960s to the mid-1990s, this was precisely the type of economic cycle the United States experienced as taxes and social investments were slashed. Structural unemployment, blighted inner cities, and rising crime rates were visible symptoms of this vicious economic cycle.

Our possibly temporary reprieve from this vicious cycle has alleviated its worst effects. But this is very likely only a temporary reprieve that has been purchased through record-high consumer debt and income gains of baby boomers who are in their highest income-earning years. At some point we will reach a limit to this economic boom without having changed some fundamental contradictions in our economy. The time to turn permanently from a vicious economic cycle toward a virtuous one is while we are experiencing fortuitous economic growth and surpluses in federal and state budgets, as the United States has been experiencing in the late 1990s and early 2000s. It is during such a period that we can generate the tax revenues necessary for sustained social investments that can ensure future economic viability and continuing revenue growth for future reinvestment. Without these investments, we could easily slide once again into a vicious economic cycle like the one witnessed from the late 1960s to the early 1990s, when structural unemployment and crime reached historically high levels.

As the leading economy in the world, the United States sets the standards for economic growth and change. Movement in the United States toward the virtuous cycle described by Robert Reich can change the dynamics of the world economy. Instead of competing for who can have the cheapest labor and lowest taxes, competition can be reset toward the nation that has the best infrastructure, greatest access to renewable and non-polluting energy sources, and most highly skilled, productive labor force. With these assets, global wealth increases in a sustainable fashion and is more equitably distributed among populations whose higher incomes raise aggregate demand for domestic and imported goods. Greater labor productivity, which is the ultimate source of improvement in the standard of living, allows for wage and income gains to occur without spurring inflation.[2] Sustained economic growth and rising incomes in one country creates opportunities for similar income growth for other countries that invest in the types of human capital and physical infrastructure that spur productivity. To help create ever-growing markets for their products and services, it is in one country's interest to ensure that other countries also have rising incomes from a virtuous economic cycle. It is for this reason that international trade agreements and foreign aid should enforce and encourage environmental protection, better working conditions, higher wages, and public investments in human capital and physical infrastructure. In the process, the dynamics of global competition change from the vicious zero-sum competition of lowering wages, environmental degradation, and stagnating infrastructure (which in the long run create the basis for worldwide economic depression), to a global virtuous cycle that raises global income and distributes it more equitably.

A comprehensive crime reduction policy must simultaneously be a plan that reshapes the economy by enhancing a nation's investment in human capital and infrastructure. The focus is less on "what to do about crime" and more on "what to do about viable competitiveness in the world economy." The latter question entails the first. Permanent crime reduction is bound up with the question of resources for human capital and human development. Enhancing human development involves radical alteration of the social reproduction process through which humans are made ready for participation in the economy and society.

Any comprehensive program affecting social reproduction processes must also aim to expand the democratic process in new and imaginative ways (Pepinsky 1991). The reduction of coercion and consequent enhancement of social bonding, self-control, self-efficacy, and other attributes, which are the keys to crime reduction, entail the maximization of democratic participation at the grass-roots level in families, schools, communities, workplaces, and governmental agencies. Throughout the following discussion, enhanced democratic participation in the activities of daily life is a key component toward building a non-coercive society.

The following specific proposals draw freely from and expand on ideas developed by Elliott Currie (1998, 1994, 1985), Francis T. Cullen and his associates (1999), Samuel Walker (1989), Lynn Curtis (1989), and the Eisenhower Foundation (1990), all of whom present a similar focus on crime prevention through addressing economic and human needs. A major problem with their approaches, in my view, is that most of their proposed programs focus exclusively on poor communities. Although such programs are a necessary part of a comprehensive approach, they risk public rejection, as many of the war on poverty programs of the 1960s did in the United States, because they are targeted at a minority of the population. To be successful and to avoid class and racial polarization, programs must receive broad-based public support by directly benefiting more than just poor people.

Many of the following proposals will be viewed by some as outrageous. That a comprehensive proposal that seeks to affect the social reproduction process in a country like the United States is viewed as "outrageous" is more a reflection of the truly outrageous state of the nation's political economy than of the proposal itself. In most industrialized democracies the development of human capital is taken as a serious public obligation and is seen as an investment in these societies' future well-being. (Although recently, the social democracies of Europe have begun to retreat from these social investments, and possibly, as a result, have witnessed rising crime rates [Weiss and South 1998].) The "privatized" nature of social reproduction in the United States, where each individual is left to fend for him or herself in the scramble for economic gain and attainment of marketable skills, creates enormous social dislocations. Future social needs are neglected as the bases for public investments are undermined by private investment decisions that on an arbitrary and unexpected basis can move capital into wild speculation, nonproductive ventures, and out of a particular nation. Much of the economic surplus that could be invested in moving young people into productive roles as adults is often wasted. In the process, these young people experience a much higher level of coercion than is necessary, and many of them get caught up in the processes that lead to crime. If my proposals seem outrageous, they need to be compared with the current set of circumstances that completely leaves future economic viability up to the whims of a volatile, impersonal global market economy.

A comprehensive plan, such as the one proposed here, will require a major change in priorities. Beginning in the 1950s, public investments in the United States were skewed toward the "military-industrial complex," which President Dwight D. Eisenhower warned, in his farewell address to the nation in 1961, threatened to overtake other important priorities in our society (Patterson 1996: 440–41). The disastrous Vietnam War, which produced the inflation that began the long wave of economic decline from 1967 to 1992, proved true the wisdom of Eisenhower's observation. The Cold War moved our nation's resources toward military investments and away from nonmilitary investments in new plants, equipment, job training, and education that would have allowed the United States to compete effectively with Asian and European nations, which increasingly captured global market shares in the 1970s and 1980s. Even with the ending of the Cold War in the late 1980s, the military-industrial complex still commands a disproportionate share of national wealth. In addition, a rising "penal-industrial complex" now drains public investments from education and other public programs that can foster viable economic growth (Donziger 1996; Schlosser 1998). National investments must be moved away from spending on the military and prisons toward education and human development. We need to establish an "educational-industrial complex" to support the web of social institutions that develop human beings for useful and productive roles in our society.

Education needs to be understood as a broader project than the formal education now offered in public schools. It must include families, schools, workplaces, and communities. And, of greatest importance for crime prevention, it must reduce the marginalization of young people and the coercion to which they are subjected in both its interpersonal and impersonal forms. Nine specific proposals make up this comprehensive approach to crime prevention.

*1. Short-term Emergency Measures.*   In the short term, to deal with those who are immediately facing joblessness and other sources of impersonal coercion, viable job training, social-skills training, and job placement programs need to be initiated and fully funded. Income subsidies for poor families can provide a stopgap measure while more comprehensive job training and job development programs are established. But a reliance on entitlement welfare programs that do not enhance human capital but only keep poor people in place is inadequate and counterproductive. Welfare reform programs instituted in the United States during the 1990s were attempts to move welfare recipients off the welfare roles and into work. The booming economy of the late 1990s facilitated the move from welfare to work for many former welfare recipients. But many faced enormous obstacles that were not removed by these reform efforts. Lack of health insurance in the new jobs meant that medical expenses increased as Medicaid benefits were eventually lost with the move to work. Expenses for childcare that were now incurred for mothers leaving for work were not provided in many states' welfare reform provisions. Transportation costs to and from work were also an added burden. Essentially, many of these former welfare recipients were moved from the roles of welfare to the ranks of the working poor who remain below the poverty line and for whom few government subsidies are available.[3] Only a growing economy in the late 1990s provided some relief. But when this economic boom ends, these will be the individuals who will be most vulnerable to increasing coercive forces. Any permanent end to welfare dependency and persistent impoverishment will necessitate the initiation of other proposals of the comprehensive program outlined in this section. Job training programs for the poor will have little impact on joblessness unless they are incorporated into a much more comprehensive approach that affects overall economic growth in the future.

In the meantime, income supplements for those who work are urgently needed so that we can bring all of the working poor up to a living wage that will allow them to provide basic needs for their families (Currie 1998). The expansion in the United States of the "earned income tax credit" and increases in the minimum wage to levels that bring people out of poverty when they work are ways of subsidizing these individuals' incomes. Providing health care insurance, especially for the children of the working poor, is a long-neglected public responsibility that can no longer be ignored in the United States. People who are unable to work because of disabilities will still need to be maintained on welfare; and for these individuals welfare benefits should be expanded. Those who are unable to work because of substance abuse problems should be provided with viable substance abuse treatment that simultaneously improves their economic and social circumstances and prepares them for the workforce (Currie 1994). Again, none of this can be done in isolation. Other aspects of the comprehensive proposal, such as improvements of workplaces (see proposal 6), must be implemented simultaneously for long-term effect. But as we move people away from welfare and substance abuse dependency, they move from being an enormous social expense that drains our public resources to being a social asset from which public revenues can be generated. And they move toward being productive members of society who will be able to participate fully in the other proposals outlined in this section.

**2. Nationwide Parent-Effectiveness Programs.**    Disciplining children in a non-coercive, consistent, and non-humiliating fashion is perhaps the most important crime prevention measure that can be instituted. Establishing a strong affective social bond between parents and children provides the basis for strong social bonds to authority figures in other social settings, especially in school. Success in school is greatly determined by early childhood experiences in families (Jencks et al. 1972). Thus effective parenting lays the groundwork for effective development of a nation's human capital.

Parent-effectiveness training should focus on teaching techniques of consistent, non-coercive discipline, and such training should emphasize the importance of prenatal care, child health care, and nutrition as the bases for healthy childhood development. (A comprehensive national health insurance system can provide the means to put much of this training into practice.) Parent training should be required in the senior year in all high schools (*before* young people become parents) and offered as an adult basic education class in all high schools to new parents. Parent-effectiveness counseling programs attached to local schools should supplement these classes. Parents can be induced to participate in these classes and in counseling programs through enhanced tax exemptions for participation. In addition, "visiting nurse" programs in which registered nurses visit mothers during their pregnancy and for two years after birth have been found to significantly reduce child abuse and neglect (Currie 1998: 82–91). These "home visiting" programs for expectant and new mothers should become a routine part of our health care system. Periods longer than two years, however, are needed for continued consultation after birth in which effective parenting, child health care, and nutrition can be provided, especially for parents who are at higher risk for abusive parenting.

Gerald Patterson's experimental programs for training parents of delinquents in effective discipline demonstrate that such programs can be effective (Bank et al. 1991; Patterson 1982; Patterson, Chamberlain, and Reid 1982). Parent-effectiveness training is geared toward initiating the child into a process of consistent, non-coercive control that provides both expressive and instrumental social supports (as in the Type 1 pattern, which is most conducive to producing pro-social behavior). Effective parenting prepares the child for the intellectual and social challenges he or she will face in school. Of course, as with each of the specific proposals included in this comprehensive plan, by itself parent-effectiveness training will have a very limited impact if basic economic and other social issues (like development of comprehensive health care programs) are left untouched.

**3. Universal "Head Start" Preschool Programs.**    All children should be prepared early for participation in school. This can be done either through parents themselves who have the time, talent, and inclination to provide preschool development or through an enhanced program modeled after the current Head Start program, which has been found to reduce school failure and delinquency (Currie 1994: 316). For parents who can provide such preschool development themselves, a program for certification and training by local schools would be a necessary prerequisite for this approach. For most working parents, however, time is too limited to provide an effective preschool experience. Certified private and public preschool centers can be coupled with daycare programs for working parents, who would receive tax exemptions for their children's enrollment in these daycare facilities or, depending on family income, receive direct public subsidies to pay for this daycare and preschool education. Combined with effective parenting, these preschool programs can provide the cognitive and emotional basis for early success in school. Because the nation as a whole eventually benefits from this enhancement of potential learning, preschool should be seen as an important public obligation and social investment in the nation's future workforce.

**4. Expanded and Enhanced Public Education.**    Public education in the United States has fallen far behind systems of education in other industrialized nations (Barrett 1990). Radical improvement and imaginative innovations in public education are the next necessary component of a comprehensive approach toward producing a non-coercive society.

A special focus on teaching problem-identification and problem-solving skills needs to be incorporated into the curriculum in all disciplines.

Such skills are a premium in the global economy and are adaptable to the changing needs of the labor market (Reich 1991). Being able to identify and solve technical and social problems are skills that will always be in demand. Giving young people these skills not only enhances their economic prospects but draws wealth to their nation from the global economy.

An essential educational reform is greatly increased teachers' salaries and changes in teacher education and certification, aimed at opening this profession up to non-education majors. Teacher education should emphasize techniques of consistent, non-coercive control of students that draws them into a process of active learning and enhances their social bonds to education. We need to attract specialists, especially in science and math, who can also teach. The current teacher education and certification process in many states precludes such specialists from entering public school classrooms until they complete often superfluous education courses (which may take more than a year to complete at their own expense) before they can receive certification. Such obstacles combined with relatively low pay makes it unlikely that many of these professionals who have the desire and talent to pass their knowledge on to the next generation will enter the teaching field. We need to attract teachers who have had not only graduate education but also practical experiences in which they have developed problem-solving and problem-identifying skills that can be passed on to their students. A conversion from a military-industrial complex (and a penal-industrial complex) to an education-industrial complex would entail the transfer of professionals with their experiences in problem solving in these fields to enhanced positions in education. In short, our brightest and best citizens need to be recruited into the teaching profession.

The school year should be lengthened to 230 days to accelerate learning in mathematics, the sciences, and humanities. Such an expansion from our current national average 180-day school year would make us competitive with the Japanese and Germans, who have about 240 days of school each year (Barrett 1990). At the same time, the school day should cover the important time period in late afternoon and early evening when the highest rates of juvenile delinquency can now be observed (Felson 1998). Starting junior and senior high school later in the morning (giving teenagers time to catch up on their sleep) and extending the school day to the early evening hours would reduce the time between the end of school and the parents' arrival home from work. Students are better served with structured educational activities during this time rather than the unstructured, unsupervised free time that often becomes a prime period for juveniles to explore deviant activities.

An expanded school year would allow enhanced learning of problem-identifying and problem-solving skills in many traditional courses and in many nontraditional educational activities, such as "outward bound" experiences in wilderness areas in which young people learn to cooperate in solving problems of living and resolving conflicts through nonviolent means. Other educational activities during an expanded school year could include paid apprenticeship programs that give young people specific role models and experiences in professions and occupations (Hamilton 1990). Tutoring, summer reading programs, financial planning classes, and parent-effectiveness training, discussed earlier, could also be part of an extended school year. Such innovative programs should be developed at the local level to address community needs and interests and include young people in the decision-making processes involved in these programs' creation.

Education can also be enhanced through the use of peer counseling programs, student-tutoring programs in which more gifted students are involved in teaching other students, and the elimination of "tracking" (Oakes 1985). Such programs and reforms are aimed at creating a cooperative educational experience in which individual success is seen to depend on group success. These educational approaches move away from the hyper-competitive nature of so many of our current educational programs and thus reduce the invidious distinctions among students that lower self-esteem for many and contribute to student alienation and marginalization.

The problem of student dropout should also be ameliorated by this more cooperative approach to education. But to further enhance the attractiveness of school, an incentive-based learning system can be instituted whereby students are paid stipends to attend school and are given "bonuses" for good school performance. These payments for attending and doing well in school would greatly reduce the need for students to work. This not only would create more time for students to concentrate on educational activities (which include educationally appropriate, paid apprenticeships) but also would free up a number of unskilled jobs for unemployed adults.

Schools can also become arenas in which responsible democratic participation and skills in conflict resolution are instilled. Students should be actively involved in developing school policies. The obvious conflicts among interested parties over school policies are not something that school administrators should avoid. Rather, such conflict should be seen as an important resource for educating students to be active participants in a democratic society. Such experiences will accustom students to democratic involvement and to the practice of identifying problems among people and solving these problems through non-coercive means. Thus, effective nonviolent methods of conflict resolution can be instilled through actual practice. An enhanced sense of empowerment among students will increase bonding to the school and decrease the sense of alienation and isolation that spurs marginalization.

In fact, schools can become the arena for community-wide involvement in the lives of young people. Local community groups, students, parents, teachers, and school administrators should all be actively involved in developing educational programs. Such grassroots involvement contributes to the development of a cohesive, cooperative community. The federal role should be limited to providing funding and ensuring that an equal distribution of educational funds is made across geographical units. The federal government can also evaluate promising programs, help publicize innovations that have been found to be effective, and coordinate the provision of technical assistance to local schools that want to implement these innovations. But the decisions should remain at the local level (within the constraints of Supreme Court decisions regarding discrimination) and with the people who are directly affected by the decisions.

The responsibility for teaching should be transferred from educational bureaucracies to classroom teachers with important input from students and parents. With professionals, who have been properly trained in consistent, non-coercive means of control and whose training and experience make them experts in their field of study, at the helm of each classroom, bureaucratic oversight becomes an unneeded expense. Teachers should be in constant communication with their peers in developing effective teaching techniques and should actively involve students and parents in assessing the effectiveness of their teaching. Those who are immediately affected (teachers, students, and parents) can open up the current stultifying bureaucracy in many schools through democratic participation. In the process we create a non-coercive atmosphere for all participants in the educational enterprise. Students are given consistent expressive and instrumental social supports in this cooperative atmosphere. Many fewer students will be alienated and marginalized; thus the pool from which future criminals are drawn is reduced.

Schools then become a true training ground for citizenship, not just in the abstract but through concrete, everyday activities. Students emerging from such an educational experience will be much better prepared to accept the challenges and deal with the conflicts inherent in a complex society. They will be better prepared to become the problem identifiers and problem solvers who can attract global capital to a nation. In the process, many of the cultural supports for coercion, discussed in chapter 4, will erode as a new generation experiences and practices non-coercive ways of interacting with others during their formative years.

*5. National Service Program.* Upon completion of secondary education, young people should have the opportunity to complete a two-year national service program, after which educational and vocational training stipends would be awarded to those participating. Each young volunteer would be involved in developing his or her own specific service commitment, although community needs will obviously influence the choice of assignments. Military service could be an option, but one that should be assigned only with the participant's consent. Payment during the national service commitment would be at the subsistence level to cover necessary expenses. The real payoffs for participants will be the gaining of positive life experiences and the opening of advanced educational opportunities.

National service can include all types of service related to environmental improvements, poverty programs, community organizing efforts, literacy programs, health care, nursing homes, construction, daycare, pre-schools, and so on. National service volunteers could provide needed labor for public works projects that are aimed at improving both our environment and infrastructure; for community development programs designed to improve social services for the poor, children, and the elderly; and for educational programs as teachers' assistants, tutors, daycare and preschool workers, and counselors' assistants. (Many of the enhanced school year activities called for in proposal 4 can be implemented with these national service volunteers.) National service volunteers would be intimately involved in the problem-identification and problem-solving processes in all these areas, thus honing their skills through practical application.

The national service program should not be mandatory. (After all, we are trying to build a non-coercive society.) But it is hoped that the incentive for participation will be quite high. For completion of two years of national service, complete tuition, room, and board should be paid for 4 years of college or for completion of vocational or technical training. Additionally, national service volunteers should be eligible for scholarships for postgraduate work if they excel as undergraduates. Those not participating in national service would receive none of these benefits. The idea is based on the G. I. Bill, which ensured returning World War II veterans an education. This governmental measure was one of the best investments of public funds ever made. While it was costly to pay for veterans' education, the money received back in the form of higher tax revenues from the increased incomes that accrued from this education more than paid for the initial outlay (Patterson 1996). In the same manner, such educational benefits for the national service commitment should be seen as an important public investment that will increase national wealth and will thus in the long run more than pay for itself.

Such a program provides at least three important benefits. First, young people between the ages of about 18 and 20 would be actively participating in the community in adult roles that lead to promising futures. During these two years they would gain experiences in life that will help them decide on their futures and give them insights that will enhance their later education. In the process, they will be deeply involved in pro-social activities at a time in life when deviant activities would normally be at their highest. It provides the basis for moving toward a life in which impersonal coercive forces are reduced. It reduces economic strain by providing a clear legitimate path toward achieving goals. Second, for a relatively low price in subsistence wages, the community can use the enormous energy of young people to enhance the life of the community, rebuild the nation's transportation and communication infrastructures, improve the environment, and contribute to the educational development of their younger brothers and sisters. Third, the program reinforces and extends young people's commitment to the community, a commitment first instilled in the educational process described earlier in proposal 4.

**6. Enhancement of Workplace Environments.**    Another important aspect of a comprehensive plan for crime-reduction through creation of a non-coercive society is the general improvement of the workplace environment for adults. Young people must know that they are eventually heading into good quality jobs; otherwise, the sense of hope that the education process is trying to instill will be undermined. In addition, as discussed in chapter 3, adults' workplace experiences have profound effects on family relationships. Coercive workplace environments create alienated workers who often duplicate these coercive relations in the home, thus recreating the cycle that produces marginalization (and crime) in our society.

Enhanced labor laws that promote workplace democracy, expanded collective bargaining, and worker participation in ownership and control of industries are needed to create the types of non-coercive work environments for which we will be educating our young people. Their experiences with democratic participation in schools should prepare them for democratically-controlled workplaces. Such workplaces are necessary for the type of self-directed and creative employees who attract capital in the global economy (Reich 1991). In the process, democracy becomes a profound everyday affair, not just an election-day exercise. The non-coercive practices of conflict resolution that take place in schools and in workplaces on an everyday basis become the model for conflict resolution in other daily interactions, which can only have a positive effect in reducing crime in the wider community.

**7. Programs for Economic Growth and Expanded Productivity.** For last-ing reduction of impersonal coercive forces, continued economic growth is essential. We saw in the late 1990s the impact of economic growth on crime reduction. Growth in employment has brought young people into the job market at somewhat better wages than we have seen in decades. But this has been the result of fortuitous circumstance, not public policy. To sustain the benefits of this economic boom, and to overcome the coun-tervailing tendency of the expected rise in the number of young people entering both the labor market and their crime-prone years (Fox 1996), public policies aimed at sustained economic growth need to be put in place soon. Enhancement of human capital (the desired outcome of the educational process) is meaningless if production and the economy are not concurrently enhanced.

Financial investments need to be publicly guided, not placed solely in the hands of a few wealthy individuals who may seek short-term profits at the expense of national growth, productivity, and true national security, as they did in the 1980s (Phillips 1990). Investment decisions of major cor-porations need to be made by boards composed of owners, managers, workers, and consumers (perhaps through greatly expanded stockholding in companies, which spreads ownership into the wider public and which would be an aspect of enhanced workplace participation discussed earlier). Public funds can be used to promote research and development of new technologies for which corporations may be reluctant to risk capital. (This has been routinely done in the military-industrial complex since World War II. Why not apply the same process in a more democratic fashion to less inflationary nonmilitary production?)

Huge investments in our basic infrastructure of transportation and communication need to be made. Private and public investments in our cities need to be made to enhance the job base in these areas, which in the United States during the last three decades of the twentieth century have been particularly hard hit by disinvestment. Many poor people in inner cities, and increasingly in older suburbs, find it difficult to get transporta-tion to jobs that are dispersed throughout metropolitan areas. Thus public transportation, which is at the core of planned efforts to reduce the out-of-control sprawl in metropolitan areas, is a key infrastructure investment, as is construction of low- and moderate-income housing nearer to trans-portation corridors and places of employment.

These public investments will serve to attract and keep private invest-ments. A smooth-flowing infrastructure and an educated, highly skilled, more productive workforce will attract businesses. During the 1980s and 1990s, the lure of short-term profits guided investments in the United States. The types of long-term investments that do not create an immediate profit, but do create a stronger economic base that attracts global capital, have only sporadically occurred. As long as we as a nation fail to make these investments, we are living on borrowed time. Much can be done with a democratically planned investment strategy that creates the human and physical infrastructure and the productive labor force that are the basis of a vibrant economy (Harrison and Bluestone 1988). This viable economic base is essential for the construction of a non-coercive society.

*8. A More Progressive Tax System.*    The tax system in the United States needs to be made truly progressive. Increasing labor productivity means growth in the general level of wealth. But a general growth in wealth does not mean that it is shared equitably. Wage stagnation for those in the bottom 40 percent of the income ladder has in the United States coincided in the last three decades of the twentieth century with rising wealth for those in the top twenty percent of the income ladder. Such inequality can eventually undercut a growing economy because consumption of goods produced reaches the limits of average people's incomes. Consumption in these circumstances can only grow through increased personal indebtedness, as has been the trend during the economic boom that started in the 1990s. A high level of personal indebtedness is a poor basis upon which to build a viable economy. More equitable distribution of wealth (coupled with higher productivity) provides a stronger basis for sustained economic health.

The wealthy in the United States are paying far lower taxes than they did in the 1960s; and middle-class citizens, if payroll deductions for Social Security are included, are paying much more (Phillips 1990). "Americans are not overtaxed. In 1989, we paid less in taxes as a percentage of GNP . . . than the citizens of any other industrialized country. Wealthy Americans, in particular, are not overtaxed. Their marginal income-tax rate is the lowest top tax rate of any industrialized nation" (Reich 1991: 51). Higher income and wealth taxes for wealthy individuals and corporations, coupled with the job training, job development, investment, and education programs proposed earlier, would pump more money into the civilian economy for purchase of basic needs and services, thus raising aggregate demand while narrowing the gap in income inequality. "Were the personal income tax as progressive as it was even as late as 1977 [in the United States], in 1989 the top tenth would have paid $93 billion more in taxes than they did. At that rate, from 1991 to 2000 they would contribute close to a trillion dollars more, even if their incomes failed to rise [and as it turned out their incomes rose dramatically]" (Reich 1991: 51). (This extra amount in government revenues from 1982 [when huge tax cuts for the wealthy and corporations went into effect] to 1999 would have been enough to cut the federal government's publicly-held debt by two-thirds from the level it stood in 1999. This estimated debt reduction does not include the extra revenues that accrued from growing incomes of the wealthy during this period. Adding this in would have provided enough government revenues to nearly eliminate this debt.)

Revenues from such tax increases can be invested in infrastructure and human capital development that keep the economy viable, growing, and producing more revenues for future investment. We thus enter the type of virtuous cycle discussed earlier (Reich 1991). A progressive tax system in conjunction with these social investments provides a sustainable and growing source of funds to finance the proposals outlined in this chapter. At the same time, economic inequality, which has been related to high crime rates (LaFree 1998a), is dramatically reduced.

### 9. Community Organizing and Criminal Opportunity Reduction.   Crime prevention efforts are most effective when strong interpersonal ties develop among members of a community. As Marcus Felson (1998) explains, capable guardians are abundant in areas where routine social interactions are common. In these areas, a more organized and structured set of routine activities reduces the opportunities for crime and reduces the number of motivated offenders, since more individuals are caught up in the positive social interactions of the area rather than being marginal to these interactions. One of the reasons that many inner city areas have higher crime is the socially disorganized nature of these areas in which social interactions and community ties are weak (Hagan 1994; Shaw and McKay 1942; Wilson 1987). Thus community organizing becomes a key tactic of any crime reduction program.

These efforts at organizing are greatly facilitated by the economic and enhanced social reproduction efforts contained in the previous eight proposals. If a stable job base reappears in an inner city area, for instance, this becomes the core around which a stable community can be built. Without this stable job base, any efforts at community organizing will be limited if not overwhelmed. So as with all of the previous proposals, community organizing should be seen as part of a larger comprehensive effort at reducing crime and the coercion from which it springs.

Efforts at community organizing go a long way toward changing the dynamics in the immediate foreground of crime. Community organizing brings people together so that they become a visible and ongoing presence on the streets as they go about their daily, legitimate activities. This increases the number of capable guardians. A key part of community organizing (especially efforts that involve community policing) includes educating people in an area on precautions to take to avoid victimization.

These efforts reduce the targets of crime. And finally, by bringing young people into an active, positive community life, instead of allowing them to drift into the cycle of coercion contained in the street culture, the number of motivated offenders in an area can be reduced. In fact, an organized community is one that intervenes effectively to prevent a criminally oriented street culture from ever emerging. Thus, all of the elements that structure criminal opportunities and motivations in the foreground of criminal events are cut short by effective community organizing.

Several successful examples of effective community organizing can be cited (Currie 1998; Silberman 1978; Smith 1999). Among these are gang violence reduction efforts such as the one at the Benning Terrace housing project in Washington, D.C. (Dickerson 1998; Smith 1999). I discuss the Benning Terrace example in some detail because it contains all the elements of a successful community organizing effort.

Benning Terrace had become such a violent neighborhood that the head of the District of Columbia Housing Authority had decided in January 1997 to tear down the housing project and disperse its residents to other locations. At about the same time, however, a group of middle aged men, many of them former convicts and drug addicts, had become alarmed at the growing gang violence in the area. They started the Alliance of Concerned Men whose aim was to stop gang violence in Washington, D.C. They chose Benning Terrace as the place to start. Their first step was to broker a truce between the neighborhood's two rival gangs whose daily shooting battles forced local residents to take cover within their apartments as early as three o'clock in the afternoon. The Alliance obtained the assistance of a professional mediator who guided the group's conflict resolution efforts with the gangs. Soon, after much talking and going back and forth between the two gangs, the Alliance was able to set up (in neutral territory) a series of face-to-face meetings between the gangs.

Rules for the meetings were not imposed on the gang members; instead, the gang members developed rules for the proceedings themselves. As the gangs talked to each other it became clear that the cycle of violence and revenge was something that both sides wanted to end, but did not know how. Significantly, no one could remember what had started the cycle of violence; both sides said that they were reacting to the threats of violence only because they felt they had no other choice. The older men of the Alliance began to explore with the youth other choices that might be available. They asked them to remember that as young children they could play in relative safety outdoors; wouldn't they like for their younger brothers and sisters to enjoy that kind of childhood as well? Since many of the gang members saw their violence as an effort to protect their younger siblings from perceived threats by the rival gang, this appeal to the safety of their younger brothers and sisters hit home. The coercive efforts by each gang to stop the violence of the other gang were only creating more violence that threatened their younger brothers and sisters. In fact, it was the killing of a twelve-year-old boy in the neighborhood that prompted the gang members to listen to the Alliance's appeal for face-to-face meetings. Finally, one of the gang members proposed that they stop the shooting. It was agreed that if one side stopped, the other side would too. No one was sure if the truce would really hold.

Word of the gang truce reached the head of the D.C. Housing Authority who decided to put on hold his plans for razing the project. Instead, he came to the next truce meeting between the gangs. While at the meeting he was asked by the gang members what he was going to do about the graffiti that defaced the walls of the project. Realizing that this question was a test (the graffiti presented not only gang markings but also memorials to dead buddies killed in the project's gang wars), he replied that he had no plans for removing the graffiti, but the gang members might want to remove it themselves. This conversation soon led to the hiring of the gang members by the D.C. Housing Authority not only to remove the graffiti but also to help renovate the project. Plans for razing the project were now completely abandoned.

Before long, young men who only a few months earlier had been shooting at each other were now acting cooperatively in efforts to better their neighborhood. Many of them became permanent employees of the Housing Authority going through extensive training programs to receive promotions; others obtained job referrals through the Housing Authority to local businesses where they began, most of them for the first time, to gain work experience. The Alliance members continued meeting with the young men, encouraging them to work, get an education, and deal with the responsibilities of becoming adults. Truce meetings were transformed into support group meetings in which training in life skills and conflict management became featured activities. In a short time, formerly hardened gang members, whom most of us would have written off as unsalvageable, were exchanging hugs and openly crying in public as each new accomplishment by individuals in the group was celebrated. The Alliance and these former gang youth had brought the neighborhood back. Children could now play in the streets safely as the number of homicides in Benning Terrace dropped from eight in 1996 to zero in 1998.

Years of coercive police crackdowns had not made the gang violence go away; for every one kid arrested and locked up, many other kids were more than willing to take his place as an urban warrior. Such coercive crackdowns did not change the dynamics in the community. In fact, these police crackdowns likely contributed to the general climate of coercion that already afflicted the neighborhood. It was the non-coercive approaches of the Alliance that broke the cycle of coercion and violence in Benning Terrace. These were men who had been through the same tough childhoods and experiences in the streets as the Benning Terrace youngsters. These experiences gave the Alliance men instant credibility with these youths. They could give permission, where no one else could, to let down the guarded suspicion and allow feelings for others to emerge. They created strong social bonding with these young men, and encouraged them to better their lives and the life of their neighborhood. The Alliance members made it clear that they were not going away; they stuck with the young men through both their triumphs and their disappointments.

In addition, the head of the Housing Authority introduced job opportunities that not only provided legitimate sources of money but also provided self-esteem, a sense of respect, and positive connections to the mainstream society and its economy. It certainly helped that these activities were taking place as the general economy was strongly improving in the late 1990s. But a stronger economy by itself did not provide the connections to these jobs. Courageous individuals who had faith in these young people were the necessary conduits to these new opportunities. Their efforts at gaining the truce and then involving these young people in organizing and improving their community set the stage so that these job and educational opportunities could be taken advantage of by young men who now believed that these opportunities were worth pursuing. The members of the Alliance and the strong community support that they were building around these young people created the context that allowed these youths to step through the doors to these opportunities. They provided the social and cultural capital that form networks to the mainstream economy and society (Hagan 1994). As their personal lives and the community itself experienced less interpersonal and impersonal coercion, they gained confidence that they could continue building a non-coercive future together.

This kind of community organizing can be replicated (and is being replicated) in other neighborhoods (Currie 1998; Smith 1999; Wood 2000). It relies on inducing cooperation through non-coercive means. It replaces a coercive cycle with a non-coercive one. Veterans of these efforts are an important resource. They can train dedicated people in other communities in organizing their neighborhoods. If other aspects of the comprehensive plan outlined in this section were also in place, many young people could be used in these types of community organizing activities as part of the National Service Program (discussed in proposal 5). These would be especially relevant national service placements for young people, like those of Benning Terrace, who had once been gang members who terrorized a neighborhood but who later contributed to reviving the same neighborhood.

Community organizing thus alters the immediate foreground in neighborhoods from one that is conducive to the cycles of coercion that produce crime to one that is based on non-coercive interchanges. In the process of reducing these criminogenic dynamics, young people in these neighborhoods are pulled away from the culture of the streets toward a viable mainstream economy and society created by the other proposals discussed earlier in this section.

The nine proposals outlined in this section constitute a comprehensive crime reduction program. They create a process that prepares children and young people for a dynamic future that they will be involved in actively planning and building. As hope for the future rises (both nationally and personally), enhanced social bonding, self-efficacy, self-control, and non-coercive behavioral modeling are created on a widespread basis. In the process, a society and culture promotes and becomes based in non-coercive relationships. A byproduct is greatly reduced crime. Throughout this chapter, the focus of these proposals is on inducing voluntary participation through positive incentives and reinforcements, not through coercion and punishments that only increase a sense of humiliation and anger and that sever social bonds. Through these positive incentives, delivered in a predictable and fair system based on democratic participation, we can produce children who are enthusiastic, imaginative, productive, and eager to participate in their community. In this environment created by this renewed socialization process, crime is reduced as individual bonding increases and national and community ties improve. Investments in physical and human capital enhance a nation's productivity and economic competitiveness, which creates the basis for a viable job base around which a non-coercive society can be constructed.

It is assumed that with these proposals in place, much crime will be prevented. Thus the need to react to crime after the fact can be greatly reduced as well. The need to expand prisons will be eliminated as we produce fewer offenders. But it will always be necessary to react to crime because no system, no matter how well designed, will ever be able to eliminate crime. But the way we react to crime needs to be dramatically altered; often this reaction only makes matters worse because it reproduces the coercive forces that lead to chronic criminality. We now turn to proposals for creating a criminal justice and corrections system for a non-coercive society.

## *A Coherent Criminal Justice and Corrections System*

In the context of a non-coercive society, as outlined in the previous section, it is much easier to introduce the kinds of criminal justice system reforms that could produce a more effective response to crime. Of course, we would not want to wait until the steps in the previous section have been implemented to begin reforming our criminal justice system. Obviously, an entire book could be written on criminal justice system reforms. In this section I merely outline some of the essential elements of these reforms that are consistent with the focus on building a non-coercive society. These criminal justice reforms are part and parcel of the changes discussed in the previous section. For instance, community organizing, discussed in proposal 9, would go hand in hand with community-oriented policing (Currie 1998).

The image of police as coercive agents in "wars on crime" has always been greatly overstated in comparison to actual policing activities, and such an image would be even less appropriate in a non-coercive society. When they are most effective, police act as facilitators of community interaction and crime prevention. Police are primarily involved in identifying and solving problems that give rise to criminal behavior and that generally affect the quality of life in local communities. As facilitators of community crime control activities, the police should come under the direct democratic control of the local neighborhood they serve. The military model of policing should be replaced with a participatory model in which police employees are actively engaged with local community members in a concerted effort to set priorities. Decentralized police agencies are most responsive to the needs of local neighborhoods and can work more effectively with members of the local community to identify and solve problems that can potentially lead to crime (Bayley 1998). While some centralized units, such as emergency response teams and criminal investigators, can serve all neighborhoods (and form the coercive back up that may be needed on occasion), the day-to-day routine police activities can be operated through decentralized storefront offices under control of the local neighborhood. The police agents who work in these offices would also live in the neighborhoods they serve, thus becoming integral members of the local community. They become the catalysts for creating organized communities in which crime prevention efforts can be enhanced and criminal acts can be responded to with greater certainty.

Criminological studies suggest that the *certainty* of being apprehended for wrongdoing is the key element of deterrence, while the *severity* of the sanction plays virtually no role in creating a deterrent effect (Krohn 1995). Such certainty is enhanced in an organized community where citizens look out for each other and maintain close cooperation with the police. These factors help explain the low crime rates in Japan (Johnson 1998). Japanese policing is organized around the *koban,* a small structure located in each neighborhood that puts police officers within the relational networks of each neighborhood (Westermann and Burfeind 1991). These officers provide a wide range of community services, while they maintain face-to-face interaction with citizens. This arrangement creates "less of the divisive 'we-they' framework that greatly informs policing in the United States. In Japan, citizens and police see themselves linked in a common cause" (Westermann and Burfeind 1991: 89). This type of community policing produces a largely non-coercive police presence aimed at understanding and responding to the community needs identified by local citizens. These community-policing efforts are an integral part of local community organizing efforts aimed at crime prevention. These efforts also create a social environment in which police can more effectively respond to those crimes that do occur, thus increasing the certainty of arresting those who victimize others and sending them to the courts and corrections systems.

Reforms in court procedures would also help produce a more coherent criminal justice system. The key product we should expect from the courts is a consistent and clear message to all types of offenders of community disapproval. Most judicial outcomes of the criminal courts are the product of plea-bargaining. These bargains are usually made through informal negotiations behind closed doors with no clear guidelines for these procedures. Charles Silberman (1978) argues that these negotiations do in fact involve predictable patterns, but are seen as mysterious and arbitrary by both victims and offenders. In this process clear and consistent messages of justice and disapproval get lost. Wealthy offenders are better able to take advantage of the plea-bargaining process because of their ability to pay for expert legal help. Poor offenders often "get the raw end of the deal" because they do not have these advantages. This situation inevitably leads to inconsistent outcomes based not of degrees of guilt or harm caused but on levels of income. The key is to open up this process and develop well-articulated guidelines for these plea-bargaining procedures. A defendant's income should play no role in this process; all persons charged with crime should have competent legal counsel that (if necessary) is fully paid for by the state and is provided the time and resources to adequately represent the defendant. If inconsistency is a key element in the production of crime (as I have argued in earlier chapters), the last thing we want is a criminal justice system that is inconsistent or even perceived as inconsistent.

The development of consistent judicial procedures must come from professionally trained judges and prosecutors who are protected from volatile political pressures. In Japan, judges and prosecutors are professionals who must undergo extensive training and education and pass professional exams directly related to their positions before they can take office. Instead of dedicating themselves to winning cases, and increasing the "body count" in their adversarial contests with defense attorneys, these prosecutors are dedicated to finding facts and restoring community harmony. The outcome in Japan is a system that is widely known for its leniency, but also for its highly certain and consistent outcomes (Johnson 1998). The non-coercive, non-adversarial approach is aimed at expressing strong community disapproval, shaming the offender, inducing remorse, and then, as quickly as possible, reintegrating the offender back into the community (Braithwaite 1989). Japan's system of "lenient" treatment has corresponded with one of the lowest national crime rates in the world.[4]

Judges and prosecutors should be selected from a pool of professionals specifically trained for these positions (perhaps appointed by legislatures and governors), rather than being directly elected. These professionally trained prosecutors and judges would serve terms of office that are renewable through voter approval in non-partisan, non-contested elections. (In Colorado, for example, voters can choose whether or not to retain a judge every few years of his term.) This would lessen the influence of politics on the judicial process (with its appeals to voters' baser instincts of fear and revenge) that often leads to wild swings in procedures, and thus greater inconsistency. Well-trained judges and prosecutors would be well-versed in, and help to create, consistent guidelines for plea-bargaining and sentencing.

Once an offender, through due process of law, has been convicted of or pled guilty to a crime, sentencing and offender classification should be based solely on the following. (1) The *seriousness of the current offense* should be ascertained through a careful assessment of actual harm to victims rather than just through reference to an offense category. This criterion would place white-collar crimes on an equal footing with ordinary street crimes; white-collar crimes often create greater harm to victims than do street crimes (Coleman 1994). In addition, basing sentences on actual harm caused to others would remove many so-called victimless crimes from the purview of the criminal justice system. Instead, these can be dealt with through appropriate social service or public health agencies, which are better designed to provide services and treatment that restore the individual to the community. For example, a person who is charged with illegal possession of drugs but has caused no criminal harm to others and needs drug addiction treatment is an obvious candidate for diversion from the criminal justice system to a public health agency.[5] (2) An assessment should be made of the offender's *prior record of criminal behavior* to discern patterns of chronic criminality. Chronic criminals may be in greater need of intensive rehabilitation services offered in institutional and community settings. (3) The *educational and social deficiencies* of the offender should be carefully assessed to determine appropriate placement and treatment. This criterion would take into consideration offender's age and maturity; the jurisdictional distinction between juveniles and adults would be replaced by a unified system that takes youth into consideration for sentencing, classification, and program placement (Feld 1999). (4) An assessment should also be made of the *offender's impact on community* members and their willingness to assist with his or her reintegration. This criterion in some ways overlaps with the first, but it takes into account other members of the community besides the victim and also is aimed at beginning the process of community involvement in the reintegration process.

A system of sentencing that produces consistency and also takes the circumstances of offenders, victims, and communities into account needs to be carefully developed. Sentencing guidelines can be mandated by state legislatures (or Congress), similar to Minnesota's presumptive sentencing system (Tonry 1995). Within these legislative guidelines set to assure some degree of consistency among cases, sentencing can be based on contracts made between the offender and the community that are developed through consultation and agreement among prosecutors, defense attorneys, crime victims, community members, and offenders. Such contracts would specify mandatory sentence lengths set in the guidelines (which can be reduced by judges with a written explanation, which is reviewed by an appeals court), fines to be paid, restitution and/or service in compensation for harm caused, and (if appropriate) treatment and educational programs to be completed.

The idea of sentencing contracts has been promoted by the restorative justice movement, which seeks to have offenders undo the harm they have caused and be restored to the community as soon as possible (Braithwaite 1999; Lerman 1999; Zehr and Mika 1998). Sentencing contracts can emerge through the plea-bargaining process or, after trial, during the pre-sentencing stage. The venue for setting these contracts (if appropriate for the type of crime) should be in the local neighborhood where the offense occurred (perhaps in the community-policing storefront). Instead of some distant austere courtroom, whose design is to impress upon the offender and the public the power of the state, the community setting impresses on the offender the connection he or she has with the community of people who have been harmed by the offense.

In the vast majority of cases, the sentence would be to a community-based alternative. As a general rule, offenders who have caused no physical harm to victims or who lack an extensive history of prior offenses should be placed in the community to fulfill the terms of their contracts. Some violent offenders may also be appropriate for community placement, but this would be contingent on prior record and other factors and the wishes of other parties considered during negotiation of the sentencing contract. For those sentenced to a community alternative, professionals from community agencies would provide intensive rehabilitation services (Gendreau, Cullen, and Bonta 1998). The most intensive rehabilitative services should be focused on those offenders who are at greater risk for repeat offending. The style and mode of treatment needs to match the offender and his or her needs. An assessment of the reasons the individual was involved in crime should be made prior to finalizing the sentencing contract; addressing these "criminogenic needs" should be the main focus of treatment and they should be specified in the sentencing contract. The community program must set a clear and consistent regimen of control that is fair but firm, rewards pro-social behavior, and disrupts contacts with any criminal networks. The program must provide predictable consequences, both positive and negative, for behavior. The individual during this process begins to understand that positive or negative outcomes are predicated on the individual's behavior, which he or she can control to produce positive outcomes. In the process, both expressive and instrumental social supports are enhanced as the individual is moved away from coercive forces that affected his or her life (Cullen 1994; Cullen et al. 1999).

Victims and other community members should be actively involved in this community-corrections effort. Community members are an essential part of the reintegration effort. At the initial hearing in which a sentencing contract is agreed upon, community members should express their strong disapproval of the criminal act and explain to the offender how he or she has harmed both the victim and the community. (This is especially important for the exploratory offenders who emerge from the permissive controls described as Type 2 in chapter 2. This strong consistent message of disapproval may by itself be enough to alter the behavior of many of these offenders.) The contract clearly states the steps that must be undertaken to achieve restoration to the community. Community members offer their support for helping the offender meet his or her responsibilities contained in the contract. This community support is essential. The offender must change his or her networks of association from criminals to the law-abiding citizens who work with the offender during the community corrections program. These community-based corrections efforts can in fact become an essential activity of the community organizing discussed earlier. Like community policing, community corrections should involve the entire community in the reintegration effort.

Successful completion of terms of the sentencing contract leads to a reintegration ceremony. In this face-to-face meeting with community members and victims, the offender discusses the harm caused by his or her criminal act, the responsibility he or she bears for this harm, and the meaning of the experience created by the correctional process. Formal apologies are made and accepted, and the ex-offender is restored to the community as a full-fledged citizen. This experience becomes a lesson in non-coercion in which compassion and caring (as opposed to vindictive-ness) are emphasized. "Using the criminal act as a catalyst on which to build" this community involvement in the corrections process helps "build relationships between alienated individuals and the wider community" (Lerman 1999: 15). The greatest victim of crime, general trust within the community, is restored through this process.

Those offenders who have committed more serious crimes causing greater harm to victims, who have more extensive prior records, or who may otherwise be deemed as not ready or suitable for community place-ments will be placed in institutional settings after going through the process of developing a sentencing contract. These contracts would clearly spell out the time to be completed in an institutional placement, the steps that must be accomplished during this institutional placement (successful completion of which can reduce institutional time served), and the inten-sive rehabilitation services to be provided in the community after release from an institution.

Institutions holding these offenders will not be like the overcrowded, brutal penal warehouses of today. First, with the comprehensive crime pre-vention efforts and community-based corrections alternatives in place, there will be a lot fewer individuals in need of incarceration. This would allow us to construct smaller facilities that are easier to control and provide services in. Second, these facilities will be run through an incentive-based control system in which prisoners are kept very busy with programs for education and treatment, paid work, and job training. Inmate idleness, prevalent in penal institutions today, would be entirely eliminated in these small, well-structured institutional settings.

Careful classification will determine the level of security needed for a particular offender, who can be placed in a more or less secure facility based on this assessment. More secure lockdown facilities would be re-served for more dangerous offenders who have longer sentences. These should be very small facilities, housing no more than 200 inmates in each facility. The small number of inmates, who are kept busy with an array of activities, helps to short-circuit the emergence of a criminally oriented in-mate subculture that can overwhelm institutional treatment programs. Staff members should be expertly trained in conflict management and methods of non-coercive control. The inmate to staff ratio should be low (perhaps 3 to 1 on any particular shift) to provide intensive supervision and support of inmates. Programs should be plentiful not only to keep inmates' time occupied but also to provide a hierarchy of incentives to encourage orderly and pro-social behavior. Various levels of programming, housing arrange-ments, and privileges within the prison allow for a graduated step system in which remunerative controls can be exercised to induce good behavior as inmates earn their way into better situations. Programs should include the full range of educational and job training activities that are available to people on the outside. (In fact, these prisons should be adjuncts to the educational-industrial complex that is the core of a non-coercive society.) Treatment of criminogenic needs, most importantly drug abuse treatment, anger control, and conflict management, should be provided in order to help offenders fulfill the treatment aspects of their sentencing contracts. Work should be provided in these institutions and inmates should be paid the prevailing minimum wage. With this money, inmates would have to pay room and board while in the prison and pay restitution to their victims or pay into a general victim compensation fund. Inmates thus have to take responsibility and pay for their own upkeep (or at least a portion of it), just like anybody else. Inmates who refuse to go along with this program will not be fulfilling the terms of their sentencing contracts, and therefore will not be advanced toward greater privileges, lower security institutions, or eventual early parole from an institutional setting.

As inmates in more secure facilities come closer to fulfilling the terms of their sentencing contracts, they are eligible for placement in less secure facilities. Again, these should be relatively small facilities with no more than 500 inmates in each, with a low inmate to staff ratio. Inmates receiving institutional sentences for less serious crimes and who have shorter sentences would be sent to these less secure facilities in the first place. Once in this less secure facility, an inmate can advance to greater privileges and eventually out to the community, or they can be set back to a more secure facility if their behavior indicates this is appropriate. As in the more secure facility, inmates are also expected to work, participate in programs, pay room and board, and compensate victims. In these less secure facilities, inmates can earn their way to better paying jobs as they complete educational and job training requirements and continue to maintain pro-social behavior. In these less secure facilities, inmates can earn a position in which they are involved in democratic participation in managing some of the programs in the prison.

Explicitly clear guidelines must be maintained for determining which steps are required to obtain these privileges. The key to the institutional program is that predictable, consistent consequences, both positive and negative, accrue from behavior. This experience is meant to instill self-control and the concept of taking responsibility for one's behavior, while at the same time providing needed education and treatment and other social supports that bond the offender to the wider community. As social supports expand and individual experience gradually becomes less affected by coercive forces, the individual's perception of reality can begin to change (Cullen et al. 1999). Cognitive-based therapies aimed at changing perceptions and attitudes about the sources of and responsibilities for behaviors and their consequences (Beck 1995; Salkovskis 1996) would have their greatest beneficial impact in this type of setting. Coercive ideation, in which the world is perceived as filled with coercive forces that can only be overcome (at least temporarily) through coercion, is slowly replaced with a realization that non-coercive, cooperative acts consistently lead to positive outcomes. This change in both experience and perception induces a move away from an external to an internal locus of control, and thus promotes stronger self-control.

In these less secure facilities, inmates participate in a wide array of pre-release programs that involve community members entering the prison to help educate prisoners in social skills and in dealing with conflict situations. These community members become conduits to family and pro-social friends in the community as well as to crime victims. The community members eventually become these ex-offenders' sponsors in the community, working closely with parole officers to assist in housing, job and educational placements, monitoring victim restitution payments, and assessments of how the individual is adapting to life in the community.

Part of the pre-release experience involves day-release programs for work and education in the community during the period prior to permanent release from an institutional setting. These day-release programs help to ease an inmate's transition back into the community and create incentives for pro-social behavior among inmates generally since day release would be seen as a highly desirable status to achieve. While on day release, the inmate would be in daily contact with his community sponsor who will help identify and solve any problems that arise during this transitional phase.

Parole from an institutional setting would be based on fulfillment of sentencing contracts, which include time served in institutions, treatment and educational programs completed, and victim compensation paid. These conditions are clearly spelled out at the beginning of the sentence. Unlike the unhappy experience with parole in the United States, in which inmates are left in the dark about exactly what they have to accomplish to make parole, these requirements are clearly spelled out in the sentencing contract. Once paroled to the community, the former inmate would enter the same intensive community-based rehabilitation services that are provided to offenders who received community alternatives. While on parole, the former prisoner can be sent back to the less secure facility if his behavior warrants this. Otherwise, the individual progresses toward a reintegration ceremony. In this face-to-face meeting with the community and crime victims, the experience of both the crime and its correction are discussed, apologies are offered and accepted, and the ex-offender is restored to the status of a full-fledged member of the community with all the rights and responsibilities of full citizenship. He or she then joins the rest of the community, as together, they take on the responsibility for constructing a non-coercive society.

These types of non-coercive correctional programs work best in a society that is based in non-coercion.[6] The crime prevention proposals discussed earlier that create a non-coercive society allow these less coercive means of corrections to work. First, they reduce the number of offenders that society has to correct. This allows resources to be concentrated to address the needs and problems that led to these individuals' criminal behavior. These programs allow an offender to earn his or her way back into the community while at the same time reducing the sources of coercion in the person's life and enhancing the social supports that maintain law-abiding behavior (Cullen et al. 1999). Second, with a viable community that is well organized, a consistent and predictable follow-through of correctional treatment can continue past the time of the sentence. Corrections, then, becomes a community responsibility, not just a job of the state. A viable community gives the ex-offender something to reintegrate back into. In today's situation, many ex-offenders, with little preparation for the transition, return to the same disorganized neighborhoods and coercive environments from which their criminal behavior emerged. Third, the incentives toward reform used in these correctional programs are intricately tied into the general incentives offered by a viable economy and effective educational process in the larger community. The hierarchy of controls in the corrections system can be raised upward toward less coercive forms when greater incentives are available in the larger society. We can thus raise the bar of incentives for those who are in the corrections system. Coercion in the corrections system can thus be much more in the background as offenders in community programs and prison calculate to a much greater extent than they do today that they have much to gain by conforming and much to lose by rebelling. This positive calculation that induces reform is based on the wide range of incentives in the larger society, which allows for a wider range of incentives within the corrections system. The incentives toward reform used in the correctional system can predictably lead an offender toward enjoying even greater economic and educational rewards when he or she rejoins the community as a full citizen. The corrections system is thus tied into the educational-industrial complex that is at the core of the non-coercive society created through the social investments in a revitalized social reproduction process.

## CONCLUSION

The response to crime outlined in this chapter is based on the understanding of the causes of crime presented in earlier chapters of this book.

If the experience of erratic coercion is a primary feature in the background and foreground of chronic criminals, then our responses to crime must involve the prevention and alteration of these coercive dynamics. The proposals for crime reduction detailed in this chapter present a means for preventing crime and correcting offenders through consistent, non-coercive control. They offer a radical departure from current practices in both our socialization and criminal justice processes. Too often these processes now create and reproduce the experience of erratic coercion that I maintain is the underlying cause of chronic criminal behavior. To have an effective and sustainable response to crime, we must build a non-coercive, democratic society that offers consistent and clear paths to future productive adult roles for young people.

The main obstacle to building this type of society is not a lack of resources. Every year, except during severe recessions, we create wealth that could be directed toward constructing the steps, like those outlined in this chapter, toward a non-coercive society. In fact, building such a society would give us the capacity to expand the production of wealth as never before, providing more resources for continual social investments. The main obstacle is political. The political process, especially in the United States, has been captured by wealthy special interests that block the types of social investments upon which a non-coercive society must be constructed. Spending is skewed toward military industries, prisons and corporate welfare because of the disproportionate influence and lobbying efforts of these special interests. Thus two key reforms that must be instituted are completely overhauling the system of political campaign financing and tightening the rules that govern the relationships between lobbyists and legislators. The specifics of such political reforms need to be worked out through democratic debate, but the essential goal should be to completely remove the influence of money from the political process, which should be guided solely by the merit of ideas. Such political reforms are an essential first step in building the type of democratic, non-coercive society that is conducive to crime reduction.

There is, of course, another apparent path toward crime reduction we could follow. It is a path that is highly appealing in a society increasingly motivated by fear and revenge, as in many American and a growing number of European nations (Weiss and South 1998). Crime could seemingly be reduced through a concerted campaign of consistent, coercive control (as in the Type 3 pattern discussed in chapter 2). We could build state structures in which individuals calculate their behavior based on fear of consistent, severe reprisals. We could intrude so deeply into the lives of individuals that any inkling of deviance is responded to with immediate, certain pain. We are developing the technological means for such intrusions, way beyond that developed by Nazi Germany or the Soviet Union in its darkest days of repression under Stalin. Communities could be developed in which constant mutual surveillance and suspicion are the guiding activities aimed at uncovering and quickly punishing any wrongdoing. We could model our communities around the design of "supermax" prisons in which constant surveillance and consistent, coercive punishments are effectively meted out (King 1999). Such a society would no doubt have reduced rates of crime, at least for the time that these coercive measures are consistently applied, which in the long run is an extremely tall order.

But these coercive measures undermine basic principles of humanity and democracy that we hold sacred, or at least we should hold such principles as sacred unless we allow our hysterical fear of crime to throw these principles out the window. If we do cast these principles aside, we have to ask, is not an incalculably greater crime being committed than the common crimes we may temporarily prevent by such a draconian resort to coercion? The greatest victim of such a coercive response to crime would be the general citizenry who would become dispirited, distrustful, and fearful of being creative. Can a society composed of such people possibly thrive either culturally or economically? And if such a society cannot thrive, then it is doubtful that a consistent regime of coercion can last very long, since such an artificial apparatus of social control would fall apart as the citizenry become atomized, fearful, uncreative, less productive, and less willing to interact in cooperative ventures. Such a regime would eventually collapse from its own weight. And the underlying causes of crime are not really affected by this coercive approach; they are merely repressed temporarily, waiting for the inevitable let up in coercion to explode to the surface. (Witness Russia today with its exploding crime rates, decaying economy, and dispirited people, which are legacies of the failure of a consistent, coercive regime that did reduce crime at least for awhile, but also contained the seeds of its own destruction.) This type of consistent, coercive response to crime offers an illusory, although to some highly appealing, solution to crime.

Thus, we can proceed in one of three ways. First, we can keep producing relatively high levels of criminal behavior by continuing to allow erratic coercion to shape the experiences of young people as they interact with the institutions of social reproduction, the economy, and the criminal justice system. Crime reduction can continue to be a mere fortuitous event that may just as erratically reverse itself. Or, second, we can give in to our fears of crime and desires for revenge and construct a society that attempts to deliver a consistent coercive response to each act of deviance. But it is not at all clear that such a response is sustainable, actually reduces crime in the long run or is desirable if we truly care about the values of freedom, democracy, and human rights. These values are not just niceties; they are the *practical* basis for a thriving society and economy that allows us to pursue our third choice. That choice is to begin taking the difficult steps, like those proposed in this chapter, to build a non-coercive and truly democratic society that provides consistent social supports for pro-social behavior and moves young people into viable and creative endeavors that strengthen our society's culture and economy. Such a society creates a sustainable basis for continuing reductions in crime because it reduces the coercive experiences that are at the root of chronic criminal behavior.

# Appendix

# A Guide to Literature on Measuring Key Variables ◉

This appendix is designed to give researchers some preliminary guidance in thinking about measurements of key variables. Such measurements have appeared in previous research. The discussion here follows the model contained in figure 4.1 located near the end of chapter 4 (which is an extension of the model contained in figure 3.1 located near the end of chapter 3). In figure 4.1, an interrelationship, leading to chronic criminality, between coercion and social-psychological deficits is outlined. Given the developmental nature of this model, a longitudinal design that follows a panel of individuals through the developmental process from early childhood into adulthood is most appropriate for a full test of the model. I will discuss first the dependent variable, chronic criminality, and then the independent variables contained in the model. The discussion does not in any way provide detailed instruments for measurement of variables. That task will have to be left for future endeavors. But the discussion does point to the types of items, and, for some variables, to precise measurements developed in existing research, which can be used for constructing questionnaires appropriate for testing the theoretical model in figure 4.1.

## CRIME AND CRIMINALITY

While criminality is understood as a potential for criminal behavior, we must infer this potentiality through the measurement of actual criminal behavior. For a survey panel design, criminal behavior can be measured through official contacts with the police (arrests) and through self-reports. Sampson and Laub (1993) use self-reports from individuals about their own behavior, as well as reports on the individual from parents, teachers, and official arrest data. These multiple sources allow them to cross-validate their measurement of delinquency. They found substantial correlation among these various indicators of criminal behavior. This is a highly useful strategy, although it is obviously difficult to obtain data from multiple sources.

The best instrument to date for self-reported crime is the one developed for the National Youth Survey (Elliott 1994; Elliott, Huizinga, and Ageton 1985). It provides an excellent means for separating chronic from exploratory offenders, at least for so-called street crimes. The response categories for the fifty-three item delinquency scale allow more precise measurement of the incidence (how often did you engage in the behavior?) and relative seriousness of criminal behavior, which are key for detecting chronic involvement in predatory street crime.

To date, there is no systematic instrument for detecting and recording white-collar crimes, especially in their various forms (as discussed in note 2 of chapter 1). Government agencies do not keep systematic records on white-collar crimes as they do on street crimes; and self-reports of these behaviors have not been used in surveys. But since the model in figure 4.1 deals with chronic involvement in street crime, this is not an important issue in the current context.

Conduct disorders and misbehavior that fall short of delinquency or crime are important to capture for a test of the model since these are seen as growing out of coercive relations experienced in early childhood and as eliciting coercive controls that push individuals further down paths toward chronic criminality. The reader is referred to studies that measure conduct disorders and connect these to early onset of delinquency (cf., Loeber and Stouthamer-Loeber 1986; Patterson, Capaldi, and Bank 1991; Sampson and Laub 1993; Simons et al. 1994. See also Parcel and Menaghan 1994: 35–36).

## COERCION

The key explanatory variable in figure 4.1 is coercion in various settings. Coercion is the force that compels or intimidates an individual to act because of the fear or anxiety it creates. It can involve the actual or threatened removal of social supports. This force can emerge from impersonal sources, such as economic compulsion or state power, or from interpersonal sources in which an individual coerces another for purposes of compliance. In any particular setting, the measurement of coercion will involve two dimensions: the strength of the force applied or threatened, and the consistency with which it is applied or experienced. Since we are looking at a developmental model and propose using a longitudinal design, we will want first to measure coercion experienced by parents, delving into their relations at work or with state agencies, the economic circumstances they face, and their own backgrounds in families and schools. In a similar way, we would want to measure coercion for children as they interact over the years of the study (toward becoming adults) with parents, schools, peers, work, and state agencies.

In the work setting, an individual can be asked what the consequences of insubordination or rule breaking would be. Perceived coercion is probably more relevant for understanding social-psychological deficits than actual application of coercion, although these should be highly correlated. It is possible to ascertain actual coercion by asking workplace managers what they would do if faced with insubordination or rule breaking. If dismissal from employment (or threatened dismissal), physical threats, demotion, pay cuts, yelling, belittlement, and humiliation are frequently cited in either employee-perceived or employer-reported responses, then the workplace can be understood as a more coercive one. The researcher can also ascertain how consistent such responses would be by asking if these happen every time, or only some of the time. In addition, aspects of the job that pertain to quality that would place the job in a secondary or primary labor market would also be important information for determining the degree to which a workplace is coercive. Robert Quinn and Graham Staines (1979) develop for their *Quality of Employment Survey* variables and indices that are highly relevant for the concept of workplace coercion. In addition, Melvin Kohn's work contains variables that are useful for measuring workplace coercion (Kohn 1977; Kohn and Schooler 1983; Kohn and Slomczynski 1990), as does the study by Parcel and Menaghan (1994).

Similarly, if an individual on welfare or under some other state agency program reports the loss of benefits as the likely potential consequence of rule breaking or failure to cooperate with agents of the state, this too can be judged as coercive. And, as with the workplace, these perceptions can be measured against actual agency rules and responses from agency personnel to questions about actions that would be taken in the face of rule violations.

Impersonal coercion from economic pressures can be ascertained by looking at the parents' or (later) the individual's income and savings from all sources and comparing this to expenses of all types, to ascertain if the person is stretched thin economically. Sampson and Laub (1993) use this type of measure in determining relative socioeconomic status among the blue-collar families in their study. Conger et al. (1994) also employ a similar index of family economic pressure. In addition, the respondent can be asked if they feel economically pressured, as has been done in some tests of classic strain theory (Agnew et al. 1996; Hagan and McCarthy 1997; Menard 1997, 1995).

Coercion of disciplinary controls over children in the family has been measured in several studies (Larzelere and Patterson 1990; Loeber and Stouthamer-Loeber 1986; McCord 1991; Rankin and Wells 1990; Sampson and Laub 1993; Simons et al. 1994; Straus 1994; Straus et al. 1991; Wells and Rankin 1988). One key problem has been to distinguish between the aspect of harsh discipline and the aspect of inconsistent discipline. These are often put together into a composite measure, which may be confounding two theoretically distinct dimensions of coercion. Both parents and children can be asked a series of questions outlining what the disciplinary consequences would be for various acts of misbehavior and the consistency with which these responses occur. In addition, the extent to which children's behavior is monitored would apply to the dimension of consistency and has also been developed as a measure in the studies cited earlier in this paragraph. Also, Agnew and White (1992) use a "parental permissiveness" scale, which is relevant for capturing Type 2 control in the family context (as discussed in chapter 2).

Oakes's (1985) study of school tracking offers some excellent examples for measuring the degree of coercion in the school setting. In addition, students can be asked about disciplinary practices encountered at school, and school officials can be asked about their use of various disciplinary strategies, such as corporal punishment and expulsion. Knowing that a juvenile is in a lower or higher track at a school may not be sufficient information for determining coercion. A lower track in a school located in a wealthy neighborhood may provide an entirely different experience of control than a lower track in a school located in a poor neighborhood. This geographic difference in school resources should be taken into account. Or better yet, the individual's actual experience in the track, not just the fact that he or she is in a particular track, needs to be captured. Here Oakes's study provides some important leads.

Oakes also provides some insights into the study of coercive peer relations in the school setting. These can be supplemented by measurements of coercive relations among peers that have emerged from several gang studies (cf., Decker and Van Winkle 1996; Klein 1995).

## CULTURAL SUPPORTS FOR COERCION

Items that measure cultural support for coercion can be built around a series of assertions about the efficacy and value of using violent force to solve problems or settle disputes. Respondents can be asked how strongly they agree or disagree with such a series of assertions. Anderson's (1994) discussion of the "code of the streets" provides an excellent source for developing such assertions, as does Wyatt-Brown's (1982) discussion of southern honor. Also relevant in this context would be items that assert the desirability of getting ahead of others no matter how this may be done. These items would capture cultural supports for competitive individualism that may justify coercive treatment of others (Messner and Rosenfeld 1997).

## SOCIAL-PSYCHOLOGICAL DEFICITS

A set of social-psychological characteristics is theorized to emerge from the experience of coercion, and these become important mediators in the relationship between coercion and chronic criminality. Most of these characteristics have been measured in existing empirical studies; some of these studies develop reliable and valid indexes that have become widely used indicators of some of these social-psychological characteristics.

"Anger" is a concept developed most thoroughly by Agnew (1985), who created a nine-item anger scale. This scale demonstrated a significant positive effect on delinquency, especially on aggressive forms of delinquency. For the overall theory of differential coercion (especially for distinguishing the Type 3 pattern from the Type 4 pattern, as discussed in chapter 2), it would be useful to measure differences in self-directed versus other-directed anger. Pioneering work by Henry and Short (1954) used a similar distinction between other-directed and self-directed aggression to explain, respectively, patterns of homicide and suicide.

"Self-control" was developed conceptually by Gottfredson and Hirschi (1990). There has been much contention about the measurement of this variable (Longshore, Stein, and Turner 1998; Piquero and Rosay 1998). Grasmick et al. (1993) test the Gottfredson and Hirschi theory using a six-item self-control scale that measures impulsiveness and risk-seeking, which are clearly related to self-control, but also includes other items like volatile temper, which probably fit better in an anger scale like the one created by Agnew (1985). A more precise measurement of self-control is presented by LaGrange and Silverman (1999) who develop a scale that taps impulsiveness, risk-taking, carelessness, present orientation, and temper. (Again the latter variable may be more appropriate in an anger index.) Another index of self-control is presented in Wright et al. (1999), who measure impulsiveness, risk-taking, lack of persistence, inattention, and hyperactivity as indicators of low self-control. These self-control indices have shown significant links in studies cited in this paragraph to crime and delinquency.

"Locus of control" has a long history as a concept in psychology. Nowicki and Strickland (1973) developed a scale that taps internal versus external control orientation. This scale, and shortened versions of it, have become standard measures of this concept.

"Self-efficacy" was conceptualized by Bandura (1982, 1977) to designate the degree of confidence one has to affect and control events or to create successful outcomes. It is operationalized by Newcomb and Harlow (1986) to tap elements of powerlessness and normlessness, which are presumed to be the opposite of self-efficacy. Agnew and White (1992) use this latter measure to capture self-efficacy in their study. Hagan and McCarthy (1997: 211) use two items to measure self-efficacy: "I can do just about anything I set my mind to" and "I am responsible for my own successes."

"Social bonding" was first conceptualized by Hirschi (1969) to include four elements: attachment, commitment, involvement, and belief. Several studies have operationalized social bonds as attachments to parents, school, friends, work, and spouse, commitments to conventional success goals in school and careers, endorsements of conventional moral beliefs, and time spent in conventional activities. Some of the important studies that have operationalized this concept include Hirschi (1969), Hindelang (1973), Wiatroski et al. (1981), LaGrange and White (1985), Wells and Rankin (1988), Sampson and Laub (1993), Burton et al. (1995), Jenkins (1997), and Wright et al. (1999). Also see Kempf (1992) for a review of this concept.

"Coercive behavioral modeling" points to the imitative behavior of individuals who witness coercion and violence being used by others. This is an important aspect of the social learning approach pioneered by Bandura (1973) and Akers (1985). Items to measure this variable would include respondents reporting that they frequently witnessed significant others (parents, friends, siblings, etc.) using coercion as a means of control and items that indicate that the respondent has learned that this is an appropriate way of exercising control over others. Exposure to media images of violence and coercion may also be an important aspect of this concept.

"Control deficit" is a concept used by Tittle (1995) to denote the amount of control to which one is subject that is in excess to the amount of control one can exercise. To date, only one attempt that I know of has been made to operationalize this concept. Piquero and Hickman (1999) asked respondents to rate the degree of control they exercised over several areas of life, including (among other things) jobs, the physical environment, other people, and one's own body. Response options ranged from 0 (no control), to 5 (medium control), to 10 (total control). Respondents were then asked to rate the degree these same things have control over them using the same response options. From these responses, a control ratio can be calculated. Piquero and Hickman (1999: 334) found that consistent with Tittle's prediction, "individuals who suffer from control deficits are likely to turn to predative acts to rebalance their control ratios." But they also found that those with control surpluses were also likely to engage in direct predation, which is contrary to Tittle, who posits that they would engage in indirect predation.

In the context of control deficits, it would also be useful to develop a measure that taps the degree to which an individual experiences debasement or humiliation. Katz's (1988) interpretation of predatory crime revolves greatly around the theme of humiliation, which may be a key emotional state created by repressive control.

## COERCIVE IDEATION

The concept of coercive ideation captures the extent to which a person conceives the world as being full of coercive forces that can only be overcome through coercion. Coercive ideation is similar to Mark S. Fleisher's *defensive worldview* concept. With very few exceptions, Fleisher (1995: 104) found that members of West Coast gang sets (Crips and Bloods) had experienced violent and neglectful home environments that pushed them into the streets. This early childhood enculturation helped create a particular mindset that is similar to what I mean by coercive ideation:

> A defensive worldview has six traits: a feeling of vulnerability and need to protect oneself; a belief that no one can be trusted; a need to maintain social distance; a willingness to use violence and intimidation to repel others; an attraction to similarly defensive people; and an expectation that no one will provide aid. . . . A defensive worldview is recognized by its emphasis on self-protection, suspicion, impulsiveness, insensitivity, reliance on physical force, propensity for risk-taking behavior, and a reluctance to become socially intimate.

Items that attempt to capture coercive ideation can be drawn from most of Fleisher's discussion. A few of the items listed by Fleisher may be more appropriate for other concepts listed earlier; for instance, impulsiveness and risk-taking fit better in a self-control index than in a coercive ideation index.

The preceding discussion is designed to provide the reader and future researcher a starting place for thinking about how key variables in figure 4.1 can be more precisely conceptualized and operationalized. Such an endeavor will require further thinking and discussion among researchers who have an interest in this subject. It is hoped that the discussion in this book will spur interest among criminologists in developing empirical studies designed to test its propositions. Hopefully the guide to literature presented here (which is by no means exhaustive) will initiate thinking and discussion about the conceptualization and measurement of key variables contained in this book.

# Notes

## CHAPTER 1: INTRODUCTION

1. Hirschi and Gottfredson (1986: 58) make a clear distinction between crime and criminality:

   Crimes are short term, circumscribed events that presuppose a peculiar set of necessary conditions (e.g., activity, opportunity, adversaries, victims, goods). Criminality, in contrast, refers to stable differences across individuals in the propensity to commit criminal (or equivalent) acts. Accordingly, criminality is only one element in the causal configuration leading to a criminal act, and criminal acts are, at best, imperfect measures of criminality.

2. This definition of white-collar crime, derived by Coleman (1994) from Sutherland's (1949) original definition, encompasses a broad range of activities that vary widely in their relative seriousness; thus its usefulness has been questioned (Braithwaite 1995). One useful way of categorizing white-collar crimes was developed by Clinard and Quinney (1970) and extended by Schrager and Short (1978), who distinguished organizational crimes from occupational crimes. *Organizational white-collar crimes* are committed by agents of an organization (a corporation or governmental agency) or by the organizational unit itself for the benefit of the organization. This category encompasses many corporate crimes including anti-trust violations, sale of unsafe products, corporate consumer fraud, false advertising, maintenance of unsafe working conditions, and manipulation of financial markets by stock brokerage firms and banks. The category also includes crimes by governmental agencies that (for instance) violate civil liberties or undermine constitutional checks and balances. Some of these involve loss of life and serious injury to victims, while others involve substantial monetary losses to victims. They all tend to undermine trust in economic and governmental institutions. Some of these activities are officially categorized as crimes, while others are handled through civil actions or regulatory agencies. Thus the categorization of some of these activities strictly as criminal is problematic, even if they cause great harm. *Occupational white-collar crimes* are committed

(sometimes against the organization for which an individual works) solely for the benefit of the individual who uses his or her occupational position to commit these crimes. These include a wide range of behaviors that vary widely in their seriousness. These occupational white-collar crimes include employees pilfering items from work, employees embezzling funds from an employer, an independent auto mechanic making unnecessary repairs, private physicians defrauding patients or performing dangerous but unneeded surgery in order to get insurance payments, and public officials taking bribes. Resolving the problems associated with the definition of white-collar crime is beyond the scope of this book. Others have dealt with these problems, and the reader is referred to these sources for detailed discussions of these issues (Coleman 1994; Frank and Lynch 1992; Geis, Meier, and Salinger 1995). The common links among all white-collar crimes are: (1) they are performed during the course of an otherwise respected and legitimate occupation or financial activity; and (2) they require that the person (or organization) be in a position of trust (either to the public, consumers, a workforce, or an employer) that is violated in the course of the criminal activity. These two elements distinguish this criminal behavior pattern from other patterns of crime.

3. Throughout this book I use the terms *crime* and *delinquency* interchangeably. Crime generally refers to illegal acts committed by adults whereas delinquency refers to illegal acts committed by juveniles. When I use the term crime I mean for this term to include delinquency as well.

## CHAPTER 2: EMERGENCE OF A DIFFERENTIAL COERCION THEORY OF CRIMINALITY

1. Recently, studies have revived Merton's classic formulation of strain theory emphasizing economic strain as a direct cause of crime (Agnew et al. 1996; Hagan and McCarthy 1997; Menard 1997, 1995). These studies do not necessarily contradict those which de-emphasize financial success goals since they tend to point to adult rather than to juvenile offending as being related to financial dissatisfaction or point to actual economic pressure rather than expectations of success in understanding the sources of strain. As I discuss in chapter 4, strain caused by economic pressure can be understood as an impersonal form of coercion that creates feelings of desperation and contributes to the production of criminality.

2. The last sentence in this quote from Tittle at first glance raises some empirical questions since studies suggest that offenders who engage in predatory crime tend to have higher rates of crime and deviance in general (Cohen 1986; Elliott 1994; Gottfredson and Hirschi 1990; Hindelang 1971; Rojek and Erickson 1982; Tracy and Kempf-Leonard 1996; Tracy et al. 1990). But Tittle might counter that he is not talking about individuals per se, but about situations in which individuals (the same ones over time) vary in the degree of control imbalance. Such variation over time and from

situation to situation translates into changes in types of deviance. So an offender may engage in predatory acts (such as robbery) when his control deficit is marginal, but engage in exploitation (as head of a drug ring) when he has a control surplus. The same individual engages in different types of deviance based on a change in his control ratio.

## CHAPTER 3: THE IMMEDIATE
## CONTEXTS OF COERCION

1. Job titles are not the best way to determine if a specific job operates according to coercive control or is in a particular working class fraction. A particular job category (like service jobs for example) may include a wide range of actual workplace experiences, especially as these relate to control. (For example, the job category "service workers" includes stockbrokers, real estate agents as well as bus boys and waitresses. "Machine operators" may be in a unionized work setting or in a sweatshop.) This is an important point since some studies that have attempted to test the Colvin-Pauly thesis (Messner and Krohn 1990; Pasternoster and Tittle 1990; Simpson and Elis 1994) have used job categories to classify workers by class fraction. (Simpson and Elis do a better job at this type of classification since they excluded job titles, like stockbroker, which clearly did not fall into fraction 1. Their study, even using this crude measure of class fractions, shows some significant but small class fraction relationships to delinquency). The use of job categories as a measure of class fractions was, unfortunately, encouraged by me in the original Colvin-Pauly article which, following Edwards, listed some examples of the types of occupations that might be included in a particular working class fraction. But the best way to measure coercion at the workplace would be to question an employee about the attributes of his or her job (as Melvin Kohn did regarding closeness of supervision) and the worker's perceptions about what would happen at work if he or she was caught breaking rules. If job loss or other severe consequences are mentioned as outcomes, then we could score this as high coercion. Paternoster and Tittle (1990) claim that these would be "impossible" to measure, but it does not seem that attributes of one's job would be insurmountable to ascertain. There are studies on work, such as the 1977 Quality of Employment Survey (Quinn and Staines 1979), that contain many of the types of questions that would be appropriate. Unfortunately, none of these studies on work contain information about family, schools, or crime and delinquency that would be needed to test the Colvin-Pauly thesis. Paternoster and Tittle lay out the possibility that a person's perception of their chances of being fired etc. may not relate to the actual practices at a workplace, but this may not be a problem and if it is it can be discovered. It is certainly less problematic than using job titles that may or may not match differences in coercion at workplaces. (See Appendix for discussion of these and other measurement issues.)

2. Delinquency studies usually combine these two dimensions of discipline, harsh and erratic, into a single measure. As should be clear from the discussion in chapter 2, where I lay out various patterns of control, harsh and erratic point to two dimensions of differential coercion. For this reason, delinquency studies that look at parental discipline do not capture potentially important differences in the two dimensions of coercion: its strength and the consistency with which it is applied and/or experienced.

3. My concept, *coercive ideation,* is similar to Mark S. Fleisher's (1995) *defensive worldview* concept. See the Appendix for a discussion of the similarity of these concepts and for a guide to their empirical measurement.

4. Under recent welfare reforms in the United States, going to work is no longer a choice. These reforms require that welfare recipients move from the welfare roles to work, which are usually in more coercive workplace environments. And under these reforms, limits are placed on the total number of months welfare can be received. Thus welfare reform has not reduced the coercive nature of the welfare system.

## CHAPTER 4: THE LARGER CONTEXTS OF COERCION: ECONOMICS AND CULTURE

1. The correlation is especially strong for homicides. From 1947 to 1997 the zero-order correlation between annual unemployment rates and annual homicide rates is .54 (Bureau of Labor Statistics 1999; National Center for Health Statistics 1999). This correspondence between unemployment and homicides is also true for earlier periods of the century. For the years 1900 through 1949, the correlation between annual unemployment rates and annual homicide rates is .46 (U.S. Bureau of Census 1975; National Center for Health Statistics 1999). (For the years 1920 through 1949, the correlation is .47). Homicide rates for the first half of the twentieth century peaked (above 9 per 100,000 population) in the years 1931 through 1934, the worst point of the Great Depression. These murder rates began receding as unemployment slowly waned and as unions began to create the basis for the non-coercive labor markets that emerged in the 1940s. During the period after 1935, government social supports inaugurated during President Franklin D. Roosevelt's New Deal cushioned the impact of unemployment, which while lower than in the early 1930s was still at historically high levels, and stayed high until the outbreak of World War II.

2. While the FBI's *Uniform Crime Reports* have been seriously criticized for possible biases, it is the only reliable source for long-term trends (prior to the late 1970s) in crime rates. (Since the mid-1970s, a possibly better gauge of crime trends, the National Crime Victimization Survey conducted jointly by the U.S. Justice Department and the U.S. Census Bureau, has become available.) There is a strong possibility that at least some

of the dramatic increase in crime reported by the FBI in the 1960s was due to greater participation by local law enforcement agencies in the gathering of crime data, which were then sent to the FBI who compiled national statistics. This reporting binge may have created an artificial increase in the crime rate (Baer and Chambliss 1997; O'Brien 1996). By the 1970s, after federal law enforcement grants made data collection at local levels more consistent and uniform, the crime statistics were probably a more accurate gauge of changes in Index crimes (the serious violent and property crimes used by the FBI). Congruency between the FBI's statistics and other sources of crime data (victimization surveys and more sophisticated self-report studies) collected since the mid-1970s lends credence to the accuracy of the FBI's official statistics on Index crimes (LaFree 1998a: 17–19).

3. This increasing global competition is also an important background force in some white-collar crimes. For instance, the decisions surrounding the manufacture of the defective and deadly Ford Pinto (which I discuss in chapter 5) were directly linked to the economic pressures created by competition from Japanese and German auto manufacturers (Cullen et al. 1987). Since there are insufficient data to discern trends in corporate white-collar crime (there is no *Uniform Crime Reports* for corporate white-collar crime), we can only speculate that as global competition has heated up since the late 1960s, corporate crime increased.

4. While violent crime rates have dropped from their historically high peaks of the late 1980s and early 1990s, they remained stubbornly high in the late 1990s as compared to the late 1960s, when the surge in crime rates began. (The exception is homicide, which by 1999 had dropped to a 30 year low. But this is the rarest type of violent crime.) An analysis by the Eisenhower Foundation (*Washington Post* 1999b) reveals that in major cities (250,000 or higher population) violent crime rates were still 40 percent higher in 1998 than they had been in 1969. For all cities (25,000 and higher population) violent crime rates in 1998 were 70 percent higher than in 1969. And in rural areas, violent crime rates in 1998 were 147 percent higher than they had been in 1969. The recent news highlighting reductions in violent crimes are comforting only in contrast to the extremely high rates reached in the late 1980s and early 1990s. Historically, however, they still remain high.

5. With the globalization of capitalism led by U.S. corporations, America's consumer culture has spread to other nations and is responsible to some extent for rising crime during the 1980s and 1990s in these nations, although they generally remain well below America's rate of violent crime. These rising crime rates are also related to a general movement toward fiscal austerity in these nations that has undercut the network of social supports that have historically been related to their lower crime rates (Weiss and South 1998). In the process of economic globalization, American culture and coercive economic pressures have also been globalized.

## CHAPTER 5: COERCION IN THE
## FOREGROUND OF CRIME

1. The structure of criminal opportunities is also shaped by the temporal and spatial patterns of labor market segmentation, which help to create a "segmented criminal labor market" (Sullivan 1989: 107).
2. The "unwitting" aspect of this partially self-created coercion is an important point for developing strategies for criminal rehabilitation. As I take up in chapter 6, a key step in rehabilitating criminals is making them conscious of how they help create the circumstances that lead to their criminal behavior. Cognitive-based rehabilitative strategies attempt to restructure the perceptions of reality in which offenders see themselves as pushed around by circumstances beyond their control toward perceptions in which they understand their own responsibility in helping to create these circumstances (Beck 1995; Salkovskis 1996). Once they understand this, then, with a lot of help and social support, they can alter their behavior so that they lessen the creation of these coercive forces in their lives.

## CHAPTER 6: A THEORY DRIVEN
## RESPONSE TO CRIME

1. The following discussion expands on arguments I presented in an article published in the journal *Crime and Delinquency* (Colvin 1991).
2. If investments, labor productivity, and rising wages are skewed toward military industries, as they were during the Vietnam War, then rising wages are associated with rising inflation. Military-based production does not create supplies of consumer goods for the civilian economy. (Most individuals do not buy tanks and missiles.) Yet the rising wages and incomes of those working for military industries chase a relatively scarce supply of civilian goods since investment in these nonmilitary industries are displaced by investments in military-based production. Thus prices for consumer goods rise rapidly, leading to a period of high inflation, as during and in the aftermath of the Vietnam War. If investments, labor productivity, and rising wages are skewed toward the civilian sector of the economy, then consumer goods are in larger supply to meet the demand from growing incomes, leading to relatively low inflation. This was the U.S. experience in the 1990s when gains in labor productivity outstripped gains in wages primarily in industries that produce goods and services consumed by average citizens. Thus, unlike the late 1960s and 1970s, in the 1990s the United States witnessed sustained non-inflationary economic growth.
3. I am grateful to Suzanne Colvin, who has extensively researched and worked on evaluations of welfare reform, for providing me with this insight about former welfare recipients moving into the ranks of the working poor.
4. In fact greater severity of punishment in worldwide comparisons does not appear to correspond to lower rates of crime (Kappler, Blumberg, and Pot-

ter 1996; Weiss and South 1998). The United States incarcerates a greater proportion of its population than any other nation (with the possible exception of Russia), but its rate of crime, especially violent crime, is among the highest in the industrialized world. It appears that social and economic factors, like income inequality, are much better predictors of international crime rates than is the severity of penal sanctions. Recent increases in Japan's crime rate are related to rising unemployment (*Washington Post* 2000a) and a rising consumer culture that has especially affected teenagers (French 2000).

5. Some jurisdictions in the United States have developed "special drug courts" that induce offenders with addiction problems into drug treatment programs; successful completion of drug treatment leads to the dropping of criminal charges (Currie 1998: 174).

6. The death penalty, of course, would have no place in a non-coercive society. The literature on the death penalty generally shows that it does not deter homicide. In fact, a number of studies suggest that executions are actually associated with subsequent *increases* in homicides (cf., Bailey 1998; Bowers 1988). This "brutalization effect" (Bowers and Pierce 1980) may indicate that the death penalty contributes to the cultural reproduction of a coercive society, which induces coercive forms of crime. This brutalization thesis argues that when the state kills someone it sends a subtle but powerful message that it is permissible to use lethal force against those who have gravely offended you. This subliminal message may overwhelm any intended deterrence message and lead to more homicides. This argument fits with my arguments in chapter 4 about the culture of violence and its contribution to creating a coercive society. States that use the death penalty extensively also tend to be those with higher homicide rates (primarily southern states in the United States). A general culture of coercion may induce both greater use of the death penalty and higher rates of homicide.

# References

Agnew, Robert. 1995. "Strain and Subcultural Theories of Criminality." Pp. 305–27 in *Criminology: A Contemporary Handbook,* 2d ed., edited by Joseph F. Sheley. Belmont, CA: Wadsworth.

———. 1992. "Foundation for a General Strain Theory of Crime and Delinquency." *Criminology* 30: 47–87.

———. 1985. "A Revised Strain Theory of Delinquency." *Social Forces* 64: 151–67.

Agnew, Robert, Francis T. Cullen, Velmer S. Burton, Jr., T. David Evans, and R. Gregory Dunaway. 1996. "A New Test of Classic Strain Theory," *Justice Quarterly* 13: 681–704.

Agnew, Robert, and Helene Raskin White. 1992. "An Empirical Test of General Strain Theory." *Criminology* 30: 475–99.

Akers, Ronald L. 1997. *Criminological Theories: Introduction and Evaluation,* 2d ed. Los Angeles: Roxbury.

———. 1985. *Deviant Behavior: A Social Learning Approach.* Belmont, CA: Wadsworth.

Allan, Emilie Anderson, and Darrell J. Steffensmeier. 1989. "Youth, Underemployment, and Property Crime: Differential Effects of Job Availability and Job Quality on Juvenile and Young Adult Arrest Rates." *American Sociological Review* 54: 107–23.

American Humane Association. 1986. *Highlights of Official Child Neglect and Abuse Reporting, 1984.* Denver, CO: American Humane Association.

Anderson, Elijah. 1994. "The Code of the Streets." *The Atlantic Monthly* 273 (May): 80–94.

Athens, Lonnie H. 1992. *The Creation of Dangerous Violent Criminals.* Urbana, IL: University of Illinois.

Aulette, Judy Root, and Raymond Michalowski. 1995. "Fire in Hamlet: A Case Study of State-Corporate Crime." Pp. 166–90 in *White-Collar Crime: Classic and Contemporary Views,* 3d ed., edited by Gilbert Geis, Robert F. Meier, and Lawrence M. Salinger. New York: Free Press.

Austin, James. 1986. "Using Early Release to Relieve Prison Crowding: A Dilemma in Public Policy." *Crime and Delinquency* 32: 391–403.

Ayers, Edward L. 1992. *The Promise of the New South: Life After Reconstruction.* New York: Oxford University Press.

———. 1984. *Vengeance and Justice: Crime and Punishment in the Nineteenth Century*

*American South.* New York: Oxford University Press.

Baer, Justin, and William J. Chambliss. 1997. "Generating Fear: The Politics of Crime Reporting." *Crime, Law and Social Change* 27: 87–107.

Bailey, William C. 1998. "Deterrence, Brutalization, and the Death Penalty: Another Examination of Oklahoma's Return to Capital Punishment." *Criminology* 36: 711–33.

Bandura, Albert. 1982. "Self-efficacy Mechanism in Human Agency." *American Psychologist* 37: 122–47.

———. 1977. "Self-efficacy: Toward a Unifying Theory of Behavioral Change." *Psychological Review* 84: 191–215.

———. 1973. *Aggression: A Social Learning Analysis.* Englewood Cliffs, NJ: Prentice-Hall.

Bank, Lew, J. Hicks Marlowe, John B. Reid, Gerald R. Patterson, and Mark R. Wienrott. 1991. "A Comparative Evaluation of Parent-Training Interventions for Families of Chronic Delinquents." *Journal of Abnormal Child Psychology* 19: 15–33.

Barak, Gregg. 1998. *Integrating Criminologies.* Boston: Allyn and Bacon.

Barber, Theodore Xenophon, David S. Calverly, Albert Forgione, John D. McPeake, John F. Chaves, and Barbara Bowen. 1969. "Five Attempts to Replicate the Experimenter Bias Effect." *Journal of Consulting and Clinical Psychology* 33: 1–6.

Barkan, Steven E. 1997. *Criminology: A Sociological Understanding.* Upper Saddle River, NJ: Prentice Hall.

Barrett, Michael J. 1990. "The Case for More School Days." *The Atlantic Monthly* 266 (November): 78–106.

Battin, Sara R., Karl G. Hill, Robert D. Abbott, Richard F. Catalano, and J. David Hawkins. 1998. "The Contribution of Gang Membership to Delinquency Beyond Delinquent Friends." *Criminology* 36: 93–115.

Bayley, David H. 1998. *What Works in Policing.* New York: Oxford.

Beck, Allen J., and Bernard Shipley. 1989. "Recidivism of Prisoners Released in 1983." *Bureau of Justice Statistics Special Report.* Washington, D.C.: U.S. Government Printing Office.

———. 1987. "Recidivism of Young Parolees." *Bureau of Justice Statistics Special Report.* Washington, D.C.: U.S. Government Printing Office.

Beck, Judith S. 1995. *Cognitive Therapy: Basics and Beyond.* New York: Guilford.

Bellah, Robert N., Richard Madsen, William M. Sullivan, Ann Swidler, and Steven M. Tipton. 1985. *Habits of the Heart: Individualism and Commitment in American Life.* New York: Harper and Row.

Bendau, Marlo Coleman (producer). 1992. *Gangs: Dreams Under Fire.* Franciscan Communications (film documentary).

Bennett, William J., John J. DiIulio, and James P. Walters. 1996. *Body Count: Moral Poverty . . . and How to Win America's War Against Crime and Drugs.* New York: Simon and Schuster.

Black, Donald. 1984. *Toward a General Theory of Social Control: Selected Problems,* Vol. 2. Orlando, FL: Academic Press.

Block, Jeanne H. 1984. *Sex Role Identity and Ego Development.* San Francisco: Josey-Bass.

Blumstein, Alfred, Jacqueline Cohen, Jeffrey A. Roth, and Christy A. Visher, eds. 1986. *Criminal Careers and Career Criminals.* Washington, D.C.: National Academy Press.

Bongiovanni, Anthony F. 1979. "An Analysis of Research on Punishment and Its Relation to the Use of Corporal Punishment in the Schools." Pp. 351–72 in *Corporal Punishment in American Education,* edited by Irwin A. Hyman and James H. Wise. Philadelphia: Temple University Press.

Bowers, William J. 1988. "The Effect of Executions is Brutalization, Not Deterrence." Pp. 49–89 in *Challenging Capital Punishment,* edited by Kenneth C. Haas and James A. Inciardi. Newbury Park, CA: Sage.

Bowers, William J., and Glenn Pierce. 1980. "Deterrence or Brutalization: What is the Effect of Executions." *Crime and Delinquency* 26: 453–84.

Bowles, Samuel, and Herbert Gintis. 1976. *Schooling in Capitalist America.* New York: Basic.

Braithwaite, John. 1999. "Restorative Justice: Assessing Optimistic and Pessimistic Accounts." Pp. 1–127 in *Crime and Justice: A Review of Research,* Vol. 25, edited by Michael Tonry. Chicago: University of Chicago Press.

———. 1997. "Charles Tittle's Control Balance and Criminological Theory." *Theoretical Criminology* 1: 77–97.

———. 1995. "White Collar Crime." Pp. 116–42 in *White-Collar Crime: Classic and Contemporary Views,* 3d ed., edited by Gilbert Geis, Robert F. Meier, and Lawrence M. Salinger. New York: Free Press.

———. 1989. *Crime, Shame and Reintegration.* New York: Cambridge University Press.

Bronfenbrenner, Urie. 1972. "Socialization and Social Class through Time and Space." Pp. 381–409 in *The Impact of Social Class: Selected Readings,* edited by Paul Blumberg. New York: Thomas Y. Crowell.

Brownfield, David. 1986. "Social Class and Violent Behavior." *Criminology* 24: 421–38.

Bryan, Janice W., and Florence W. Freed. 1982. "Corporal Punishment: Normative Data and Sociological and Psychological Correlates in a Community College Population." *Journal of Youth and Adolescence* 11: 77–87.

Bureau of Labor Statistics. 1999. *Labor Statistics from the Current Population Survey.* Washington, D.C.: U.S. Department of Labor.

Bursik, Robert J., Jr., and Harold G. Grasmick. 1993. "Economic Deprivation and Neighborhood Crime Rates, 1960–1980." *Law and Society Review* 27: 263–83.

Bursik, Robert J., Jr., Don Merten, and Gary Schwartz. 1985. "Approximate Age-Related Behavior for Male and Female Adolescents: Adult Perceptions." *Youth and Society* 17: 115–30.

Burton, Velmer, Francis T. Cullen, T. David Evans, R. Gregory Dunaway, Sesha Kethineni, and Gary Payne. 1995. "The Impact of Parental Controls on Delinquency." *Journal of Criminal Justice* 23: 111–26.

Bushnell, Timothy. 1991. *State Organized Terror: The Case of Violent Internal Repression.* Boulder, CO: Westview.

Butterfield, Fox. 1995. *All God's Children: The Bosket Family and the American Tradition of Violence.* New York: Alfred A. Knopf.

Caspi, Avshalom, Terrie E. Moffitt, Phil A. Silva, Magda Stouthamer-Loeber, Robert F. Krueger, and Pamela S. Schmutte. 1994. "Are Some People Crime-Prone? Replications of the Personality-Crime Relationship Across Countries, Races, and Methods." *Criminology* 32: 163–95.

Carlson, Susan M., and Raymond J. Michalowski. 1997. "Crime, Unemployment, and Social Structures of Accumulation: An Inquiry into Historical Contingency." *Justice Quarterly* 14: 101–33.

Cernkovich, Stephen A., and Peggy C. Giordano. 1992. "School Bonding, Race, and Delinquency." *Criminology* 30: 261–91.

Cernkovich, Stephen A., Peggy C. Giordano, and Meredith D. Pugh. 1985. "Chronic Offenders: The Missing Cases in Self-Report Delinquency Research." *Journal of Criminal Law and Criminology* 76: 705–32.

Chesney-Lind, Meda, and Randal G. Shelden. 1998. *Girls, Delinquency, and Juvenile Justice.* 2d ed. Belmont, CA: Wadsworth.

———. 1992. *Girls, Delinquency, and Juvenile Justice.* Pacific Grove, CA: Brooks/Cole.

Chiricos, Theodore G. 1987. "Rates of Crime and Unemployment: An Analysis of Aggregate Research Evidence." *Social Problems* 34: 187–212.

Clark, John P., and Richard C. Hollinger. 1983. *Theft by Employees in Work Organizations.* Washington, D.C.: National Institute of Justice.

Clark, Ronald V., and Derek B. Cornish. 1985. "Modeling Offenders' Decisions: A Framework for Research and Policy." Pp. 147–85 in *Crime and Justice: An Annual Review,* Vol. 6, edited by Michael Tonry and Norval Morris. Chicago: University of Chicago Press.

Clinard, Marshall B., and Richard Quinney. 1970. *Criminal Behavior Systems: A Typology.* 2d ed. New York: Holt, Rinehart and Winston.

Cloward, Richard A., and Lloyd E. Ohlin. 1960. *Delinquency and Opportunity.* New York: Free Press.

Coburn, David, and Virginia L. Edwards. 1976. "Job Control and Child-rearing Values." *Review of Sociology and Anthropology* 13: 337–44.

Cohen, Albert K. 1955. *Delinquent Boys: The Culture of the Gang.* New York: Free Press.

Cohen, Jacqueline. 1986. "Research in Criminal Careers: Individual Frequency Rates and Offense Seriousness." Pp. 292–418 in *Criminal Careers and Career Criminals,* edited by Alfred J. Blumstein, Jacqueline Cohen, Jeffrey A. Roth, and Christy A. Visher. Washington, D.C.: National Academy Press.

Coleman, James William. 1995. "Motivation and Opportunity: Understanding the Causes of White-Collar Crime." Pp. 360–81 in *White-Collar Crime: Classic and Contemporary Views,* 3d ed., edited by Gilbert Geis, Robert F. Meier, and Lawrence M. Salinger. New York: Free Press.

———. 1994. *The Criminal Elite: The Sociology of White-Collar Crime.* 3d ed. New York: St. Martin's Press.

Colvin, Mark. 1997. *Penitentiaries, Reformatories, and Chain Gangs: Social Theory and the History of Punishment in Nineteenth-Century America.* New York: St. Martin's Press.

———. 1992. *The Penitentiary in Crisis: From Accommodation to Riot in New Mexico.* Albany, NY: State University of New York Press.

———. 1991. "Crime and Social Reproduction: A Response to the Call for 'Outrageous' Proposals." *Crime and Delinquency* 37: 436–48.

———. 1982. "The 1980 New Mexico Prison Riot." *Social Problems* 29: 449–63.

Colvin, Mark, and John Pauly. 1983. "A Critique of Criminology: Toward an Integrated Structural-Marxist Theory of Delinquency Production." *American Journal of Sociology* 89: 513–51.

Conger, Rand D., Xiaojia Ge, Glen H. Elder, Jr., Frederick O. Lorenz, and Ronald L. Simons. 1994. "Economic Stress, Coercive Family Process, and Developmental Problems of Adolescents." *Child Development* 65: 541–61.

Cornish, Derek B., and Ronald V. Clark. 1986. *The Reasoning Criminal.* New York: Springer-Verlag.

Covey, Herbert C., Scott Menard, and Robert J. Franzese. 1992. *Juvenile Gangs.* Springfield, IL: Charles C. Thomas.

Cressey, Donald. 1953. *Other People's Money.* New York: Free Press.

Crutchfield, Robert D. 1989. "Labor Stratification and Violent Crime." *Social Forces* 69: 489–512.

Crutchfield, Robert D., and Susan R. Pitchford. 1997. "Work and Crime: The Effects of Labor Stratification." *Social Forces* 76: 93–118.

Cullen, Francis T. 1994. "Social Support as an Organizing Concept for Criminology: Presidential Address to the Academy of Criminal Justice Sciences." *Justice Quarterly* 11: 527–59.

———. 1983. *Rethinking Crime and Deviance Theory.* Totowa, NJ: Rowman and Allanheld.

Cullen, Francis T., William J. Maakestad, and Gary Cavender. 1987. *Corporate Crime Under Attack: The Ford Pinto Case and Beyond.* Cincinnati, Ohio: Anderson.

Cullen, Francis T., Nicolas Williams, and John Paul Wright. 1997. "Work Conditions and Juvenile Delinquency: Is Youth Employment Criminogenic?" *Criminal Justice Policy Review* 8: 119–43.

Cullen, Francis T., John Paul Wright, and Mitchell B. Chamlin. 1999. "Social Support and Social Reform: A Progressive Crime Control Agenda." *Crime and Delinquency* 45: 188–207.

Currie, Elliott. 1998. *Crime and Punishment in America.* New York: Metropolitan Books.

———. 1994. *Reckoning: Drugs, the Cities, and the American Future.* New York: Hill and Wang.

———. 1985. *Confronting Crime.* New York: Pantheon.

Curtis, Lynn A. 1989. "Race and Violent Crime: Toward a New Policy." Pp. 139–70 in *Violent Crime, Violent Criminals,* edited by Neil A. Weiner and Marvin E. Wolfgang. Newbury Park, CA: Sage.

Decker, Scott H., and Barrik Van Winkle. 1996. *Life in the Gang.* New York: Cambridge University Press.

Devine, John. 1996. *Maximum Security: The Culture of Violence in Inner-City Schools.* Chicago: University of Chicago Press.

Dewey, John. 1929. *Experience and Nature.* La Salle, WI: Open Court Press.

Dickerson, Debra. 1998. "Cease-fire in Simple City." *U.S. News and World Report* March 16: 22–27.

Donziger, Steven R., ed. 1996. *The Real War on Crime.* New York: Harper Perennial.

Durkheim, Emile. 1952 [1897]. *Suicide.* New York: Free Press.

Edwards, Richard. 1979. *Contested Terrain: The Transformation of the Workplace in the Twentieth Century.* New York: Basic.

Eisenhower Foundation. 1990. *Youth Investment and Community Reconstruction.* Washington, D.C.: Milton S. Eisenhower Foundation.

Elder, Glen H., and Charles E. Bowerman. 1963. "Family Structure and Child Rearing Patterns: The Effect of Family Size and Sex Composition." *American Sociological Review* 28: 891–905.

Elias, Norbert. 1982 [1939]. *The Civilizing Process II: Power and Civility.* New York: Pantheon.

———. 1978 [1939]. *The Civilizing Process I: The History of Manners.* New York: Urizen Books.

Elliott, Delbert S. 1994. "Serious Violent Offenders: Onset, Developmental Course, and Termination—The American Society of Criminology 1993 Presidential Address." *Criminology* 32: 1–21.

Elliott, Delbert S., David Huizinga, and Suzanne Ageton. 1985. *Explaining Delinquency and Drug Use.* Beverly Hills, CA: Sage.

Elliott, Delbert S., David Huizinga, and Scott Menard. 1989. *Multiple Problem Youth: Delinquency, Substance Use, and Mental Health Problems.* New York: Springer-Verlag.

Empey, LaMar T. 1967. "Delinquency Theory and Recent Research." *Journal of Research in Crime and Delinquency* 4: 28–42.

Erickson, Maynard L., and Lamar T. Empey. 1965. "Class Position, Peers and Delinquency." *Sociology and Social Research* 49: 268–82.

Erickson, Maynard L., and Gary F. Jensen. 1977. "Delinquency Is Still Group Behavior! Toward Revitalizing the Group Premise in the Sociology of Deviance." *Journal of Criminal Law and Criminology* 68: 262–73.

Erlanger, Howard S. 1974. "Social Class and Corporal Punishment in Child-rearing: A Reassessment." *American Sociological Review* 39: 92–107.

Esbensen, Finn-Aage, and David Huizinga. 1993. "Gangs, Drugs, and Delinquency in a Survey of Urban Youth." *Criminology* 31: 565–87.

Etzioni, Amitai. 1970. "Compliance Theory." Pp. 103–26 in *The Sociology of Organizations,* edited by Oscar Grusky and George A. Miller. New York: Free Press.

Fagan, Jeffrey. 1989. "The Social Organization of Drug Use and Drug Dealing Among Urban Gangs." *Criminology* 27: 633–69.

Fagan, Jeffrey, and Richard B. Freeman. 1999. "Crime and Work." Pp. 225–90 in *Crime and Justice: A Review of Research,* Vol. 25, edited by Michael Tonry. Chicago: University of Chicago Press.

Fagan, Jeffrey, Elizabeth Piper, and Melinda Moore. 1986. "Violent Delinquents and

Urban Youths." *Criminology* 24: 439–71.

Farnworth, Margaret, Terrence P. Thornberry, Marvin D. Krohn, and Alan J. Lizotte. 1994. "Measurement in the Study of Class and Delinquency: Integrating Theory and Research." *Journal of Research in Crime and Delinquency* 31: 33–61.

Farrington, David P. 1997. "Human Development and Criminal Careers." Pp. 361–408 in *The Oxford Handbook of Criminology,* 2d ed., edited by Mike Maguire, Rod Morgan, and Robert Reiner. New York: Oxford University Press.

Feeney, Floyd. 1986. "Robbers as Decision-Makers." Pp. 53–71 in *The Reasoning Criminal,* edited by Derek B. Cornish and Ronald V. Clarke. New York: Springer-Verlag.

Feld, Barry C. 1999. *Bad Kids: Race and the Transformation of the Juvenile Court.* New York: Oxford University Press.

Felson, Marcus. 1998. *Crime and Everyday Life,* 2d ed. Thousand Oaks, CA: Pine Forge.

Fischer, Claude S., Michael Hout, Martín Sánchez Jankowski, Samuel R. Lucas, Ann Swidler, and Kim Voss. 1996. *Inequality by Design: Cracking the Bell Curve Myth.* Princeton, NJ: Princeton University Press.

Fleisher, Mark S. 1995. *Beggars & Thieves: Lives of Urban Street Criminals.* Madison, WI: University of Wisconsin Press.

Fox, James A. 1996. *Trends in Juvenile Violence: A Report to the United States Attorney General on Current and Future Rates of Juvenile Offending.* Boston: Northeastern University Press.

Frank, Nancy K., and Michael J. Lynch. 1992. *Corporate Crime, Corporate Violence: A Primer.* New York: Harrow and Heston.

Franklin, Jack I., and Joseph E. Scott. 1970. "Parental Values: An Inquiry into Occupational Setting." *Journal of Marriage and the Family* 32: 406–9.

Franklin, John Hope, and Loren Schweninger. 1999. *Runaway Slaves: Rebels on the Plantation.* New York: Oxford University Press.

Freeman, Richard B. 1995. "The Labor Market." Pp. 171–92 in *Crime and Public Policy,* 2d ed., edited by James Q. Wilson and Joan Petersilia. San Francisco: Institute for Contemporary Studies.

———. 1994. *Working under Different Rules.* New York: Russell Sage Foundation.

Freeman, Richard B., and William M. Rodgers III. 1999. "Area Economic Conditions and the Labor Market Outcomes of Young Men in the 1990s Expansion." Working Paper # 7073. Cambridge, MA: National Bureau of Economic Research. [www.nber.org/w7073].

French, Howard W. 2000. "Tokyo Dropouts' Vocation: Painting the Town." *New York Times* March 5: 1, 6.

Fukuyama, Francis. 1999. "The Great Disruption." *The Atlantic Monthly* 283 (May): 55–80.

Gans, Herbert J. 1996. *The War Against the Poor: The Underclass and Anti-Poverty Policy.* New York: Basic.

Garbarino, James. 1989. "The Incidence and Prevalence of Child Mistreatment." Pp. 219–61 in *Family Violence: Crime and Justice, A Review of Research,* Vol. 11, edited by Lloyd Ohlin and Michael Tonry. Chicago: University of Chicago Press.

Gecas, Victor. 1979. "The Influence of Social Class on Socialization." Pp. 365–404 in *Contemporary Theories about the Family,* Vol. 1, edited by Wesley R. Burr, Ruben Hill, F. Ivan Nye, and Ira L. Reiss. New York: Free Press.

Gecas, Victor, and F. Ivan Nye. 1974. "Sex and Class Differences in Parent-Child Interaction: A Test of Kohn's Hypothesis." *Journal of Marriage and the Family* 36: 742–49.

Geis, Gilbert, Robert F. Meier, and Lawrence M. Salinger, eds. 1995. *White-Collar Crime: Classic and Contemporary Views,* 3d ed. New York: Free Press.

Gendreau, Paul, Francis T. Cullen, and James Bonta. 1998. "Intensive Rehabilitation Supervision: The Next Generation in Community Corrections?" Pp. 198–206 in *Community Corrections,* edited by Joan Petersilia. New York: Oxford University Press.

Gephart, William J. 1970. "Will the Real Pygmalion Please Stand Up?" *American Educational Research Journal* 7: 473–74.

Gil, David G. 1970. *Violence Against Children: Physical Child Abuse in the United States.* Cambridge, MA: Harvard University Press.

Gilbert, James. 1986. *A Cycle of Outrage: America's Reaction to the Juvenile Delinquent in the 1950s.* New York: Oxford University Press.

Giles-Sims, Jean, Murray A. Straus, and David B. Sugarman. 1995. "Child, Maternal, and Family Characteristics Associated with Spanking." *Family Relations* 44: 170–76.

Glenn, Myra C. 1984. *Campaigns Against Corporal Punishment: Prisoners, Sailors, Women, and Children in Antebellum America.* Albany, NY: State University of New York Press.

Glueck, Sheldon, and Eleanor Glueck. 1950. *Unraveling Juvenile Delinquency.* New York: The Commonwealth Fund.

Gordon, David M., Richard Edwards, and Michael Reich. 1982. *Segmented Work, Divided Workers.* New York: Cambridge University Press.

Gottfredson, Don M., Mark G. Neithercutt, Joan Nuffield, and Vincent O'Leary. 1973. *Four Thousand Lifetimes: A Study of Time Served and Parole Outcome.* Hackensack, NJ: National Council on Crime and Delinquency.

Gottfredson, Michael R., and Travis Hirschi. 1990. *A General Theory of Crime.* Stanford, CA: Stanford University Press.

Gould, Eric D., Bruce A. Weinberg, and David B. Mustard. 1999. "Crime Rates and Local Labor Market Opportunities in the United States: 1979–1995." Working Paper, Ohio State University [http://economics.sbs.ohio-state.edu/weinberg/crime_sep17_99.pdf].

Grasmick, Harold G., Charles R. Tittle, Robert J. Bursik, Jr., and Bruce J. Arneklev. 1993. "Testing the Core Empirical Implications of Gottfredson and Hirschi's General Theory of Crime." *Journal of Research in Crime and Delinquency* 30: 5–29.

Greenberg, Jerald. 1990. "Employee Theft as a Reaction to Underpayment Inequity: The Hidden Costs of Pay Cuts." *Journal of Applied Psychology* 75: 561–68.

Greenfield, Lawrence. 1985. "Examining Recidivism." *Bureau of Justice Statistics Special Report*. Washington, D.C.: U.S. Government Printing Office.

Greenland, Cyril. 1987. *Preventing CAN Deaths: An International Study of Deaths Due to Child Abuse and Neglect*. London: Travistock.

Hagan, John. 1994. *Crime and Disrepute*. Thousand Oaks, CA: Pine Forge.

Hagan, John, and Bill McCarthy. 1997. *Mean Streets*. New York: Cambridge University Press.

Hagedorn, John M. 1994. "Homeboys, Dope Fiends, Legits, and New Jacks." *Criminology* 32: 197–219.

———. 1988. *People and Folks: Gangs, Crime and the Underclass in a Rustbelt City*. Chicago: Lake View Press.

Halberstam, David. 1993. *The Fifties*. New York: Fawcett Columbine.

Hamilton, Stephen F. 1990. *Apprenticeship for Adulthood: Preparing Youth for the Future*. New York: Free Press.

Harrison, Bennett, and Barry Bluestone. 1988. *The Great U-Turn*. New York: Basic.

Henry, Andrew F., and James F. Short, Jr. 1954. *Suicide and Homicide: Some Economic, Sociological, and Psychological Aspects of Aggression*. New York: Free Press.

Henry, Stuart, and Dragan Milovanovic. 1996. *Constitutive Criminology: Beyond Postmodernism*. Thousand Oaks, CA: Sage.

Hickey, Eric W. 1991. *Serial Murderers and Their Victims*. Pacific Grove, CA: Brooks/Cole.

Hindelang, Michael J. 1973. "Causes of Delinquency: A Partial Replication." *Social Problems* 20: 471–87.

———. 1971. "Age, Sex, and the Versatility of Delinquent Involvement." *Social Problems* 18: 522–35.

Hirschi, Travis. 1969. *Causes of Delinquency*. Berkeley: University of California Press.

Hirschi, Travis, and Michael Gottfredson. 1986. "The Distinction Between Crime and Criminality." Pp. 55–69 in *Critique and Explanation*, edited by Timothy F. Hartnagel and Robert A. Silverman. New Brunswick, NJ: Transaction Books.

Hirschi, Travis, and Michael J. Hindelang. 1977. "Intelligence and Delinquency: A Revisionist Review." *American Sociological Review* 42: 571–87.

Holmes, Ronald M., and James De Burger. 1988. *Serial Murder*. Newbury Park, CA: Sage.

Horowitz, Ruth. 1983. *Honor and the American Dream: Culture and Identity in a Chicano Community*. New Brunswick, NJ: Rutgers University Press.

Hotaling, Gerald T., and Murray A. Straus, with Alan J. Lincoln. 1989. "Intrafamily Violence, and Crime and Violence Outside the Family." Pp. 315–75 in *Family Violence: Crime and Justice, A Review of Research*, Vol. 11, edited by Lloyd Ohlin and Michael Tonry. Chicago: University of Chicago Press.

Hyman, Irwin A. 1990. *Reading, Writing, and the Hickory Stick*. Lexington, MA: D.C. Heath.

Irwin, John. 1980. *Prisons in Turmoil*. Boston: Little, Brown.

Jacobs, Bruce A. 1999. *Dealing Crack: The Social World of Streetcorner Selling*. Boston: Northeastern University Press.

Jacobs, Bruce A., and Richard Wright. 1999. "Stick-up, Street Culture, and Offender Motivation." *Criminology* 37: 149–73.

Jacobs, James B. 1977. *Stateville: The Penitentiary in Mass Society.* Chicago: University of Chicago Press.

Jencks, Christopher, Marshall Smith, Henry Acland, Mary Jo Bane, David Cohen, Herbert Gintis, Barbara Heyns, and Stephan Michelson. 1972. *Inequality: A Reassessment of the Effect of Family and Schooling in America.* New York: Basic.

Jenkins, Henry. 1999. "Professor Jenkins Goes to Washington." *Harper's* 299 (July): 19–23.

Jenkins, Patricia. 1997. "School Delinquency and the School Social Bond." *Journal of Research in Crime and Delinquency* 34: 337–67.

Johnson, Elmer H. 1998. "The Japanese Experience: Effects of Decreasing Resort to Imprisonment." Pp. 337–65 in *Comparing Prison Systems,* edited by Robert P. Weiss and Nigel South. Amsterdam: Gordon and Breach.

Johnson, Richard E. 1979. *Juvenile Delinquency and Its Origins.* New York: Cambridge University Press.

Kappeler, Victor E., Mark Blumberg, and Gary W. Potter. 1996. *The Mythology of Crime and Criminal Justice.* 2d ed. Prospect Heights, IL: Waveland Press.

Katz, Jack. 1991. "The Motivation of the Persistent Robber." Pp. 277–305 in *Crime and Justice: A Review,* Vol. 13, edited by Michael Tonry. Chicago: University of Chicago Press.

———. 1988. *The Seductions of Crime.* New York: Basic.

Katz, Michael B. 1997. *Improving the Poor: The Welfare State, The "Underclass," and Urban Schools as History.* Princeton, NJ: Princeton University Press.

———. 1990. *The Undeserving Poor: From War on Poverty to War on Welfare.* New York: Pantheon.

Kelly, Delos H. 1977. "How the School and Teachers Create Deviants." *Contemporary Education* 48: 202–5.

———. 1974. "Track Position and Delinquent Involvement: A Preliminary Analysis." *Sociology and Social Research* 58: 380–86.

Kempf, Kimberly. 1992. "The Empirical Status of Hirschi's Control Theory." Pp. 111–29 in *Advances in Criminological Theory,* Vol. 4, edited by William S. Laufer and Freda Adler. New Brunswick, NJ: Transaction.

King, Roy. 1999. "The Rise and Rise of Supermax: An American Solution in Search of a Problem?" *Punishment & Society* 1: 163–86.

Klein, Malcolm. 1995. *The American Street Gang.* New York: Oxford University Press.

Kohn, Melvin L. 1977. *Class and Conformity.* Chicago: University of Chicago Press.

———. 1976. "Social Class and Parental Values: Another Confirmation of the Relationship." *American Sociological Review* 41: 538–45.

Kohn, Melvin L., and Carmi Schooler. 1983. *Work and Personality: An Inquiry Into the Impact of Social Stratification.* Norwood, NJ: Ablex Publishing.

———. 1973. "Occupational Experience and Psychological Functioning: An Assessment of Reciprocal Effects." *American Sociological Review* 38: 97–118.

Kohn, Melvin L., and Kazimierz M. Slomczynski. 1990. *Social Structure and Self-Di-*

rection: *A Comparative Analysis of the United States and Poland.* Cambridge, MA: Basil Blackwell.

Kolata, Gina. 1989. "Despite Its Promise of Riches, The Crack Trade Seldom Pays." *New York Times* November 26: 1, 42.

Kolchin, Peter. 1993. *American Slavery, 1619–1877.* New York: Hill and Wang.

Komarovsky, Mirra. 1962. *Blue Collar Marriage.* New York: Random House.

Kozol, Jonathon. 1995. *Amazing Grace.* New York: Crown.

———. 1991. *Savage Inequalities: Children in America's Schools.* New York: Crown.

———. 1989. *Rachel and Her Children.* New York: Fawcett Columbine.

Kraus, John. 1987. "Homicide While at Work: Persons, Industries and Occupations at High Risk." *American Journal of Public Health* 77: 1285–89.

Krohn, Marvin. 1995. "Control and Deterrence Theories of Criminality." Pp. 329–48 in *Criminology,* 2d ed., edited by Joseph F. Sheley. Belmont, CA: Wadsworth.

Kruttschnitt, Candace, Jane D. McLeod, and Maude Dornfeld. 1994. "The Economic Environment of Child Abuse." *Social Problems* 41: 299–315.

Kutler, Stanley I. 1990. *The Wars of Watergate.* New York: Norton.

LaFree, Gary. 1998a. *Losing Legitimacy: Street Crime and the Decline of Social Institutions in America.* Boulder, CO: Westview.

———. 1998b. "Social Institutions and the Crime 'Bust' of the 1990s." *Journal of Criminal Law and Criminology* 88: 1325–68.

LaGrange, Randy L., and Helen Raskin White. 1985. "Age Differences in Delinquency: A Test of Theory." *Criminology* 23: 19–45.

LaGrange, Teresa C., and Robert A. Silverman. 1999. "Low Self-Control and Opportunity: Testing the General Theory of Crime as an Explanation for Gender Differences in Delinquency." *Criminology* 37: 41–72.

Lane, Roger. 1999. "Murder in America." Pp. 191–224 in *Crime and Justice: A Review of Research,* Vol. 25, edited by Michael Tonry. Chicago: University of Chicago Press.

Larzelere, Robert E., and Gerald R. Patterson. 1990. "Parental Management: Mediator of the Effect of Socioeconomic Status on Early Delinquency." *Criminology* 28: 301–24.

Lasch, Christopher. 1991. *Culture of Narcissism: American Life in an Age of Diminishing Expectations.* New York: Norton.

Lauritsen, Janet L., Robert J. Sampson, and John H. Laub. 1991. "The Link Between Offending and Victimization among Adolescents." *Criminology* 29: 265–92.

Lawrence, Richard. 1998. *School Crime and Juvenile Justice.* New York: Oxford University Press.

Leacock, Eleanor. 1969. *Teaching and Learning in City Schools.* New York: Basic.

Lerman, David. 1999. "Restoring Justice." *Tikkun,* September/October, 13–15.

Levine, Lawrence W. 1977. *Black Culture and Black Consciousness.* New York: Oxford University Press.

Loeber, Rolf, and Magda Stouthamer-Loeber. 1986. "Family Factors as Correlates and Predictors of Juvenile Conduct Problems and Delinquency." Pp. 29–149 in

*Crime and Justice: An Annual Review of Research,* Vol. 7, edited by Michael Tonry and Norval Morris. Chicago: University of Chicago Press.

Longshore, Douglas, Judith A. Stein, and Susan Turner. 1998. "Reliability and Validity of a Self-control Measure: Rejoinder." *Criminology* 36: 175–82.

Luckenbill, David F. 1984. "Murder and Assault." Pp. 19–45 in *Major Forms of Crime,* edited by Robert F. Meier. Beverly Hills, CA: Sage Publications.

———. 1977. "Criminal Homicide as a Situated Transaction." *Social Problems* 25: 176–86.

Maccoby, Eleanor E., and Carol N. Jacklin. 1974. *The Psychology of Sex Differences.* Stanford, CA: Stanford University Press.

MacCoun, Robert, and Peter Reuter. 1992. "Are the Wages of Sin $30 an Hour? Economic Aspects of Street-Level Drug Dealing." *Crime and Delinquency* 38: 477–91.

MacDonald, A. P. 1971. "Internal-External Locus of Control: Parental Antecedents." *Journal of Consulting and Clinical Psychology* 37: 141–47.

Maguire, Kathleen, and Ann L. Pastore, eds. 1995. *Sourcebook of Criminal Justice Statistics—1994.* Washington, D.C.: U.S. Bureau of Justice Statistics.

Marvell, Thomas B., and Carlisle E. Moody, Jr. 1991. "Age Structure and Crime Rates: The Conflicting Evidence." *Journal of Quantitative Criminology* 7: 237–73.

Massey, James L., and Marvin D. Krohn. 1986. "A Longitudinal Examination of an Integrated Social Process Model of Deviant Behavior." *Social Forces* 65: 135–61.

Matza, David. 1964. *Delinquency and Drift.* New York: John Wiley.

Matza, David, and Gresham Sykes. 1961. "Juvenile Delinquency and Subterranean Values." *American Sociological Review* 26: 712–20.

McCord, Joan. 1995. "Introduction: Coercion and Punishment in the Fabric of Social Relations." Pp. 1–5 in *Coercion and Punishment in Long-Term Perspectives,* edited by Joan McCord. New York: Cambridge University Press.

———. 1991. "Family Relationships, Juvenile Delinquency, and Adult Criminality." *Criminology* 29: 397–417.

McDowell, Eileen, and Robert H. Friedman. 1979. "An Analysis of Editorial Opinion Regarding Corporal Punishment: Some Dynamics of Regional Differences." Pp. 329–34 in *Corporal Punishment in American Education,* edited by Irwin A. Hyman and James H. Wise. Philadelphia: Temple University Press.

Menard, Scott. 1997. "A Developmental Test of Cloward's Differential Opportunity Theory." Pp. 142–86 in *The Future of Anomie Theory,* edited by Nikos Passas and Robert Agnew. Boston: Northeastern University Press.

———. 1995. "A Developmental Test of Mertonian Anomie Theory." *Journal of Research in Crime and Delinquency* 32: 136–74.

Menard, Scott, and Barbara J. Morse. 1984. "A Structural Critique of the IQ-Delinquency Hypothesis: Theory and Evidence." *American Journal of Sociology* 89: 1347–78.

Merton, Robert K. 1990 [1938.] "Social Structure and Anomie." Pp. 227–36 in *Criminal Behavior: Text and Readings,* 2d ed., edited by Delos H. Kelly. New York: St. Martin's Press [originally published, 1938, *American Sociological Review* 3: 672–82].

Messner, Steven F., and Marvin D. Krohn. 1990. "Class Compliance Structures and Delinquency: Assessing Integrated Structural-Marxist Theory." *American Journal of Sociology* 96: 300–28.

Messner, Steven F., Marvin D. Krohn, and Allen E. Liska, eds. 1989. *Theoretical Integration in the Study of Deviance and Crime: Problems and Prospects.* Albany, NY: State University of New York Press.

Messner, Steven F., and Richard Rosenfeld. 1997. *Crime and the American Dream.* 2d ed. Belmont, CA: Wadsworth.

———. 1994. *Crime and the American Dream.* Belmont, CA: Wadsworth.

Messner, Steven F., and Rodney Stark. 1999. *Criminology: An Introduction Using Explorit.* 4th ed. Bellevue, WA: MicroCase Corporation.

Michalowski, Raymond J., and Susan M. Carlson. 1999. "Unemployment, Imprisonment, and Social Structures of Accumulation: Historical Contingency in the Rusche-Kirchheimer Hypothesis." *Criminology* 37: 217–49.

Miethe, Terance D., and Richard McCorkle. 1998. *Crime Profiles: The Anatomy of Dangerous Persons, Places, and Situations.* Los Angeles, CA: Roxbury.

Miller, Jody. 1998. "Up It Up: Gender and the Accomplishment of Street Robbery." *Criminology* 36: 37–65.

Miller, Walter B. 1958. "Lower Class Culture as a Generating Milieu of Gang Delinquency." *Journal of Social Issues* 14: 5–19.

Moffitt, Terrie E. 1997. "Adolescent-Limited and Life-Course Persistent Offending: A Complementary Pair of Developmental Theories." Pp. 11–54 in *Developmental Theories of Crime and Delinquency, Advances in Criminological Theory,* Vol. 7, edited by Terence P. Thornberry. New Brunswick, NJ: Transaction Books.

Moore, Joan W. 1991. *Going Down to the Barrio: Homeboys and Homegirls in Change.* Philadelphia: Temple University Press.

Morash, Merry. 1986. "Gender, Peer Group Experiences, and Seriousness of Delinquency." *Journal of Research in Crime and Delinquency* 23: 43–67.

Morash, Merry, and Meda Chesney-Lind. 1991. "A Re-Formulation and Partial Test of the Power Control Theory of Delinquency." *Justice Quarterly* 8: 347–77.

Nasar, Sylvia, and Kirsten B. Mitchell. 1999. "Booming Job Market Draws Young Black Men Into Fold: Surprisingly Big Gain for Low-Wage Group—Link Seen to Falling Crime Rates." *New York Times* May 23: 1, 21.

National Center for Health Statistics. 1999. *Vital Statistics.* Washington, D.C.: U.S. Department of Health and Human Services.

Newcomb, Michael D., and L. L. Harlow. 1986. "Life Events and Substance Use among Adolescents: Mediating Effects of Perceived Loss of Control and Meaninglessness in Life." *Journal of Personality and Social Psychology* 51: 564–77.

Newman, Barbara M., and Colleen I. Murray. 1983. "Identity and Family Relations in Early Adolescence." *Journal of Early Adolescence* 3: 293–303.

Nowicki, Stephen, and Bonnie R. Strickland. 1973. "A Locus of Control Scale for Children." *Journal of Consulting and Clinical Psychology* 40: 148–54.

Oakes, Jeannie. 1985. *Keeping Track: How Schools Structure Inequality.* New Haven, CN: Yale.

O'Brien, Robert M. 1996. "Police Productivity and Crime Rates: 1973–1992."

*Criminology* 34: 183–207.

Osgood, D. Wayne, Lloyd D. Johnston, Patrick M. O'Malley, and Jerald G. Bachman. 1988. "The Generality of Deviance in Late Adolescence and Early Adulthood." *American Sociological Review* 53: 81–93.

Palladino, Grace. 1996. *Teenagers: An American History.* New York: Basic.

Parcel, Toby L., and Elizabeth G. Menaghan. 1994. *Parents' Jobs and Children's Lives.* New York: Aldine De Gruyter.

Paternoster, Raymond, and Charles R. Tittle. 1990. "Parental Work Control and Delinquency: A Theoretical and Empirical Critique." Pp. 39–70 in *Advances in Criminological Theory,* Vol. 2, edited by William S. Laufer and Freda Adler. New Brunswick, NJ: Transaction.

Patterson, Gerald R. 1995. "Coercion as a Basis for Early Age of Onset for Arrest." Pp. 81–105 in *Coercion and Punishment in Long-Term Perspective,* edited by Joan McCord. New York: Cambridge University Press.

———. 1990. *Depression and Aggression in Family Interaction.* Hillsdale, NJ: Lawrence Erlbaum Associates.

———. 1982. *Coercive Family Process.* Eugene, Oregon: Castalia.

———. 1980. "Children Who Steal." Pp. 73–90 in *Understanding Crime: Current Theory and Research,* edited by Travis Hirschi and Michael Gottfredson. Beverly Hills, CA: Sage.

Patterson, Gerald R., Deborah Capaldi, and Lou Bank. 1991. "An Early Starter Model for Predicting Delinquency." Pp. 139–68 in *The Development and Treatment of Childhood Aggression,* edited by Debra J. Pepler and Kenneth H. Rubin. Hillsdale, NJ: Erlbaum.

Patterson, Gerald R., Patricia Chamberlain, and John B. Reid. 1982. "A Comparative Evaluation of a Parent-Training Program." *Behavior Therapy* 13: 636–50.

Patterson, Gerald R., and Karen Yoerger. 1993. "Developmental Models for Delinquent Behavior." Pp. 140–72 in *Mental Disorder and Crime,* edited by Sheilagh Hodgins. Newbury Park, CA: Sage.

Patterson, James. 1996. *Grand Expectations: The United States, 1945–1974.* New York: Oxford University Press.

Pearlin, Leonard I. 1970. *Class Context and Family Relations: A Cross-national Study.* Boston: Little, Brown.

Peiser, Nadine C., and Patrick C. L. Heaven. 1996. "Family Influences on Self-reported Delinquency among High School Students." *Journal of Adolescence* 19: 557–68.

Pelton, Leroy H. 1981. *The Social Context of Child Abuse and Neglect.* New York: Human Sciences Press.

Pepinsky, Harold E. 1991. *The Geometry of Violence and Democracy.* Bloomington: Indiana University Press.

———. 1988. "Violence as Unresponsiveness: Toward a New Conception of Crime." *Justice Quarterly* 4: 539–63.

Petersilia, Joan, Peter Greenwood, and Martin Levin. 1978. *Criminal Careers of Habitual Felons.* Washington, D.C.: National Institute of Law Enforcement and Criminal Justice.

Phillips, Kevin. 1990. *The Politics of Rich and Poor.* New York: Random House.

Piquero, Alex R., and Mathew Hickman. 1999. "An Empirical Test of Tittle's Control Balance Theory." *Criminology* 37: 319–41.

Piquero, Alex R., and Andre B. Rosay. 1998. "The Reliability and Validity of Grasmick et al.'s Self-control Scale: A Comment on Longshore et al." *Criminology* 36: 157–73.

Piven, Frances Fox, and Richard A. Cloward. 1997. *The Breaking of the American Social Compact.* New York: New Press.

———. 1993. *Regulating the Poor: The Functions of Public Welfare.* 2d ed. New York: Vintage.

Quinn, Robert, and Graham Staines. 1979. *Quality of Employment Survey, 1977: Cross-Section* [ICPSR # 7689]. Ann Arbor, MI: Inter-University Consortium for Political and Social Research.

Rankin, Joseph H., and L. Edward Wells. 1990. "The Effect of Parental Attachments and Direct Controls on Delinquency." *Journal of Research in Crime and Delinquency* 27: 140–65.

Ray, JoAnn, and Katherine Hooper Briar. 1999. "Economic Motivators for Shoplifting." Pp. 354–60 in *Crime and Criminals: Contemporary and Classic Readings in Criminology,* edited by Frank R. Scarpitti and Amie L. Nielson. Los Angeles, CA: Roxbury.

Reardon, Francis J., and Robert N. Reynolds. 1979. "A Survey of Attitudes Toward Corporal Punishment in Pennsylvania Schools." Pp. 301–28 in *Corporal Punishment in American Education,* edited by Irwin A. Hyman and James H. Wise. Philadelphia: Temple University Press.

Regoli, Robert M., and John D. Hewitt. 1997. *Delinquency in Society.* 3d ed. New York: McGraw-Hill.

Reich, Robert B. 1991. "The Real Economy." *The Atlantic Monthly* 267 (February): 35–52.

Reiman, Jeffrey. 1995. *The Rich Get Richer and the Poor Get Prison: Ideology, Crime and Criminal Justice.* 4th ed. Boston: Allyn & Bacon.

Rist, Ray C. 1970. "Student Social Class and Teacher Expectations: The Self-fulfilling Prophecy in Ghetto Education." *Harvard Educational Review* 40: 411–51.

Rojek, Dean G., and Maynard L. Erickson. 1982. "Delinquent Careers: A Test of the Career Escalation Model." *Criminology* 20: 5–28.

Rose, Terry L. 1984. "Current Uses of Corporal Punishment in American Public Schools." *Journal of Educational Psychology* 76: 427–41.

Rosenbaum, Jill Leslie. 1987. "Social Control, Gender, and Delinquency: An Analysis of Drug, Property and Violent Offenders." *Justice Quarterly* 4: 117–42.

Rosenthal, Robert. 1973. "Pygmalion Effect Lives." *Psychology Today* 7: 56–63.

Rosenthal, Robert, and Lenore Jacobson. 1968. *Pygmalion in the Classroom.* New York: Holt, Rinehart & Winston.

Rubin, Lillian B. 1976. *Worlds of Pain.* New York: Basic.

Rubovits, Pamela C., and Martin L. Maehr. 1971. "Pygmalion Analyzed: Toward an Explanation of the Rosenthal-Jacobson Findings." *Journal of Personality and Social Psychology* 19: 197–203.

Sacks, Howard R., and Charles H. Logan. 1984. "Does Parole Make a (Lasting) Difference?" Pp. 362–78 in *Criminal Justice: Law and Politics*, edited by George F. Cole. Pacific Grove, CA: Brooks/Cole.

Salkovskis, Paul M., ed. 1996. *Frontiers of Cognitive Therapy.* New York: Guilford.

Sampson, Robert J., and John H. Laub. 1993. *Crime in the Making: Pathways and Turning Points Through Life.* Cambridge, MA: Harvard University Press.

Schaefer, Walter E., Carol Olexa, and Kenneth Polk. 1972. "Programmed for Social Class: Tracking in High School." Pp. 33–54 in *Schools and Delinquency*, edited by Kenneth Polk and Walter E. Schaefer. Englewood Cliffs, NJ: Prentice-Hall.

Schlosser, Eric. 1998. "The Prison-Industrial Complex." *The Atlantic Monthly* 282 (December): 51–77.

Schrager, Laura S., and James F. Short, Jr. 1978. "Toward a Sociology of Organizational Crime." *Social Problems* 25: 407–19.

Sellers, Charles. 1991. *Market Revolution: Jacksonian America, 1815–1845.* New York: Oxford University Press.

Shannon, Lyle W. 1988. *Criminal Career Continuity: Its Social Context.* New York: Human Sciences Press.

———. 1982. "Reassessing the Relationship of Adult Careers to Juvenile Careers: A Summary." *Report for the U.S. Department of Justice.* Washington, D.C.: U.S. Government Printing Office.

Shaw, Clifford R., and Henry D. McKay. 1942. *Juvenile Delinquency in Urban Areas.* Chicago: University of Chicago Press.

Shaw, Janis. M., and William. A. Scott. 1991. "Influence of Parent Discipline Style on Delinquent Behavior: the Mediating Role of Control Orientation." *Australian Journal of Psychology* 43: 61–67.

Sherman, Lawrence W. 1993. "Defiance, Deterrence, and Irrelevance: A Theory of the Criminal Sanction." *Journal of Research in Crime and Delinquency* 30: 445–73.

Short, James F., Jr. 1998. "The Level of Explanation Problem Revisited—the Amercian Society of Criminology 1997 Presidential Address." *Criminology* 36: 3–36.

———. 1996. "Exploring Integration of Theoretical Levels of Explanation: Notes on Gang Delinquency." Pp. 198–204 in *Juvenile Delinquency: Readings*, edited by Joseph G. Weiss, Robert D. Crutchfield, and George S. Bridges. Thousands Oaks, CA: Pine Forge Press.

———. 1958. "Differential Association with Delinquent Friends and Delinquent Behavior." *Pacific Sociological Review* 1: 20–25.

Short, James F., Jr., Ramon Rivera, and Ray A. Tennyson. 1965. "Perceived Opportunities, Gang Membership and Delinquency." *American Sociological Review* 30: 56–67.

Short, James F., Jr., and Fred L. Strodtbeck. 1974. *Group Process and Gang Delinquency.* Chicago: University of Chicago Press.

Shover, Neal. 1996. *Great Pretenders: Pursuits and Careers of Persistent Thieves.* Boulder, CO: Westview.

Shover, Neal, and David Honaker. 1992. "The Socially Bounded Decision Making of Persistent Property Offenders." *Howard Journal of Criminal Justice* 31: 276–93.

Silberman, Charles E. 1978. *Criminal Violence, Criminal Justice.* New York: Vintage.

Simons, Ronald L., Chyi-In Wu, Rand D. Conger, and Frederick O. Lorenz. 1994. "Two Routes to Delinquency: Differences Between Early and Late Starters in the Impact of Parenting and Deviant Peers." *Criminology* 32: 247–75.

Simpson, Sally S., and Lori Elis. 1994. "Is Gender Subordinate to Class? An Empirical Assessment of Colvin and Pauly's Structural Marxist Theory of Delinquency." *The Journal of Criminal Law and Criminology* 85: 453–80.

Smith, Carolyn, and Terence P. Thornberry. 1995. "The Relationship Between Childhood Maltreatment and Adolescent Involvement in Delinquency." *Criminology* 33: 451–81.

Smith, Hedrick (executive producer). 1999. *Seeking Solutions.* Hedrick Smith Productions, Inc. (film documentary).

Snyder, James, and Gerald Patterson. 1987. "Family Interaction and Delinquent Behavior." Pp. 216–43 in *Handbook of Juvenile Delinquency,* edited by Herbert C. Quay. New York: John Wiley.

Spergel, Iriving A. 1995. *The Youth Gang Problem.* New York: Oxford University Press.

Straus, Murray A. 1994. *Beating the Devil Out of Them: Corporal Punishment in American Families.* New York: Lexington Books.

Straus, Murray A., Richard J. Gelles, and Suzanne K. Steinmetz. 1980. *Behind Closed Doors: Violence in the American Family.* New York: Doubleday/Anchor.

Straus, Murray A., Demie Kurz, Donileen Loseke, and Joan McCord. 1991. "Discipline and Defense: Physical Punishment of Children and Violence and Other Crime in Adulthood." *Social Problems* 38: 133–54.

Steffensmeier, Darrell. 1989. "On the Causes of 'White-Collar' Crime: An Assessment of Hirschi and Gottfredson's Claims." *Criminology* 27: 345–58.

Steffensmeier, Darrell, and Emilie Allan. 1995. "Criminal Behavior: Gender and Age." Pp. 83–113 in *Criminology: A Contemporary Handbook,* 2d ed., edited by Joseph F. Sheley. Belmont, CA: Wadsworth.

Steffensmeier, Darrell, and Miles Harer. 1991. "Did Crime Rise or Fall During the Reagan Presidency?: The Effects of an 'Aging' U.S. Population on the Nation's Crime Rate." *Journal of Research in Crime and Delinquency* 28: 330–39.

Sugrue, Thomas J. 1996. *The Origins of the Urban Crisis: Race and Inequality in Postwar Detroit.* Princeton, NJ: Princeton University Press.

Sullivan, Mercer T. 1989. *"Getting Paid": Youth Crime and Work in the Inner City.* Ithaca, NY: Cornell University Press.

Sutherland, Edwin H. 1949. *White Collar Crime.* New York: Dryden.

Sutherland, Edwin H., and Donald R. Cressey. 1978. *Criminology.* Philadelphia: Lippincott.

Sykes, Gresham M., and David Matza. 1957. "Techniques of Neutralization." *American Sociological Review* 22: 664–70.

Thornberry, Terence P., Marvin D. Krohn, Alan J. Lizotte, and Deborah Chard-Wierschem. 1993. "The Role of Juvenile Gangs in Facilitating Delinquent Behavior." *Journal of Research in Crime and Delinquency* 30: 55–87.

Time. 1999. "The Columbine Tapes." December 20: 40–59.

Tittle, Charles R. 1995. *Control Balance: Toward a General Theory of Deviance.* Boulder, CO: Westview.

Tonry, Michael. 1995. *Malign Neglect: Race, Crime, and Punishment in America.* New York: Oxford University Press.

Tracy, Paul E., and Kimberly Kempf-Leonard. 1996. *Continuity and Discontinuity in Criminal Careers.* New York: Plenum Press.

Tracy, Paul E., Marvin E. Wolfgang, and Robert M. Figlio. 1990. *Delinquency Careers in Two Birth Cohorts.* New York: Plenum Press.

Tunnel, Kenneth D. 1999. "The Motivation to Commit Property Crime." Pp. 345–53 in *Crime and Criminals: Contemporary and Classic Readings in Criminology,* edited by Frank R. Scarpitti and Amie L. Nielson. Los Angeles, CA: Roxbury.

U.S. Bureau of Census. 1975. *Historical Statistics of the United States: Colonial Times to 1970.* Washington, D.C.: U.S. Government Printing Office.

Vigil, James D. 1988. *Barrio Gangs.* Austin: University of Texas Press.

Visher, Christy A. 1995. "Career Offenders and Crime Control." Pp. 515–33 in *Criminology: A Contemporary Handbook,* 2d ed., edited by Joseph F. Sheley. Belmont, CA: Wadsworth.

Voss, Harwin L. 1964. "Differential Association and Reported Delinquent Behavior: A Replication." *Social Problems* 12: 78–85.

Walker, Samuel. 1989. *Sense and Nonsense about Crime.* Pacific Grove, CA: Brooks/Cole.

*Washington Post.* 2000a. "Japan's Violent Turn." February 2: A17–A18.

———. 2000b. "This Time, Boom Benefits the Poor." February 11: A14.

———. 1999a. "Crime Rates Down for 7th Straight Year." October 18: A2.

———. 1999b. "Despite Rhetoric, Violent Crime Climbs." December 5: A3.

Wauchope, Barbara A., and Murray A. Straus. 1990. "Physical Punishment and Physical Abuse of American Children: Incidence Rates by Age, Gender, and Occupational Class." Pp. 133–65 in *Physical Violence in American Families: Risk Factors and Adaptations to Violence in 8,145 Families,* edited by Murray A. Straus and Richard J. Gelles. New Brunswick, NJ: Transaction Publishers.

Weinberg, Daniel H. 1996. "A Brief Look at Postwar U.S. Income Inequality." *Current Population Reports* (report no. P60–191, June). Washington, D.C.: U.S. Bureau of the Census.

Weiss, Robert P., and Nigel South. 1998. *Comparing Prison Systems.* Amsterdam: Gordon and Breach.

Welch, Ralph S. 1979. "Severe Parental Punishment and Aggression: The Link between Corporal Punishment and Delinquency." Pp. 126–42 in *Corporal Punishment in American Education,* edited by Irwin A. Hyman and James H. Wise. Philadelphia: Temple University Press.

Wells, L. Edward, and Joseph H. Rankin. 1988. "Social Control Theories of Delinquency: Direct Parental Controls." *Criminology* 26: 263–85.

Westermann, Ted D., and James W. Burfeind. 1991. *Crime and Justice in Two Societies: Japan and the United States.* Pacific Grove, CA: Brooks/Cole.

Wiatrowski, Michael D., David Griswold, and Mary K. Roberts. 1981. "Social

Control Theory and Delinquency." *American Sociological Review* 46: 525–41.

Wiatrowski, Michael D., Stephen Hansell, Charles R. Massey, and David L. Wilson. 1982. "Curriculum Tracking and Delinquency." *American Sociological Review* 47: 151–60.

Widom, Cathy Spatz. 1992. *The Cycle of Violence*. Washington, D.C.: National Institute of Justice.

———. 1989. "Child Abuse, Neglect, and Violent Criminal Behavior." *Criminology* 27: 251–71.

Williams, Nicolas, Francis T. Cullen, and John Paul Wright. 1996. "Labor Market Participation and Youth Crime: The Neglect of 'Working' in Delinquency Research." *Social Pathology* 2: 195–217.

Wilson, William Julius. 1987. *The Truly Disadvantaged*. Chicago: University of Chicago Press.

Witkin, Gordon. 1998. "The Crime Bust: What's Behind the Dramatic Drop in Crime? The Prime Suspect is Not Police, Nor Prison, Nor Prevention." *U.S. News and World Report* May 25: 28–37.

Wolfgang, Marvin E. 1958. *Patterns of Criminal Homicide*. Philadelphia: University of Pennsylvania Press.

Wolfgang, Marvin E., Robert M. Figlio, and Thorsten Sellin. 1972. *Delinquency in a Birth Cohort*. Chicago: University of Chicago Press.

Wood, Daniel B. 2000. "Inside America's 'Safest' Cities." *The Christian Science Monitor* January 7: 1, 8, 9.

Wright, Bradley R. Entner, Avshalom Caspi, Terrie E. Moffitt, and Phil A. Silva. 1999. "Low Self-Control, Social Bonds, and Crime: Social Causation, Social Selection, or Both." *Criminology* 37: 479–514.

Wright, John Paul, Francis T. Cullen, and Nicolas Williams. 1997. "Working While in School and Delinquent Involvement: Implications for Social Policy." *Crime and Delinquency* 43: 203–21.

Wright, Richard T., and Scott H. Decker. 1997. *Armed Robbers in Action: Stickups and Street Culture*. Boston: Northeastern University Press.

———. 1994. *Burglars on the Job: Street Life and Residential Break-ins*. Boston: Northeastern University Press.

Wright, James D., and Sonia R. Wright. 1976. "Social Class and Parental Values for Children: A Partial Replication and Extension of the Kohn Thesis." *American Sociological Review* 41: 527–37.

Wyatt-Brown, Bertram. 1982. *Southern Honor*. New York: Oxford University Press.

Yablonsky, Lewis. 1966. *The Violent Gang*. Baltimore, MD: Penguin Books.

Zehr, Howard, and Harry Mika. 1998. "Fundamental Concepts of Restorative Justice." *Contemporary Justice Review* 1: 47–55.

Zieger, Robert H. 1986. *American Workers, American Unions, 1920–1985*. Baltimore, MD: Johns Hopkins University Press.

Zimring, Franklin E. 1998. *American Youth Violence*. New York: Oxford University Press.

# Index